DIAGRAPHICS

THE BEST IN

GRAPHS,

CHARTS,

MAPS

AND

TECHNICAL

ILLUSTRATION

P·I·E BOOKS

DIAGRAM GRAPHICS

Copyright ©1992 by P•I•E BOOKS

First published in Japan

in 1992 by:

P•I•E BOOKS

Villa Phoenix Suite 407, 4-14-6, Komagome,

Toshima-ku, Tokyo 170, Japan

Tel: 03-3949-5010 Fax: 03-3949-5650

ISBN 4-938586-34-7 C3070 P16000E

First published in

Germany in 1992 by:

Nippan

Nippon Shuppan Hanbai Deutschland GmbH

Krefelder Str. 85

D-4000 Düsseldorf 11 (Heerdt)

Tel: 0211-5048089 Fax: 0211-5049326

ISBN 3-910052-17-7

The design used for the front cover was

provided by Grundy & Northedge Designers,

commissioned by Blueprint magazine.

CONTENTS

DIAGRAM GRAPHICS

3

現在、私たちはきわめて多様なメディアの吐きだす膨大な量の情報に取り囲まれて生きている。

新聞雑誌に代表される活字メディアが提供する文字情報、ラジオ・テレビに代表される電波メディアが提供する映像情報と音声情報、そして、活字メディア未来形ともいうべきパソコン通信等の電子メディアを介して交換される言語情報、加えて、ビデオの普及で完全に一般家庭への浸透を果たした映画等の高品質の画像情報……等々。

ともかく膨大な量の情報が、おそろしく多様な表現手段によって、私たちのもとへ送られてくるのが今日である。

こうした日々の生活は、知らずのうちに、私たちの情報というものに接する態度自体を根本から変えてしまっている。私たちの情報に対する感受性そのものが、飛躍的に多様化してしまい、もはや、文字情報のみによるコミュニケーション手段や、音声情報のみによるコミュニケーション手段では、新鮮な感動を得ることも、強い影響力をこうむることもむずかしい状況になっているのである。

こうした高度情報化社会に特有の、情報に対する感受性の多様化は、当然、印刷および映像の分野におけるデザインのありかたにも大きな影響を及ぼすことになる。

文字だけ、絵だけでは、こちらの思うような関心を示してくれなくなった読者たちの目を引き、気を引くために、印刷メディア、映像メディアを問わず、今後ますますデザイン需要を増すのが、本書で取り上げたダイアグラムというものである。

ダイアグラムとは、図表、図解など、文字情報だけでは伝わりにくい内容を、図形的なデザイン処理の力を借りて行なうものの総称である。

手法から見ても主題から見てもそのジャンルは多岐にわたるが、本書では、とりあえず、収録作品を下記の通りに分類し紹介してある。

1．表・グラフ：統計や比較のためにデータを視覚化したもの
2．チャート・スコア：ものごとの関係や流れを視覚化したもの
3．マップ：空間や地域を視覚化したもの
4．建築プラン：建築設計、都市計画等のための図解全般
5．製品イラストレーション：製品、商品を紹介するための図解全般
6．科学イラストレーション：現象、知識を解説するための図解全般

各ジャンルのダイアグラムの特徴等については、各章の扉のガイダンスを参照して頂きたい。

ダイアグラムの語源は、ギリシア語で「作図されたもの、図形」をいう「ｄｉａｇｒａｍｍａ」にある。

「線を引くこと、描くこと」を表わす動詞「ｇｒａｐｈｅｉｎ」に、「〜を通して」という意味を持つ「ｄｉａ」がついて、「ｄｉａｇｒａｐｈｅｉｎ」で、図形を指すようになった。

一目してわかる通り、「ｇｒａｐｈｅｉｎ」は、グラフィックの語源でもあり、グラフィック・デザインの分野そのものが、視覚化的な素材を効果的に利用してコミュニケーション効率の増大をはかるという姿勢において、「ｄｉａｇｒａｐｈｅｉｎ」すなわちダイアグラムをその基本精神としているのである。

先にも述べたように、高度情報化社会のなかで多様化する一方の人々の情報感受性に的確に訴求するためには、この図形化されコミュニケーションとしてのダイアグラムは、ますますその真価を発揮するであろうし、また、いよいよ本格化する国際化社会においても、各国言語の障壁を超えるデザイン手法としてのダイアグラムの可能性は、さらに強い関心の的になるに違いない。

多様化し国際化するコミュニケーション環境における視覚言語の未来像を探り、出版に広告に、より説得力に富んだコミュニケーション手段の導入を模索する読者のために、本書が一助になれば幸いである。

DIAGRAM GRAPHICS

西岡文彦

 序　文

FOREWORD

Fumihiko Nishioka

DIAGRAM GRAPHICS

The origin of the word "diagram" is the Greek "diagramma" which simply means, "Something drawn." The prefix "dia" means "via" and was attached to the verb "graphein" which means, "To draw a line, to draw." Obviously, "graphein" is also the origin of the word graphic.

Today we are surrounded by a staggering amount of information. It pours into our lives through a variety of diverse channels including text information via the printed media such as newspapers and magazines, visual and sound information via the broadcast media such as radio and TV and information which comes in new formats via new channels, such as the data exchanged via electronic networks of personal computers. In addition, information in the form of high-quality motion pictures and video documentaries, etc., has penetrated into the homes of ordinary families.

In short, the amount of information coming in through the mix of media to which we are all exposed, is vast. Living within this flood of input has become a way of life for most of us and without realizing it we have entirely changed our attitude towards information. The basic structure of our receptivity toward information has itself been diversified. In this new state we are unlikely to be moved or inspired or strongly influenced by any communication which depends upon, for example, text information only or sound information only. This diversification of human sensory mechanisms, which is undoubtedly inherent to life in a highly advanced information society, naturally has important ramifications in design for print and other visual media.

We have chosen to feature diagrams in this book, in part because it is clear that they are going to be of increasing importance in the future of print and visual media. More and more, diagrams will be required to attract the attention of, to stimulate and hold the interest of readers who will show less and less inclination to embrace a message delivered in plain text.

The word diagram is a general term for that which uses graphic design as an expository tool to convey something which would be difficult to explain with text alone. There are any number of genres of graphical communication which might fall under the general heading of diagrams, as viewed from the perspective of methodology, theme, intention and so forth. For this book, they have been classified and showcased in the following manner:

1. **Statistical Tables & Graphs: Visualize data for the purpose of statistical comparison.**
2. **Charts & Scores: Visualize the relationships among and the flow of elements.**
3. **Maps: Visualize space and regions.**
4. **Architectural Plans & Drawings: A range of illustrations for architectural design, city planning etc.**
5. **Instructional Diagrams for Products: A range of illustrations which introduce products.**
6. **Scientific Illustrations: A range of illustrations that explain phenomena and knowledge.**

Refer to the guide at the head of each chapter for detailed descriptions of the characteristics of the diagrams in each genre.

We might say that the graphic design field as a whole has the same fundamental objective as does the making of any individual diagram. That is, it reflects the attempt to increase the efficiency of communication by the effective use of visual material.

As mentioned before, in the future, diagrams will play an even greater role in communication by accurately focusing on the information receptors of contemporary people. In the borderless world of modern communication methods, the potential for diagrams as a design technique which overcomes language barriers, looms ever larger.

Amid the diversification and internationalization of our rapidly changing communication environment, we stumble forward in our attempts, largely by trial and error, to bring about more persuasive means of communication in publishing and advertising. We hope that this book will in some way help the reader who is interested in the images of a visual language for the future, to understand this exciting and dynamic process.

Das Wort "Diagramm" leitet sich vom dem griechischen Wort "diagramma" ab, das "etwas Gezeichnetes" bedeutet und durch Voranstellen der Vorsilbe "dia" (entspricht "via") vor das Verb "graphein" entstand. "Graphein" heißt "zeichnen, eine Linie ziehen" und aus diesem Begriff hat sich auch unser Wort "Graphik" entwickelt.

Wir sind heutzutage von einer erstaunlichen Menge an Informationen umgeben. Sie durchdringen unser Leben über eine Vielzahl von Kanälen, sowohl als Textinformation über die Printmedien wie Zeitungen und Zeitschriften, als visuelle und akustische Information über die Funkmedien Radio und Fernsehen und auch in neuer Form, wie es mit Datenübertragung in Computer-Netzwerken möglich ist. Der Video-Berelch hat sich als zusätzlicher Informationskanal mit Unterhaltung und Dokumentation etabliert, der bis in die Wohnzimmer vordringt.

Kurz, wir stehen einer unermeßlichen Informationsflut gegenüber. Wir haben uns daran gewöhnt, mit diesem Überangebot zu leben und ohne es zu bemerken, haben wir unsere Einstellung zu Informationen selbst verändert. Die Grundstruktur unserer Aufnahmefähigkeit für Informationen ist modifiziert. In diesem neuen Stadlum ist es sehr unwahrscheinlich, daß wir durch Informationen bewegt, beeinflußt oder inspiriert werden, deren Kommunikationsfähigkeit zum Beispiel nur von Text oder nur von Ton abhängt. Diese Veränderung der Wahrnehmungsfähigkeit, die mit dem Leben in einer hochentwickelten Informationsgesellschaft zwangsläufig einhergeht, hat natürlich weitreichende Auswirkungen im Design für Print- und andere Medien.

Wir haben uns entschlossen, in diesem Buch Diagramme vorzustellen, da sie eine steigende Bedeutung für die Zukunft der Print-und visuellen Medien haben werden. In zunehmendem Maße werden Diagramme notwendig sein, um Aufmerksamkeit und Interesse eines Leser zu wecken und zu binden, der immer weniger geneigt sein wird, eine Nachricht zu erfassen, die nur mit Text kommunizieren kann.

"Diagramm" steht als allgemeine Bezeichnung für alle Gestaltungen, die sich graphischer Techniken als Werkzeug bedienen, um etwas zu vermitteln, was mit Text allein nur schwer zu erklären ist. Es gibt daher eine Reihe von Genres graphischer Kommunikation, die unter den Oberbegriff "Diagramm" fallen, unterteilt nach Gesichtspunkten von Methodlk, Thematik, Intention etc. In diesem Buch werden die folgenden Einteilungen vorgestelit:

1. Tabellen-Graphiken: Visualisieren Daten zum statistischen Vergleich.

2. Übersichten, Flußdiagramme: Visualisieren den Zusammenhang zwischen und den Fluß von Elementen.

3.Landkarten: Visualisieren Landschaftsräume und Regionen.

4. Architektur-Pläne: Eine Reihe von Illustrationen für Architektur-Entwürfe, Stadtplanung etc.

5. Produkt-Illustration: Eine Reihe von Illustrationen, die Produkte vorstellen.

6. Wissenschaftliche Illustrationen: Eine Reihe von Illustrationen, die Phänomene und Sachzusammenhänge erklären.

In der Einleitung zu jedem Kapiteln werden detailliert die Charakteristiken der Graphiken in ihrem Genre vorgestellt. Wir möchten noch bemerken, daß Graphik-Design generell dieselben fundamentalen Vorgaben aufweist, wie das Erstellen eines individuellen Diagramms, nämlich die Reflexion des Versuches, die Effizienz der Kommunikation durch effektiven Einsatz visueller Mittel zu verbessern.

Wie bereits erwähnt, werden Diagramme im Kommunikationssystem eine immer größere Rolle spielen, da sie präzise auf die Rezeptoren der Information ausgerichtet werden können. In der grenzenlosen Welt der modemen Kommunikationsmethoden wird das Potential von Diagrammen, die Sprachgrenzen problemlos überwinden können, immer bedeutungsvoller.

Inmitten der Diversifikation und Internationalisierung unserer rasch wechselnden kommunikativen Umgebung bemühen wir uns ständig, Kommunikationsmittel mit größerer Überzeugungskraft für die Publikation und Werbung zu entwickeln-oftmals mittels Versuch und Irrtum. Wir hoffen, daß dieses Buch dem an den Bildern einer zukünftigen visuellen Sprache interessierten Leser auf die eine oder andere Art hilft, diesen aufregenden und faszinierenden Vorgang zu verstehen.

Fumihiko Nishioka

DIAGRAM GRAPHICS

VORWORT

EDITORIAL NOTE:

CD: Creative Director

AD: Art Director

D: Designer

P: Photographer

I: Illustrator

PR: Producer

DF: Design Firm

クレジットのタイトルに関しては、クライアント名を
また、国名の表示に関しては出品者の居住国を表記しています。
作品説明は出品者より送られたものを記載し、それ以外のものについては小社で作成しました。

The title of each credit indicates the name of the commissioning client.
The country indicated for each entry is the country in which the artist resides.
Most of the descriptions accompanying the diagrams
in this book have been reproduced as received from the artists themselves.
The others were prepared by the Editorial Department of P·I·E Books.

STATISTICAL
TABLES & GRAPHS

表＆グラフ

データは整理されていなければ、単なる情報の寄せ集めである。ここで紹介する表とグラフは、データを整理、分類し、一定の法則に従って図形的に配置し、視覚的に変換したダイアグラムのことをいう。

　表は、普通、タテ軸とヨコ軸の二系列にそれぞれ別の項目を設定し、データを配置する形式をとる。整理、分類されたデータを体系的に配列し、データ相互の対応関係を確認するためのダイアグラムであり、グラフをはじめとする他のダイアグラムを作成するための基本となる作業でもある。

　作成にあたっては、データの読み取りやすい明快な構成を心がけたい。線と文字による表組みは、ともすれば単調な画面となりやすいだけに、デザイン上の工夫が求められる。ただし、データの読み取りやすさをそこなっては、本来の表の機能が果たせないので、タイポグラフィにせよ、色彩設計にせよ、表本来の明確な性格を損なわない抑制した処置が望まれる。

　グラフは、単に、データを整理、分類するのではなく、一定の法則に従って視覚的に変換されたものを配置したダイアグラムのことをいう。

　数字を線に変換すれば線グラフ、面に変換すれば面グラフというように、データを視覚的な「量」に置き換えることで、具体的な比較を容易にするためのダイアグラムである。グラフの特徴は、抽象的な情報を具体的な形に変換して、明確なイメージとして提示し、データを直観的に把握し比較できるようにする点にある。

　したがって、グラフの制作にあたっては、棒グラフのようにデータを線の長さに置き換えるのか、円グラフのように面の広さに置き換えて、量を比較するのか、あるいは折れ線グラフのように点を結んだ線として示し、データの量の変化を示すか、データの性格とグラフの目的にかなった視覚的要素の、的確な選定がカギとなる。

　単なる棒の代わりに鉛筆を使ったり、単なる面の代わりに具体的な地図を使ったりして、ややもすれば統計的、数学的な冷たい表情を示しやすいグラフに、よりソフトな表情を加えることも大切な工夫である。

STATISTICAL TABLES & GRAPHS

表 & グラフ

Data which have not been sorted and classified are merely a chaotic hodgepodge of raw information. The tables and graphs introduced here are examples of the type of diagrams in which data are sorted and classified and then laid-out according to certain graphical rules to form a visual presentation.

Normally, such a diagram basically takes the form of intersecting vertical and horizontal axes, whereupon the separate items are set out on the respective scales; the *rank* and *file*, or the *x* axis and *y* axis. It is a diagram for arranging sorted and classified data systematically and for verifying the corresponding relationships among different sets of data. A table can be a finished presentation, or it might be a preparatory arrangement of data that serves as a basis for a graph or some other kind of diagram.

In creating a table, one should bear in mind that it should have a clear structure that facilitates reading the data. The composition of a table featuring lines and text tends to be somewhat monotonous and that is why you have to be as innovative as possible. However, if, because of your designer's contrivances, you detract from the readability of the data, then the table will fail in its original function. In terms of general design, choice of typefaces, overall color scheme and so forth, a degree of restraint must be exercised so that the diagram will not lose its essential characteristic; that of a precision visual instrument for conveying information.

A graph, then, is a diagram in which data are not simply sorted and classified but also converted to a visual form in accordance with certain pictorial rules. If a set of numbers is converted to lines, for example, this will constitute a line graph, if converted to areas, then perhaps, a pie graph. The purpose of this sort of diagram, of course, is to make it easier to compare data by converting it into a clear visual form which represents quantitative information.

One of the main characteristics of a graph is that it offers easy and direct visual understanding and comparison of abstract numerical data. Once converted to simple shapes and forms, a definite and clear image of the meaning of the data becomes apparent. When producing graphs, therefore, the key is to choose the visual elements carefully so that they will be appropriate to the nature of the data you are working with. If your terms are expressed in percentages, for example, a pie graph might be the most accessible way of presenting it. On the other hand, if you want to demonstrate they way your values have changed over time, a polygonal line graph might work best.

It is of the utmost importance, in any case, that a graph be rendered in a viewer-friendly format. One effective design choice is to employ familiar representative objects as the main visual elements; pencils instead of bars, for example, or maps instead of featureless areas. Without this sort of effort, a graph will tend to wear a rather cold statistical image and will remain unappealing.

STATISTICAL
TABLES & GRAPHS

CHARTS & SCORES

MAPS

ARCHITECTURAL
PLANS & DRAWINGS

INSTRUCTIONAL DIAGRAMS
FOR PRODUCTS

SCIENTIFIC
ILLUSTRATIONS

AMERICAN PACIFIC CORPORATION
USA 1991
CD:Thomas Page
AD:Don Kano
D,I:Faith Ishibashi
DF:Kano Design Group

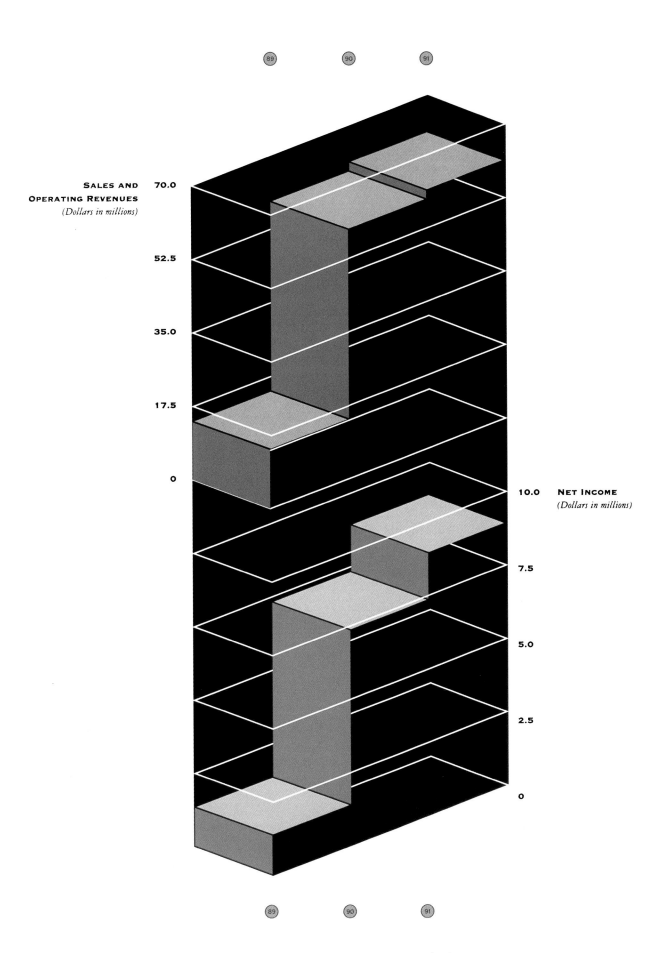

Graphs showing sales & operating revenues and net income.
The grid lines in these graphs create an environment as well as a strong sense of structure. From an American Pacific Corporation annual report.
アメリカン・パシフィック社のアニュアルリポートより、販売や営業による収益と純利益を表したグラフ。グラフ中の格子線は正確かつ印象的なデザイン表現のポイントとなっている。

STATISTICAL
TABLES & GRAPHS

CHARTS & SCORES

MAPS

ARCHITECTURAL
PLANS & DRAWINGS

INSTRUCTIONAL DIAGRAMS
FOR PRODUCTS

SCIENTIFIC
ILLUSTRATIONS

CLABIR CORPORATION
USA 1983
CD:Jack Hough
AD,D:Tom Morin
I:Jerry Hablitzel
DF:Jack Hough Associates, Inc.

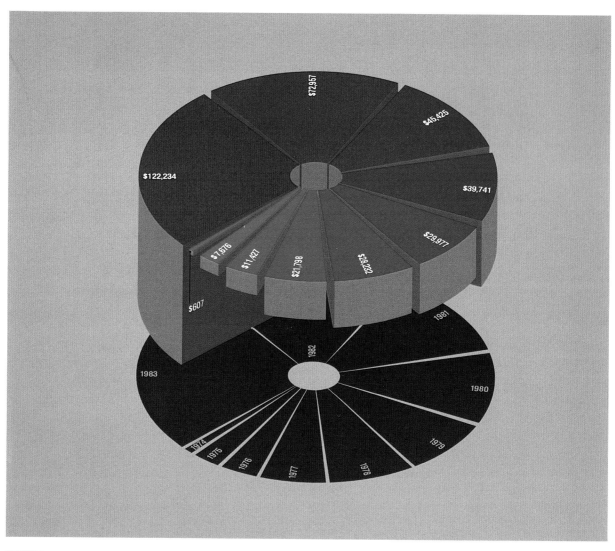

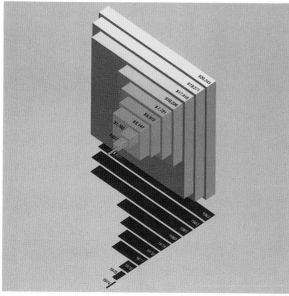

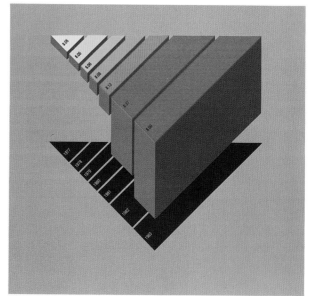

Graphs highlighting Clabir Corporation's financial success over the previous decade. From a corporate annual report.
クラビル社のアニュアルリポートより、同社の過去10年間の財政上の成功に焦点を当てたグラフ。

GENERAL DEFENSE CORPORATION
USA 1984
CD,AD:Jack Hough
D:Henry Goerke
P:Jerry Sarpochiello
I:Nick Fasciano
DF:Jack Hough Associates, Inc.

STATISTICAL
TABLES & GRAPHS

CHARTS & SCORES

MAPS

ARCHITECTURAL
PLANS & DRAWINGS

INSTRUCTIONAL DIAGRAMS
FOR PRODUCTS

SCIENTIFIC
ILLUSTRATIONS

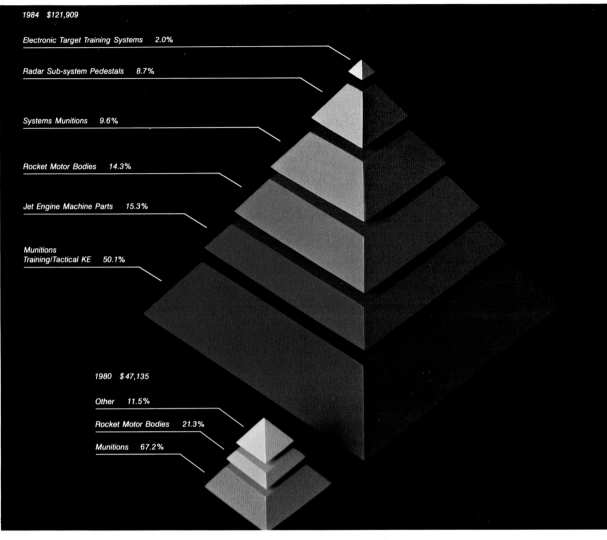

1984 $121,909

Electronic Target Training Systems   2.0%

Radar Sub-system Pedestals   8.7%

Systems Munitions   9.6%

Rocket Motor Bodies   14.3%

Jet Engine Machine Parts   15.3%

Munitions
Training/Tactical KE   50.1%

1980 $47,135

Other   11.5%

Rocket Motor Bodies   21.3%

Munitions   67.2%

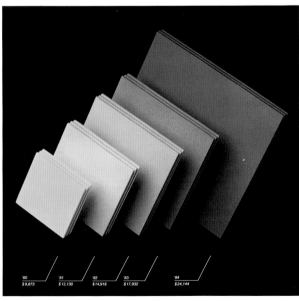

'80
$9,673   '81
$12,130   '82
$14,918   '83
$17,932   '84
$24,144

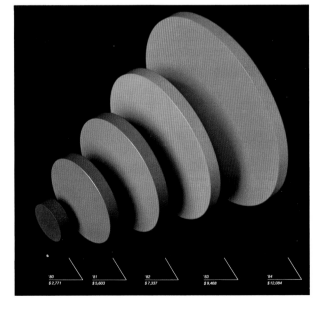

'80
$2,771   '81
$5,603   '82
$7,337   '83
$9,468   '84
$12,084

These financial graphs were constructed out of plastic, painted and displayed as full-page illustrations. From a General Defense Corporation annual report.
ジェネラル・ディフェンス社のアニュアルリポートより、プラスチック素材を使用してページいっぱいに表現した財務に関するグラフ。

CHARTS & SCORES

MAPS

ARCHITECTURAL
PLANS & DRAWINGS

INSTRUCTIONAL DIAGRAMS
FOR PRODUCTS

SCIENTIFIC
ILLUSTRATIONS

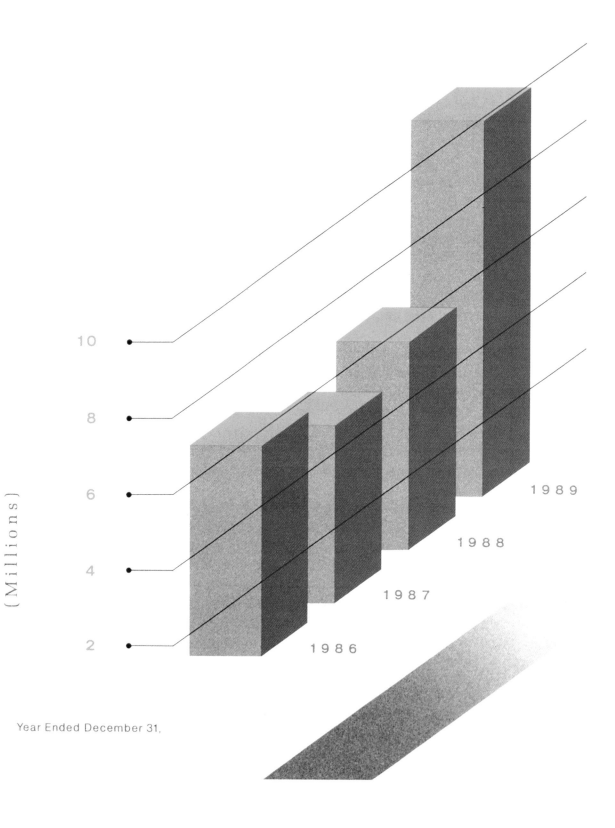

(Millions)

10

8

6

4

2

1989

1988

1987

1986

Year Ended December 31,

STATISTICAL
TABLES & GRAPHS

CHARTS & SCORES

MAPS

ARCHITECTURAL
PLANS & DRAWINGS

INSTRUCTIONAL DIAGRAMS
FOR PRODUCTS

SCIENTIFIC
ILLUSTRATIONS

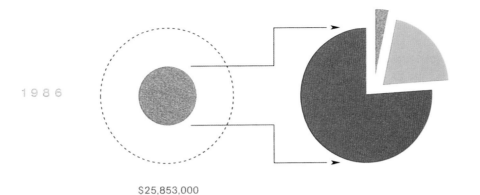

1986

$25,853,000

Premiums Earned 76%

Commissions & Fees 21%

Net Investment Income 3%

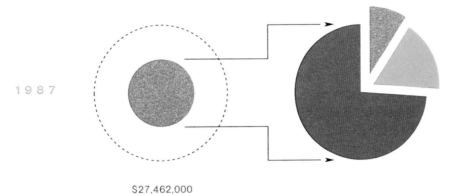

1987

$27,462,000

Premiums Earned 74%

Commissions & Fees 17%

Net Investment Income 9%

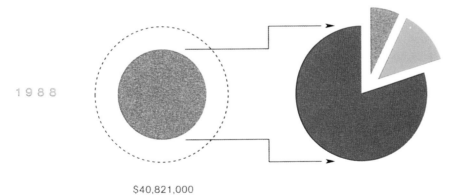

1988

$40,821,000

Premiums Earned 80%

Commissions & Fees 13%

Net Investment Income 7%

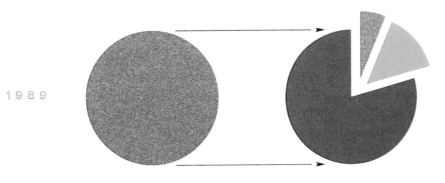

1989

$62,941,000

Premiums Earned 79%

Commissions & Fees 15%

Net Investment Income 6%

Three-dimensional bar graph appears to hover over a drop shadow that represents the base line.
Graphs showing the growth in revenues while demonstrating the composition of revenues by source. From a U.S. Facilities Corp. annual report.
USファシリティーズ社のアニュアルリポートより、ベースラインを影で表し、その上に浮かせるデザインを採用した立体棒グラフ、及び資金源と対比して表した歳入のグラフ。

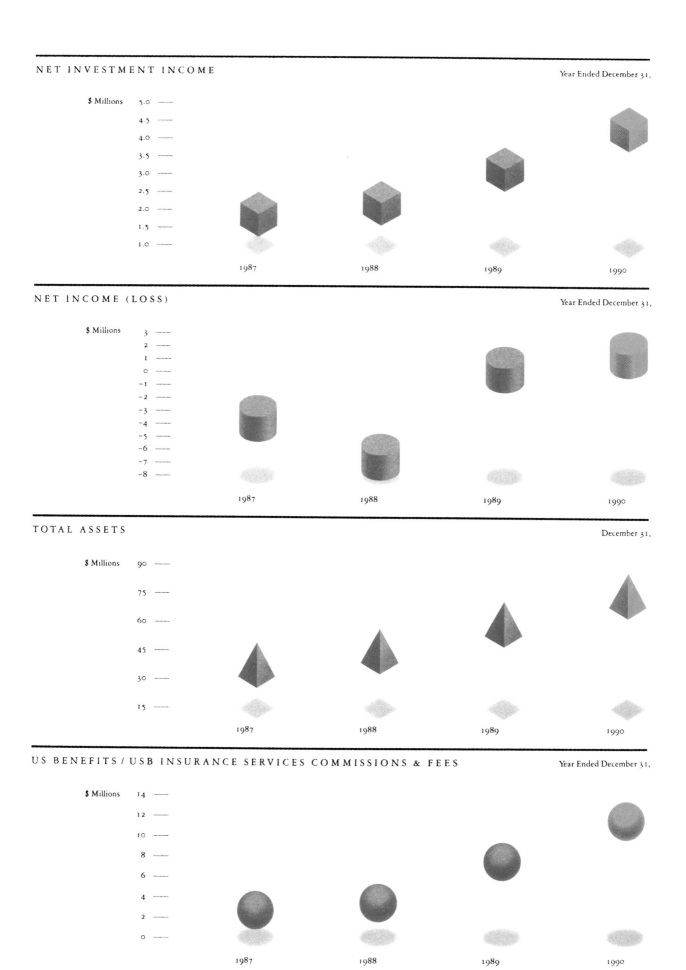

NET INVESTMENT INCOME

Year Ended December 31,

NET INCOME (LOSS)

Year Ended December 31,

TOTAL ASSETS

December 31,

US BENEFITS / USB INSURANCE SERVICES COMMISSIONS & FEES

Year Ended December 31,

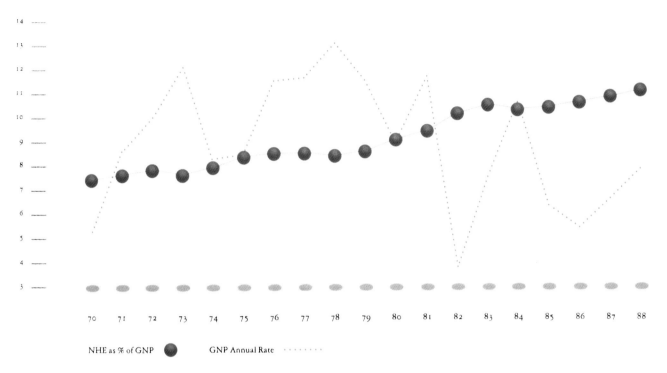

Percent   Years 1970–1988

COMPARISON OF GROWTH RATES OF GNP AND NATIONAL HEALTH EXPENDITURES

NHE as % of GNP ●   GNP Annual Rate ·········

Sources: U.S. Department of Health and Human Services, Health Care Financing Administration, Health Care Financing Notes, July 1989 and unpublished data from the U.S. Department of Commerce.

TOTAL REVENUES

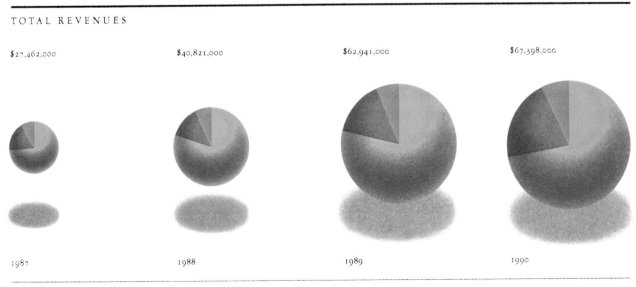

$27,462,000 $40,821,000 $62,941,000 $67,398,000

1987   1988   1989   1990

BY SOURCE

Premiums Earned 74%   Premiums Earned 80%   Premiums Earned 79%   Premiums Earned 73%
Commissions & Fees 17%   Commissions & Fees 13%   Commissions & Fees 15%   Commissions & Fees 20%
Net Investment Income 9% Net Investment Income 7% Net Investment Income 6% Net Investment Income 7%

The basic geometry of the cube, sphere, pyramid and cylinder was employed as a simple but effective way to satisfy a wide range of chart requirements including bar graphs, a mountain graph and pie graphs. From a U.S. Facilities Corp. annual report.

USファシリティーズ社のアニュアルリポートより、より印象的な表現のために立方体・球・三角錐・円筒などを利用した棒グラフ、山型グラフ、円グラフ。

NYNEX CORPORATION
USA 1991
CD:Meera Singh
AD:Lynn Martin
D:Jennifer Choi
DF:Inc Design

STATISTICAL
TABLES & GRAPHS

CHARTS & SCORES

MAPS

ARCHITECTURAL
PLANS & DRAWINGS

INSTRUCTIONAL DIAGRAMS
FOR PRODUCTS

SCIENTIFIC
ILLUSTRATIONS

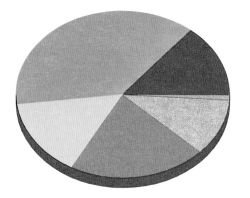

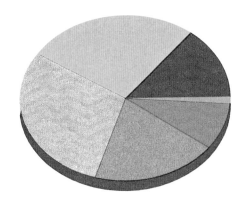

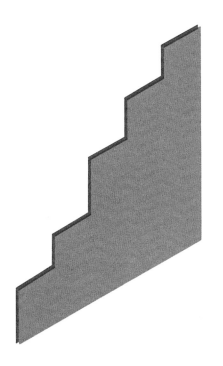
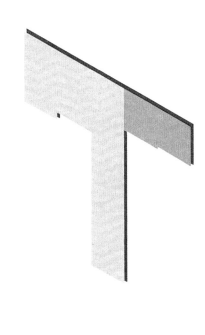
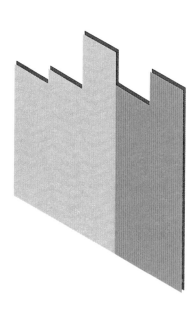

Fiscal graphs from a Nynex Corporation annual report.
ナイネックス社のアニュアルリポートより、財務に関するグラフ。

BANPONCE CORPORATION
USA 1990
AD:Howard Belk
D:Carin Benger
I:In House
DF:Belk Mignogna Associates Ltd.

STATISTICAL
TABLES & GRAPHS

CHARTS & SCORES

MAPS

ARCHITECTURAL
PLANS & DRAWINGS

INSTRUCTIONAL DIAGRAMS
FOR PRODUCTS

SCIENTIFIC
ILLUSTRATIONS

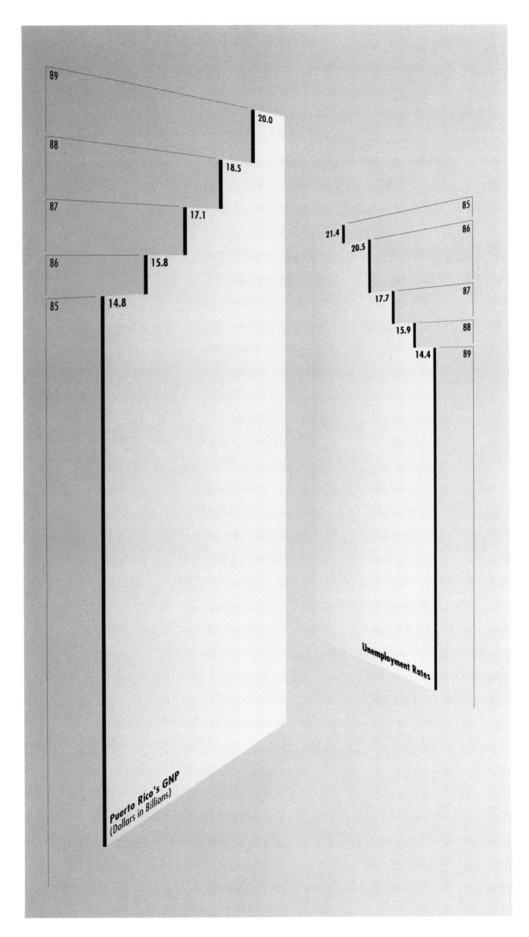

Graphs showing Puerto Rico's GNP and unemployment rate. From a Banponce Corporation annual report.
バンポンス社のアニュアルリポートより、プエルトリコのGNP、及び失業率を表したチャート。

STATISTICAL
TABLES & GRAPHS

CHARTS & SCORES

MAPS

ARCHITECTURAL
PLANS & DRAWINGS

INSTRUCTIONAL DIAGRAMS
FOR PRODUCTS

SCIENTIFIC
ILLUSTRATIONS

GOLD PEAK
INDUSTRIES(HOLDINGS)LIMITED
HONG KONG 1990,1991
CD,AD:Kan Tai-Keung
AD,D:Eddy Yu Chi Kong
DF:Kan Tai-Keung Design & Associates Ltd.

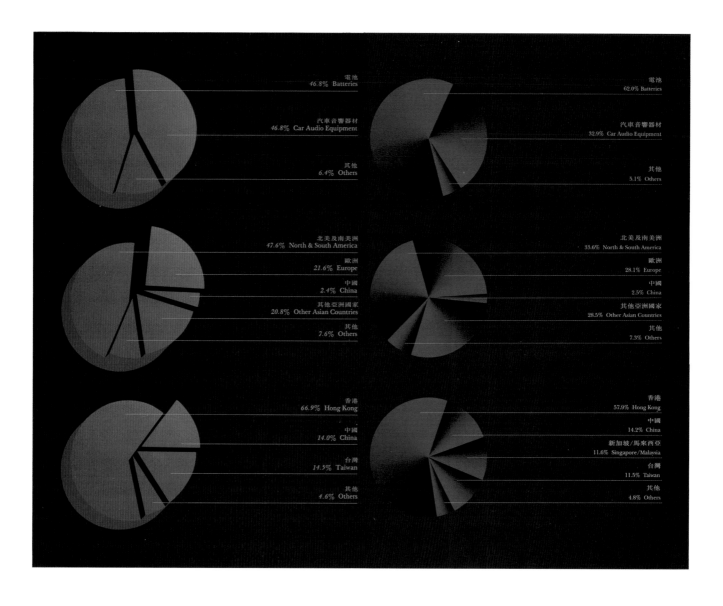

Financial graphs from a Gold Peak Industries Ltd. annual report.
ゴールドピーク・インダストリーズ社のアニュアルリポートより、財務に関するグラフ。

STATISTICAL
TABLES & GRAPHS

CHARTS & SCORES

MAPS

ARCHITECTURAL
PLANS & DRAWINGS

INSTRUCTIONAL DIAGRAMS
FOR PRODUCTS

SCIENTIFIC
ILLUSTRATIONS

1. SEIYU CO., LTD.
JAPAN 1982
CD,AD,D:Tetsuya Ohta

**2. THE SEIBU GROUP OF
RETAIL ENTERPRISES**
JAPAN 1985
CD,AD,D:Tetsuya Ohta

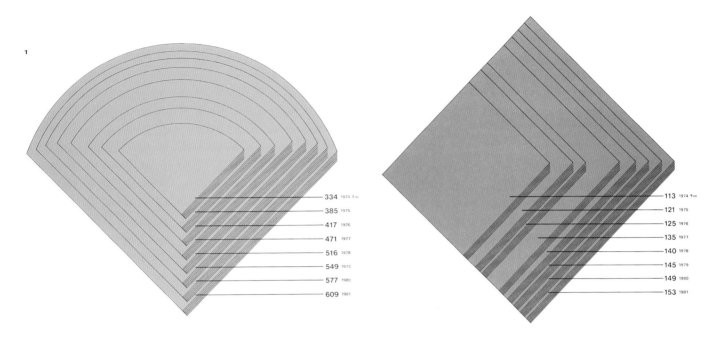

1
334 1974 干㎡
385 1975
417 1976
471 1977
516 1978
549 1979
577 1980
609 1981

113 1974 千㎡
121 1975
125 1976
135 1977
140 1978
145 1979
149 1980
153 1981

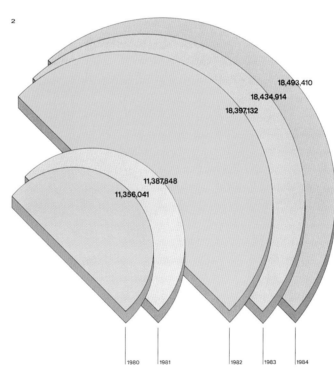

2
18,493,410
18,434,914
18,397,132
11,387,848
11,356,041

1980 1981 1982 1983 1984

1. Annual changes of sales floor area of the supermarket chain, Seiyu.
スーパーマーケット「西友」の年間売場面積推移図。

2. Changes in the land area developed by the real estate
department of Seibu Group of Retail Enterprises.
西武流通グループ/不動産部門の開発面積推移図。

STATISTICAL
TABLES & GRAPHS

CHARTS & SCORES

MAPS

ARCHITECTURAL
PLANS & DRAWINGS

INSTRUCTIONAL DIAGRAMS
FOR PRODUCTS

SCIENTIFIC
ILLUSTRATIONS

CIRCUS CIRCUS ENTERPRISES, INC.
USA 1989
CD,AD,D:Don Kano
I:Carlos Delgado
DF:Kano Design Group

LONG ISLAND SAVINGS BANK
USA 1988
AD,D:Georgna Leaf
DF:Lintas Marketing Communications

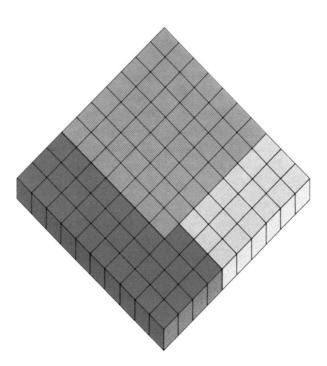

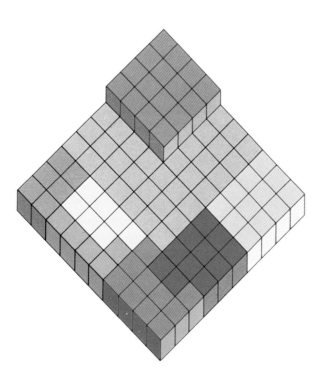

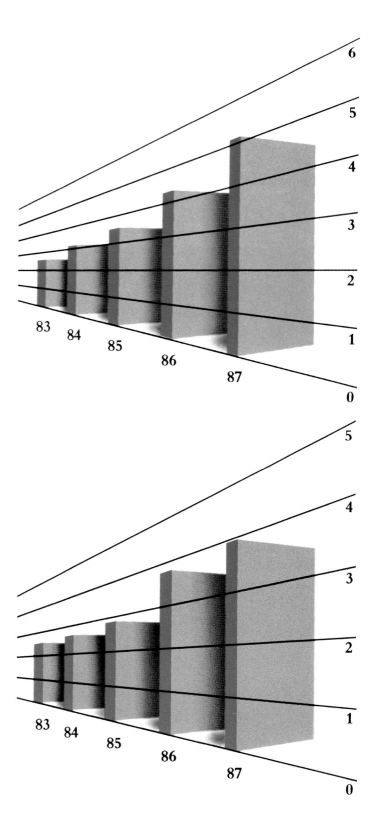

An alternative to the traditional pie chart.
There are 100 cubes in each graph with each cube representing one percent of the total.
From a Circus Circus Enterprises, Inc. annual report.
サーカス・サーカス・エンタープライズ社のアニュアルリポートより、
一般的に使用される円グラフに代わって100個のキューブを採用したグラフ。1個のキューブが1パーセントを表す。

Fiscal graphs from a Long Island Savings Bank annual report.
ロングアイランド貯蓄銀行のアニュアルリポートより、財務報告のためのグラフ。

STATISTICAL
TABLES & GRAPHS

CHARTS & SCORES

MAPS

ARCHITECTURAL
PLANS & DRAWINGS

INSTRUCTIONAL DIAGRAMS
FOR PRODUCTS

SCIENTIFIC
ILLUSTRATIONS

**CHAMPION INTERNATIONAL
CORPORATION**
USA 1985
CD:Jack Hough
AD,D:Tom Morin
I:Paul Giovanopoulos
DF:Jack Hough Associates, Inc.

LOCKHEED CORPORATION
USA 1990
CD,AD,D:Carl Seltzer
DF:Carl Seltzer Design Office

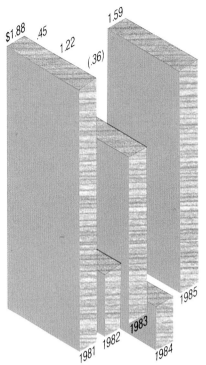

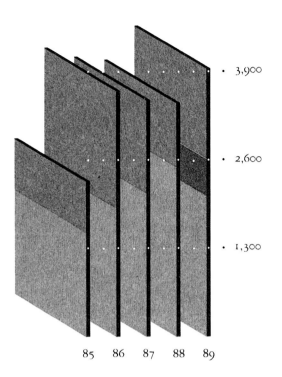

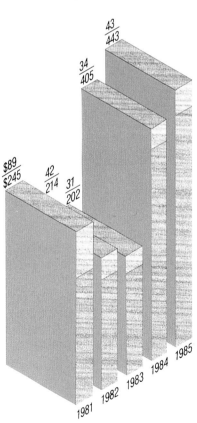

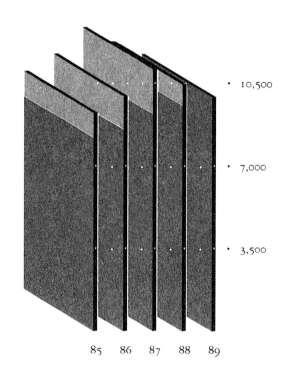

The Champion International annual report focused primarily
on the company's financial results. To make the report more interesting,
an artist was commissioned to draw the graphs with colored pencils.
チャンピオン・インターナショナル社のアニュアルリポートより、
色鉛筆を使用することでより印象を高めている財務関連のグラフ。

In these fiscal graphs, subtle but distinctive colors were
chosen to make each section of the bar clear.
From a Lockheed Corporation annual report.
ロッキード社のアニュアルリポートより、各棒の配色が微妙でありながら、
はっきりと判別できるよう工夫された財務関連のグラフ。

STATISTICAL
TABLES & GRAPHS

CHARTS & SCORES

MAPS

ARCHITECTURAL
PLANS & DRAWINGS

INSTRUCTIONAL DIAGRAMS
FOR PRODUCTS

SCIENTIFIC
ILLUSTRATIONS

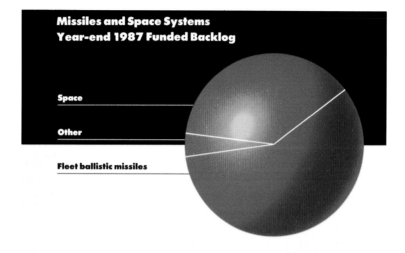

Missiles and Space Systems
Year-end 1987 Funded Backlog

Space

Other

Fleet ballistic missiles

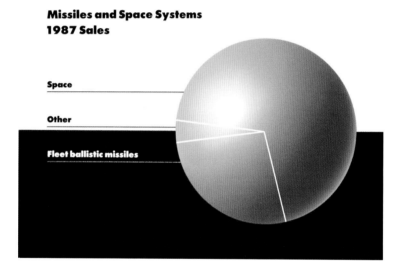

Missiles and Space Systems
1987 Sales

Space

Other

Fleet ballistic missiles

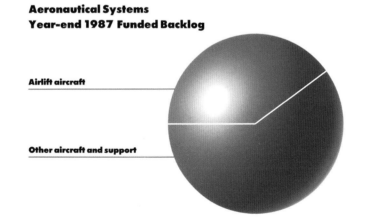

Aeronautical Systems
Year-end 1987 Funded Backlog

Airlift aircraft

Other aircraft and support

Graphs illustrating corporate operating state. From a Lockheed Corporation annual report.
ロッキード社のアニュアルリポートより、同社の経営状況に関するグラフ。

STATISTICAL
TABLES & GRAPHS

CHARTS & SCORES

MAPS

ARCHITECTURAL
PLANS & DRAWINGS

INSTRUCTIONAL DIAGRAMS
FOR PRODUCTS

SCIENTIFIC
ILLUSTRATIONS

MOUNTAIN BELL
(U.S. WEST COMMUNICATIONS)
USA 1985
CD,AD,D:Errol Beauchamp
P:Paul Peregrine
I:Martin Miller
DF:Beauchamp Group/Denver

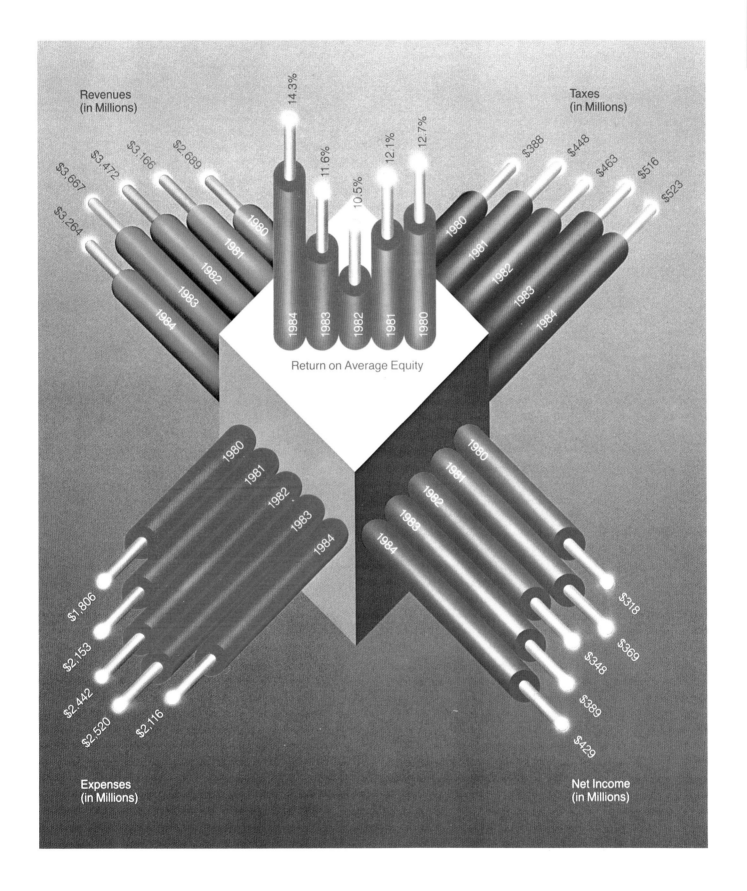

Diagram of selected financial data using fiber optic cable technology as the primary picture element. From a Mountain Bell annual report.
マウンテン・ベル社のアニュアルリポートより、光ファイバーケーブルをモチーフにして財務データを表したグラフ。

STATISTICAL
TABLES & GRAPHS

CHARTS & SCORES

MAPS

ARCHITECTURAL
PLANS & DRAWINGS

INSTRUCTIONAL DIAGRAMS
FOR PRODUCTS

SCIENTIFIC
ILLUSTRATIONS

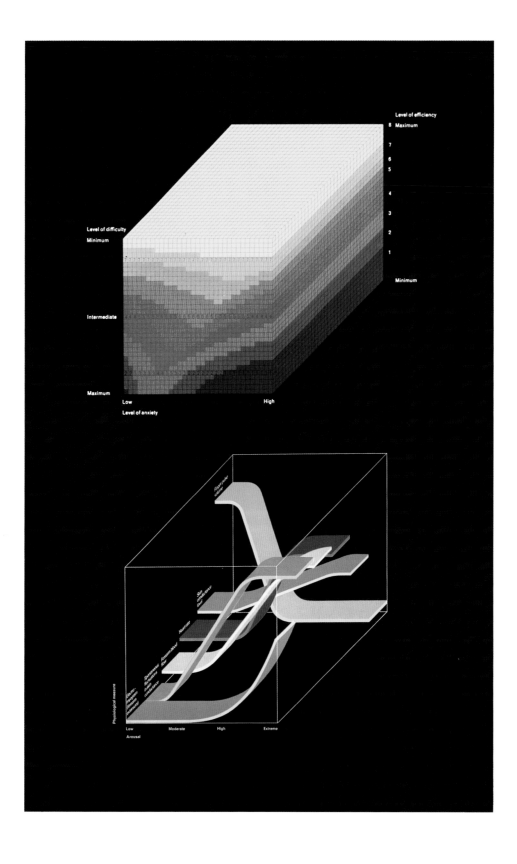

Illustration showing the effect anxiety has on the efficiency with which tasks are carried out.
From a Roche Products Limited promotional brochure for a new tranquillizer.
ロッシュ・プロダクツ社の新精神安定剤プロモーション用パンフレットより、
不安が遂行中の仕事に及ぼす影響を示すグラフ。

A physical profile of anxiety
- steepness of the curve indicates the speed of change taking place.
心理的不安が肉体に及ぼす影響のグラフ。曲線の傾斜が変化の速度を示している。

FEDERAL EXPRESS CORPORATION
USA 1989
CD:Stephen Ferrari
I:Javier Romero
DF:The Graphic Expression, Inc.

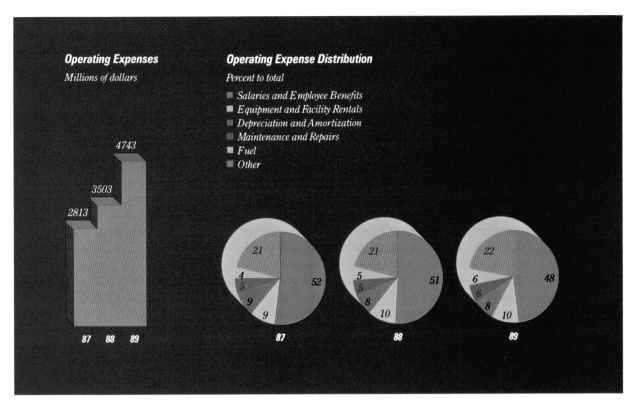

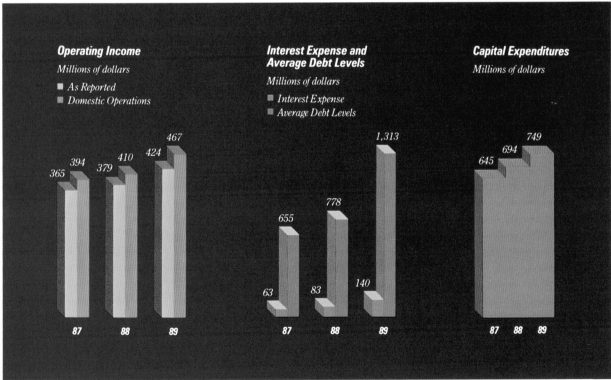

Graphs visualizing important financial measures which accompanied the management discussion and analysis of operating results.
From a Federal Express Corporation annual report.
フェデラル・エクスプレス社のアニュアルリポートより、経営論議や運営結果の分析にともなった重要な財政方策を視覚化するチャート。

STATISTICAL
TABLES & GRAPHS

CHARTS & SCORES

MAPS

ARCHITECTURAL
PLANS & DRAWINGS

INSTRUCTIONAL DIAGRAMS
FOR PRODUCTS

SCIENTIFIC
ILLUSTRATIONS

1977	1978	1979	1980	1981	1982	1983	1984	
								168
								164
								161
								153
								149
								145
								140
								135

Annual changes in the performance of the supermarket chain, Seiyu.
スーパーマーケット「西友」の年間業績推移図。

BOSTON UNIVERSITY MEDICAL CENTER
USA 1991
CD,D:Michael McPherson
I:Fred Lynch
DF:Corey McPherson Nash

HARVARD LAW SCHOOL
USA 1990
CD,AD,D:Michael McPherson
DF:Corey McPherson Nash

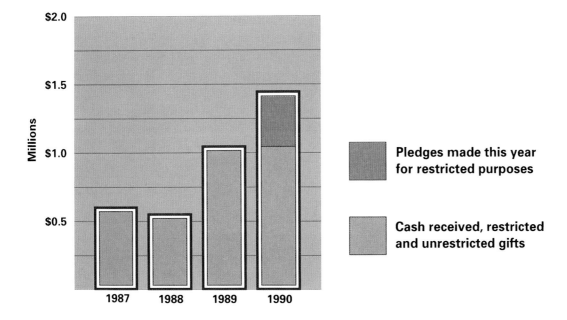

Pledges made this year
for restricted purposes

Cash received, restricted
and unrestricted gifts

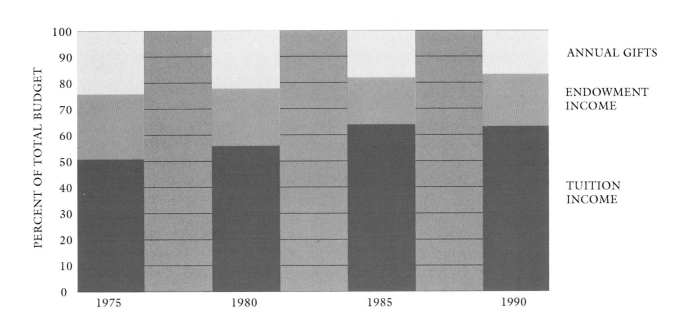

ANNUAL GIFTS

ENDOWMENT
INCOME

TUITION
INCOME

Graph of fund raising achievement.
From a Boston University Medical Center annual report.
ボストン大学医療センターのアニュアルリポートより、基金開発の成功を示すグラフ。

Graph of annual gifts and endowment income.
From a Harvard Law School promotional brochure.
ハーバード・ロウ・スクールのプロモーション用パンフレットより、年間の寄贈収益のグラフ。

STATISTICAL
TABLES &
GRAPHS

CHARTS & SCORES

MAPS

ARCHITECTURAL
PLANS & DRAWINGS

INSTRUCTIONAL DIAGRAMS
FOR PRODUCTS

SCIENTIFIC
ILLUSTRATIONS

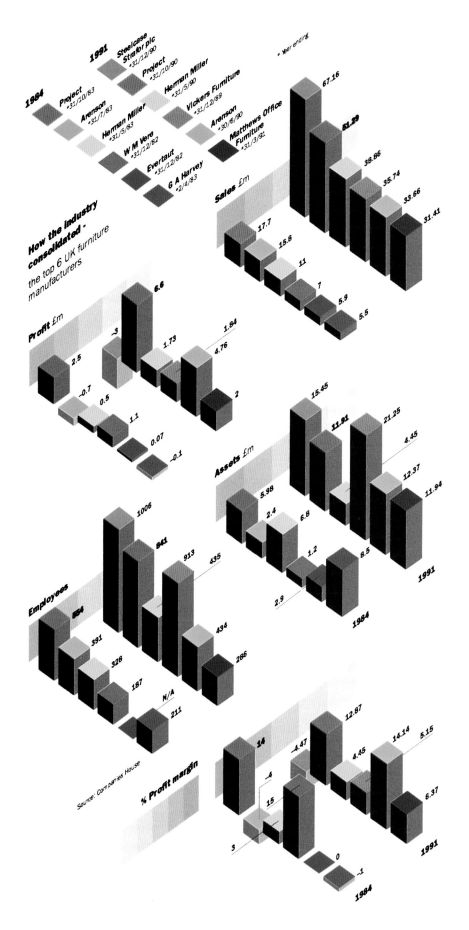

Graph of the top 6 UK furniture manufacturers showing how the industry consolidated. From Design magazine.
「デザインマガジン」より、英国の家具産業がいかに整理統合されてきたかを示す上位 6 社のグラフ。

STATISTICAL
TABLES & GRAPHS

CHARTS & SCORES

MAPS

ARCHITECTURAL
PLANS & DRAWINGS

INSTRUCTIONAL DIAGRAMS
FOR PRODUCTS

SCIENTIFIC
ILLUSTRATIONS

FORBES MAGAZINE
USA 1992
AD:Everett Halvorsen
D,I:Andy Christie

CENTOCOR, INC.
USA 1990
CD:Charles C. Cabot III
AD,D:Joel Katz
I:Stacey Lewis
DF:Katz Wheeler Design

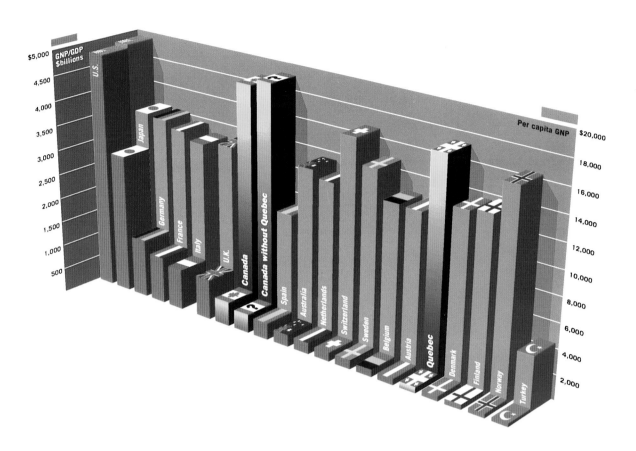

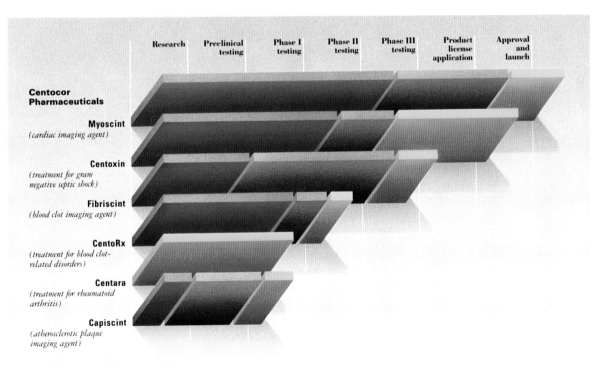

Graphs showing the GNP and GDP of various countries.
From an article on the present economic situation in Canada, in Forbes magazine.
「フォーブスマガジン」より、"カナダ経済の現況"の記事に使用された各国のGNPとGDPを表すグラフ。

Phase diagram showing the progressive development of pharmaceutical products.
From a Centocor, Inc. annual report.
セントコア社のアニュアルリポートより、医薬品の製造過程を示す段階図。

STATISTICAL
TABLES & GRAPHS

CHARTS & SCORES

MAPS

ARCHITECTURAL
PLANS & DRAWINGS

INSTRUCTIONAL DIAGRAMS
FOR PRODUCTS

SCIENTIFIC
ILLUSTRATIONS

1. BOSTON UNIVERSITY
MEDICAL CENTER
USA 1992
CD,AD,D:Michael McPherson
DF:Corey McPherson Nash

2. UNOCAL CORPORATION
USA 1986
CD,AD,I:Ray Engle
D,I:Debra Hampton
DF:Ray Engle & Associates

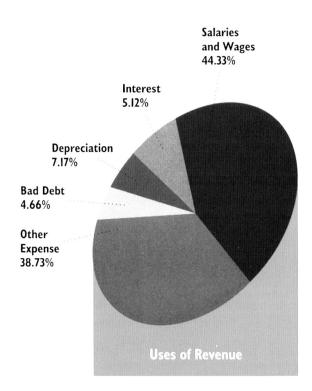

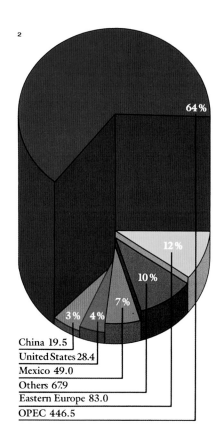

1. Graphs of 1991 Funds by Donor Source and Uses of Revenue.
From a Boston University Medical Center annual report.
ボストン大学医療センターのアニュアルリポートより、
1991年度基金源、及び歳入の使途についてのグラフ。

2. Graph showing estimated world crude oil reserves.
From a magazine article on America's energy future.
"アメリカのエネルギー事情の今後"についての雑誌記事より、
全世界の原油推定埋蔵量を表すグラフ。

STATISTICAL
TABLES & GRAPHS

CHARTS & SCORES

MAPS

ARCHITECTURAL
PLANS & DRAWINGS

SCIENTIFIC
INSTRUCTIONAL DIAGRAMS
FOR PRODUCTS

SCIENTIFIC
ILLUSTRATIONS

1. HARVARD LAW SCHOOL
USA 1990
CD,AD,D:Michael McPherson
DF:Corey McPherson Nash

**2. FREMONT GENERAL
CORPORATION**
USA 1991
CD,AD,D:Carl Seltzer
D:Chris Wevers
DF:Carl Seltzer Design Office

**3. GREAT WESTERN FINANCIAL
CORPORATION**
USA 1992
CD,AD,D:Carl Seltzer
D:Luis Alvarado
DF:Carl Seltzer Design Office

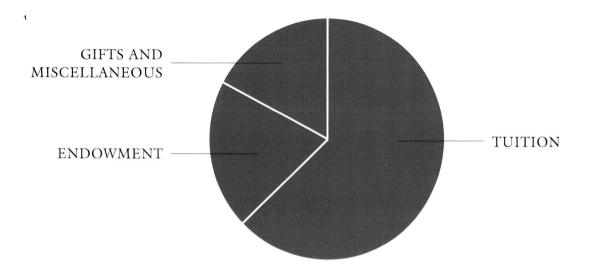

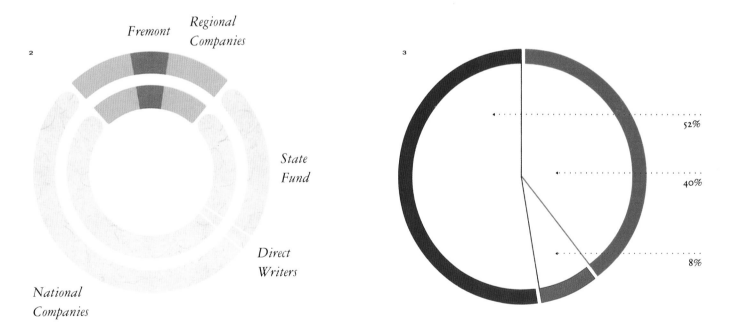

1. Graph of Income
from a Harvard Law School promotional brochure.
ハーバード・ロウ・スクールの
プロモーション用パンフレットより、収益のグラフ。

2. Graph clearly showing the company's percentage of the
California market in worker's compensation insurance.
From a Fremont General Corporation annual report.
フリーモント・ジェネラル社のアニュアルリポートより、
勤労者保証保険のカリフォルニア・マーケットにおける
同社の占める割合を示したグラフ。

3. Graph showing new adjustment rate mortgages.
The bright colors and legible type add to the overall
'upbeat' feeling. From a Great Western Financial
Corporation annual report.
グレートウエスタン・ファイナンシャル社の
アニュアルリポートより、明るい配色で軽快に表現された
新調整金利抵当に関するグラフ。

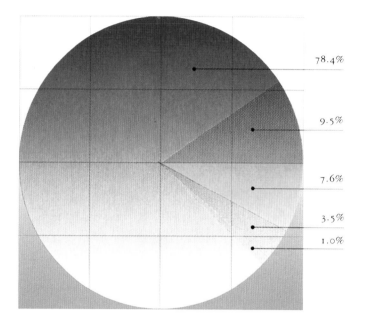

78.4%

9.5%

7.6%

3.5%

1.0%

These bar, pie, line and mountain financial graphs were all designed to work together with subtle gradations in both the backgrounds and foregrounds.
From a Great Western Financial Corporation annual report.
グレートウエスタン・ファイナンシャル社のアニュアルリポートより、デザインに微妙なグラデーションを採用し、印象的に表現された財務関連のグラフ。

STATISTICAL
TABLES & GRAPHS

CHARTS & SCORES

MAPS

ARCHITECTURAL
PLANS & DRAWINGS

INSTRUCTIONAL DIAGRAMS
FOR PRODUCTS

SCIENTIFIC
ILLUSTRATIONS

STAR PAGING
(INTERNATIONAL HOLDING)LIMITED
HONG KONG 1992
CD,AD:Kan Tai-Keung
AD:Clement Yick Tat Wa
D:Janny Lee Yin Wa
DF:Kan Tai-Keung Design & Associates Ltd.

THE WCRS GROUP PLC
ENGLAND
AD:Amanda Tatham
D,I:Gill Davies
DF:Tatham Pearce Ltd.

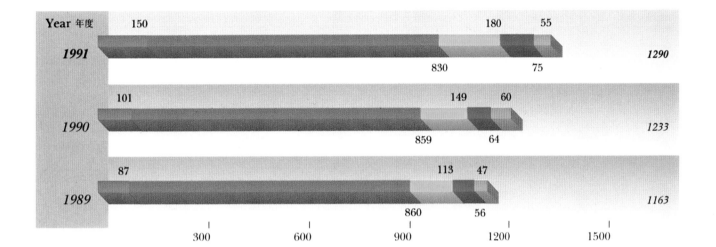

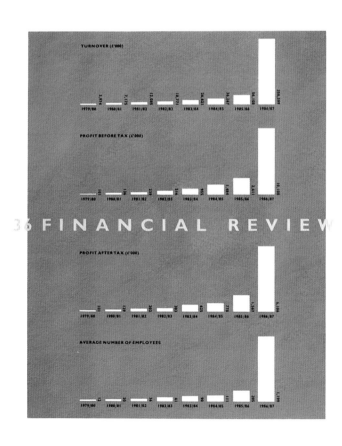

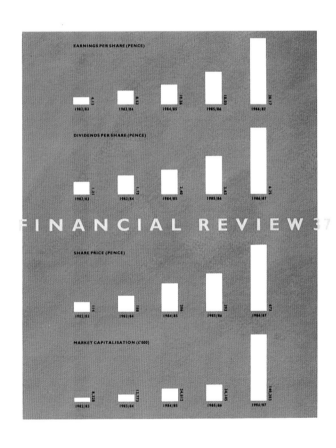

Graph showing the number of subscribers. From Star Paging Ltd. annual report.
スター・ページング社のアニュアルリポートより、労働者数を表したグラフ。

Financial review from the WCRS Group's annual report.
WCRSグループのアニュアルリポートより、財務評論のためのグラフ。

STATISTICAL
TABLES & GRAPHS

CHARTS & SCORES

MAPS

ARCHITECTURAL
PLANS & DRAWINGS

INSTRUCTIONAL DIAGRAMS
FOR PRODUCTS

SCIENTIFIC
ILLUSTRATIONS

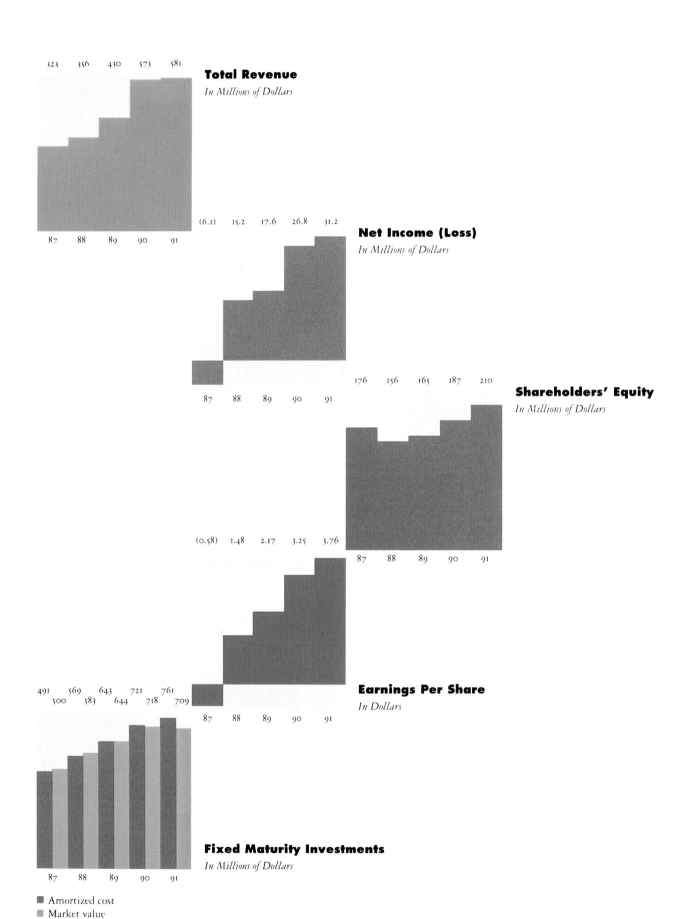

Total Revenue
In Millions of Dollars

323 356 430 573 581
87 88 89 90 91

Net Income (Loss)
In Millions of Dollars

(6.1) 15.2 17.6 26.8 31.2
87 88 89 90 91

Shareholders' Equity
In Millions of Dollars

176 156 165 187 210
87 88 89 90 91

Earnings Per Share
In Dollars

(0.58) 1.48 2.17 3.25 3.76
87 88 89 90 91

Fixed Maturity Investments
In Millions of Dollars

491 569 643 721 761
500 583 644 718 709
87 88 89 90 91

■ Amortized cost
■ Market value

The design and colors used in these graphs are coordinated with the photos and other elements in the report. From a Fremont General Corporation annual report.
フリーモント・ジェネラル社のアニュアルリポートより、本文中の写真などの要素と調和がとれるよう留意して制作された財務関連のグラフ。

STATISTICAL
TABLES & GRAPHS

CHARTS & SCORES

MAPS

ARCHITECTURAL
PLANS & DRAWINGS

INSTRUCTIONAL DIAGRAMS
FOR PRODUCTS

SCIENTIFIC
ILLUSTRATIONS

Graphs illustrating the financial position of a real estate company. From a Kuwait Real Estate Company annual report.

クウェート不動産会社のアニュアルリポートより、同社の財政状態を表すグラフ。

STATISTICAL
TABLES & GRAPHS

CHARTS & SCORES

MAPS

ARCHITECTURAL
PLANS & DRAWINGS

INSTRUCTIONAL DIAGRAMS
FOR PRODUCTS

SCIENTIFIC
ILLUSTRATIONS

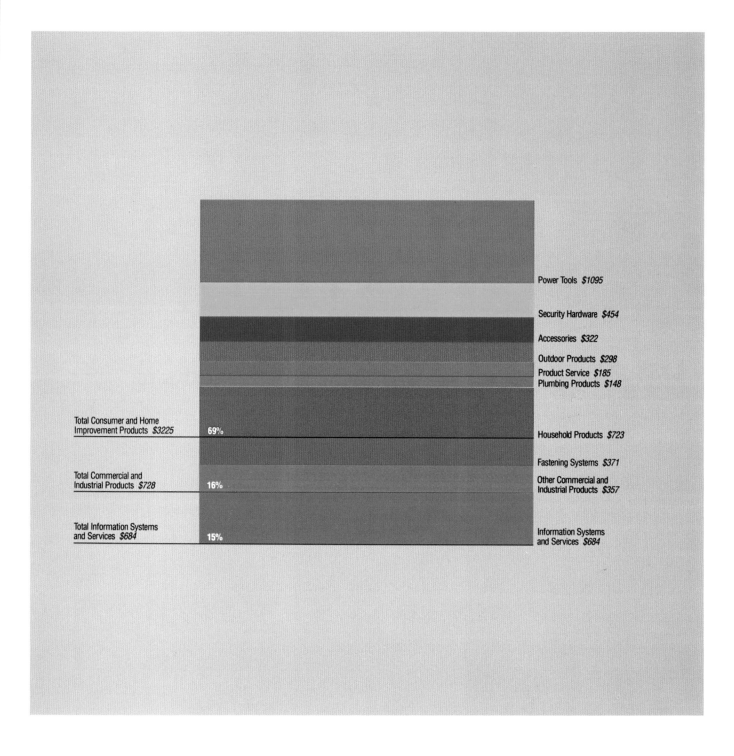

Power Tools *$1095*

Security Hardware *$454*

Accessories *$322*

Outdoor Products *$298*

Product Service *$185*
Plumbing Products *$148*

Total Consumer and Home
Improvement Products *$3225*   **69%**   Household Products *$723*

Fastening Systems *$371*

Total Commercial and
Industrial Products *$728*   **16%**   Other Commercial and
Industrial Products *$357*

Total Information Systems
and Services *$684*   **15%**   Information Systems
and Services *$684*

Black & Decker 1991 worldwide revenues, in millions of dollars. From an annual report.
アニュアルリポートより、1991年度ブラック&デッカー社の全世界からの蔵入を表したグラフ。

STATISTICAL
TABLES & GRAPHS

CHARTS & SCORES

MAPS

ARCHITECTURAL
PLANS & DRAWINGS

INSTRUCTIONAL DIAGRAMS
FOR PRODUCTS

SCIENTIFIC
ILLUSTRATIONS

LOCKHEED CORPORATION
USA 1988
CD,AD,D:Carl Seltzer
DF:Carl Seltzer Design Office

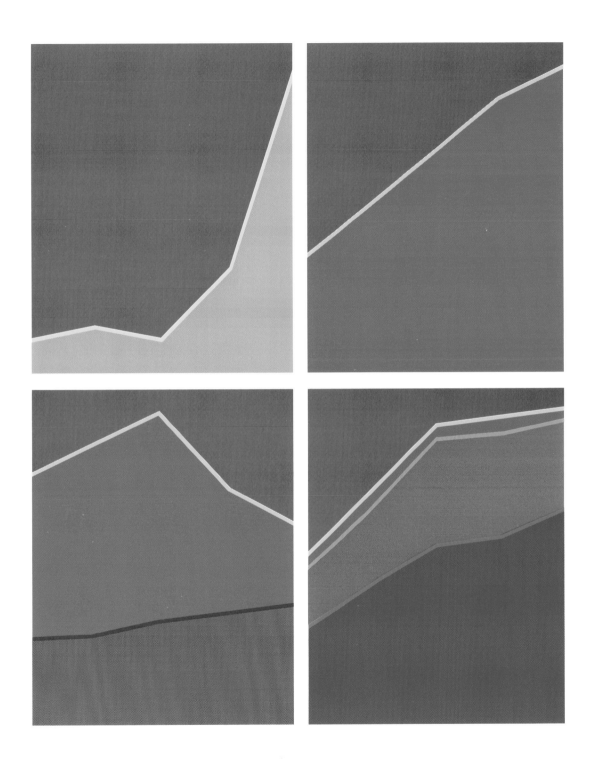

Fiscal graphs as part of the overall design of the color spread. From a Lockheed Corporation annual report.
ロッキード社のアニュアルリポートより、配色に工夫して表現した財務に関するグラフ。

STATISTICAL
TABLES & GRAPHS

CHARTS & SCORES

MAPS

ARCHITECTURAL
PLANS & DRAWINGS

INSTRUCTIONAL DIAGRAMS
FOR PRODUCTS

SCIENTIFIC
ILLUSTRATIONS

MEDICAL INTER-INSURANCE EXCHANGE
OF NEW JERSEY
USA 1992
AD:Roger Cook/Don Shanosky
D:Cathryn L. Cook
DF:Cook and Shanosky Associates, Inc.

Four medical insurance graphs. From a Medical Inter-Insurance Exchange annual report.
メディカル・インターインシュランス・エスクチェンジ社のアニュアルリポートより、医療保険に関する4つのグラフ。

JANNOCK LIMITED
CANADA 1992
AD,D:Roslyn Eskind
D:Sandi King
I:Gary Mansbridge
DF:Eskind Waddell

STATISTICAL
TABLES & GRAPHS

CHARTS & SCORES

MAPS

ARCHITECTURAL
PLANS & DRAWINGS

INSTRUCTIONAL DIAGRAMS
FOR PRODUCTS

SCIENTIFIC
ILLUSTRATIONS

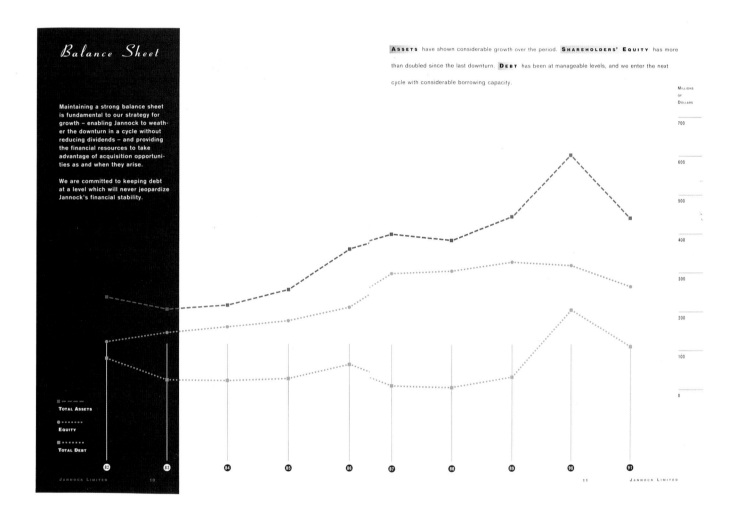

Graph illustrating the company's long-term growth record issued during a down-turn cycle. From a Jannock Limited annual report.
ジャノック社のアニュアルリポートより、不景気時におけるクライアントの長期的な成長を表すグラフ。

STATISTICAL
TABLES &
GRAPHS

CHARTS & SCORES

MAPS

ARCHITECTURAL
PLANS & DRAWINGS

INSTRUCTIONAL DIAGRAMS
FOR PRODUCTS

SCIENTIFIC
ILLUSTRATIONS

CENTOCOR, INC.
USA 1987
CD:Charles C. Cabot III
AD,D:Joel Katz
DF:Katz Wheeler Design

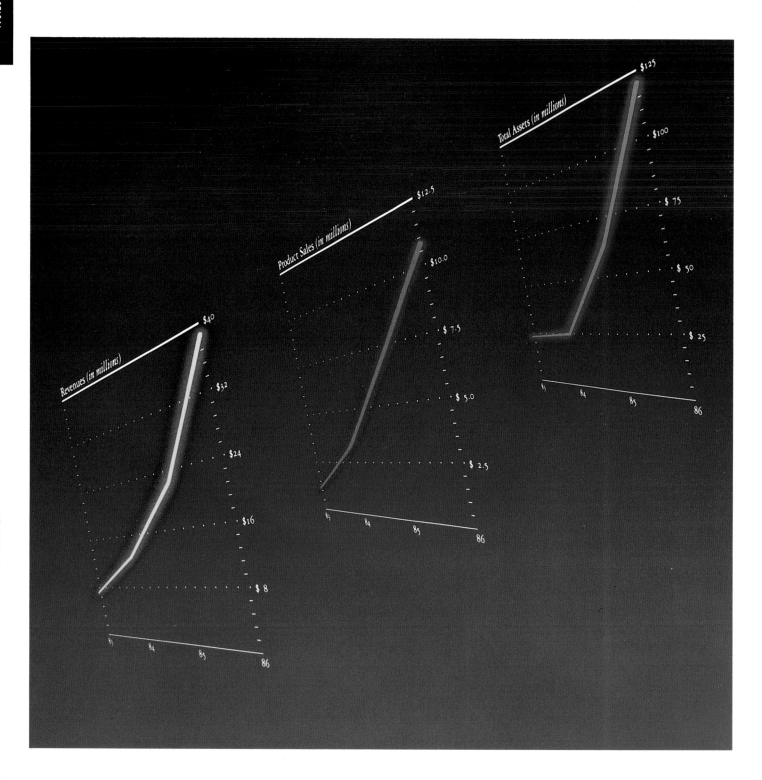

Graph of financial highlights. From a Centocor, Inc. annual report.
セントコア社のアニュアルリポートより、強調して見せたい財務データのグラフ。

STATISTICAL
TABLES & GRAPHS

CHARTS & SCORES

MAPS

ARCHITECTURAL
PLANS & DRAWINGS

INSTRUCTIONAL DIAGRAMS
FOR PRODUCTS

SCIENTIFIC
ILLUSTRATIONS

1. UNOCAL CORPORATION
USA 1986
CD,AD,I:Ray Engle
D,I:Debra Hampton
DF:Ray Engle & Associates

2. PERMANENT TRUSTEE COMPANY LIMITED
AUSTRALIA 1989
CD,AD:Raymond Bennett
D,I:Joanne Delves
DF:Raymond Bennett Design

3. BAKER HUGHES INCORPORATED
USA 1992
CD:Ron Jefferies
D,I:Scott Lambert
DF:The Jefferies Association

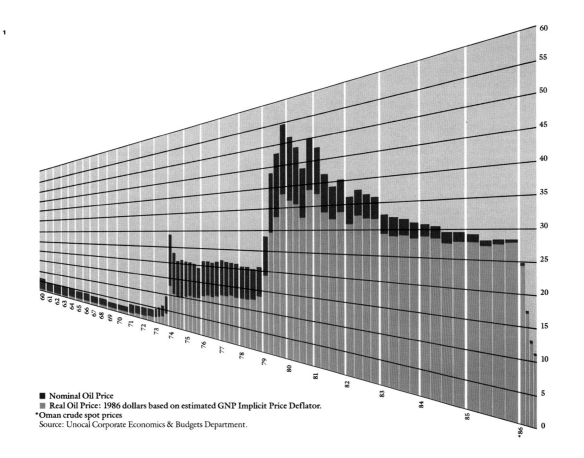

1

■ Nominal Oil Price
■ Real Oil Price: 1986 dollars based on estimated GNP Implicit Price Deflator.
*Oman crude spot prices
Source: Unocal Corporate Economics & Budgets Department.

2

Shareholders' Funds
$ million

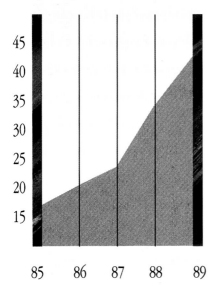

3

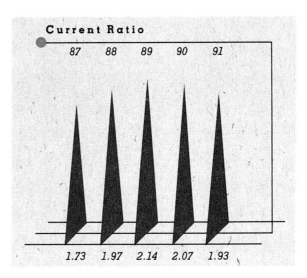

1. Graph showing crude oil spot prices.
From a magazine article on America's energy future.
"アメリカのエネルギー事情の今後"についての雑誌記事より、
原油スポット価格を示したグラフ。

2. Graph showing the growth in shareholders' funds
over five years. From a Permanent Trustee
Company Limited annual report.
パーマネント・トラスティー社のアニュアルリポートより、
5カ年内の自己資本の成長ぶりを示すグラフ。

3. Graph of current ratio created to look inspiring during
a down year, hence the broad bases and pointed tops
of the bars. From a Baker Hughes Inc. annual report.
ベーカー・ヒューズ社のアニュアルリポートより、景気下降期を
励ますように楽しい要素を盛り込んだ流動比率のグラフ。

STATISTICAL
TABLES & GRAPHS

CHARTS & SCORES

MAPS

ARCHITECTURAL
PLANS & DRAWINGS

INSTRUCTIONAL DIAGRAMS
FOR PRODUCTS

SCIENTIFIC
ILLUSTRATIONS

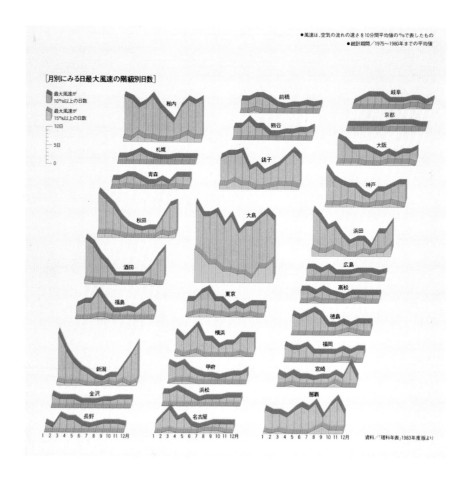

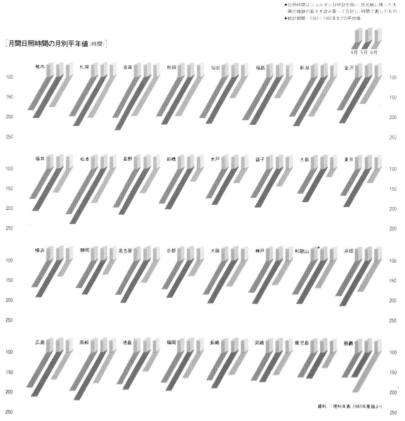

Graph showing meteorological data. Appeared on the cover of the architectural magazine, "Building".

建築専門誌「施工」の表紙を飾る、気象データのグラフ。

STATISTICAL
TABLES & GRAPHS

CHARTS & SCORES

MAPS

ARCHITECTURAL
PLANS & DRAWINGS

INSTRUCTIONAL DIAGRAMS
FOR PRODUCTS

SCIENTIFIC
ILLUSTRATIONS

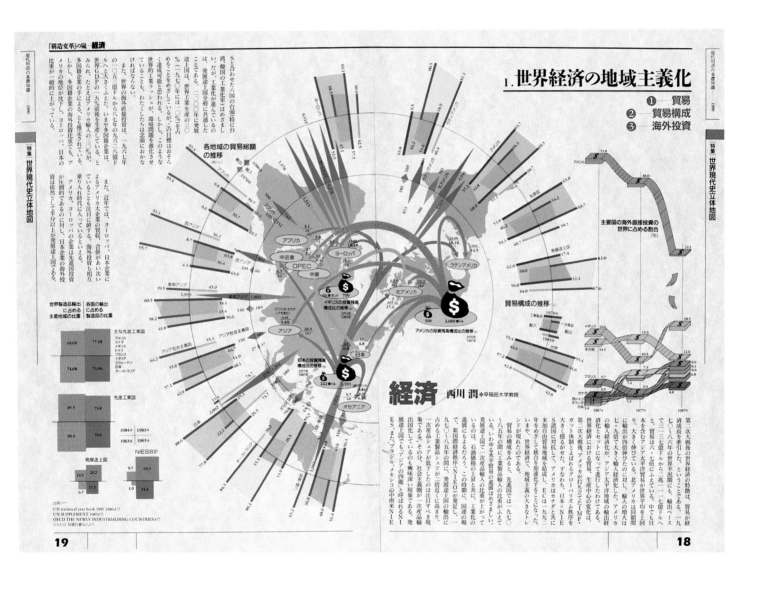

Graph showing "the Regionalization of the Global Economy". From an article in the terminology dictionary, "Basic Knowledge of Contemporary Terminology".
用語辞典「現代用語の基礎知識」の記事より、"世界経済の地域主義化"という題材を効果的に表現するグラフ。

STATISTICAL
TABLES & GRAPHS

CHARTS & SCORES

MAPS

ARCHITECTURAL
PLANS & DRAWINGS

INSTRUCTIONAL DIAGRAMS
FOR PRODUCTS

SCIENTIFIC
ILLUSTRATIONS

SEIYU CO., LTD.
JAPAN 1976
CD, AD, D: Tetsuya Ohta

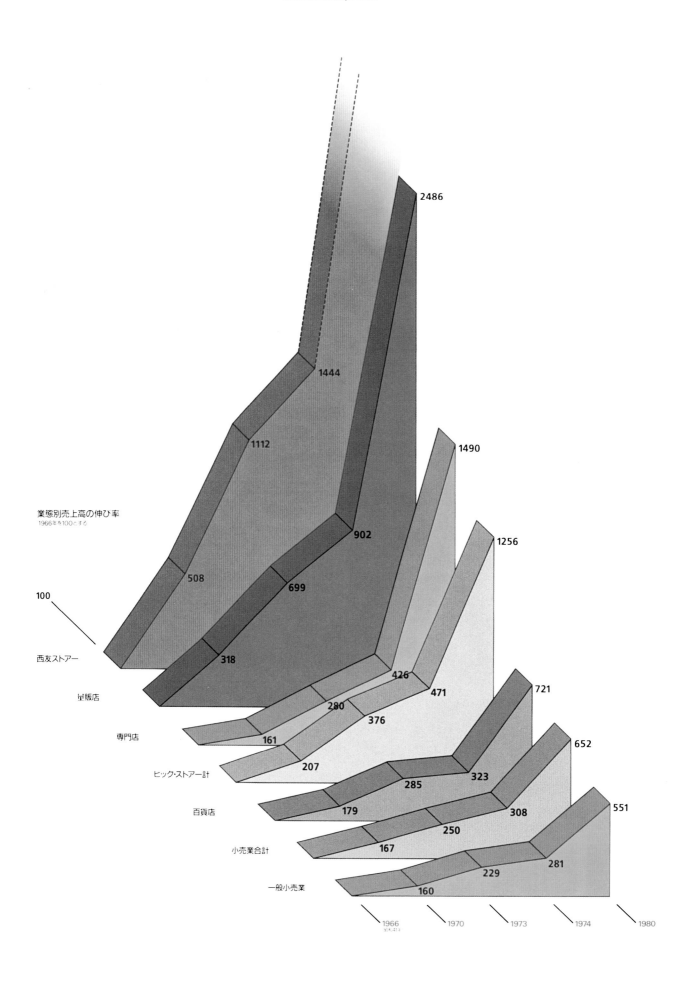

業態別売上高の伸び率
1966年を100とする

100

西友ストアー

量販店

専門店

ビック・ストアー計

百貨店

小売業合計

一般小売業

2486
1490
1256
1444
1112
902
721
699
652
551
508
471
426
376
323
318
308
285
281
280
250
229
207
179
167
161
160

1966
1970
1973
1974
1980

Comparison of performance between the supermarket chain Seiyu and other retailers.
スーパーマーケット「西友」の他小売業との業績比較図。

STATISTICAL
TABLES & GRAPHS

CHARTS & SCORES

MAPS

ARCHITECTURAL
PLANS & DRAWINGS

INSTRUCTIONAL DIAGRAMS
FOR PRODUCTS

SCIENTIFIC
ILLUSTRATIONS

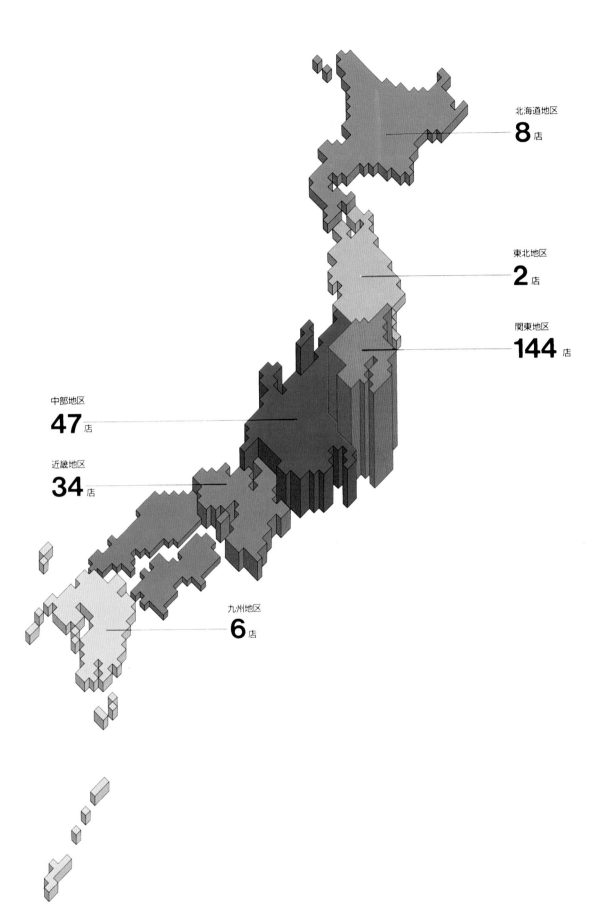

北海道地区
8店

東北地区
2店

関東地区
144店

中部地区
47店

近畿地区
34店

九州地区
6店

Graph showing the number of stores by region of the supermarket chain, Seiyu.
スーパーマーケット「西友」の地域別店舗数グラフ。

STATISTICAL
TABLES & GRAPHS

CHARTS & SCORES

MAPS

ARCHITECTURAL
PLANS & DRAWINGS

INSTRUCTIONAL DIAGRAMS
FOR PRODUCTS

SCIENTIFIC
ILLUSTRATIONS

ASSURANCEFORENINGEN
GARD-GJENSIDIG
ENGLAND 1988
CD,AD,D:David Pearce
I:Grundy Northedge
DF:Tatham Pearce

Table H. Nature of claims (paid claims, gross)

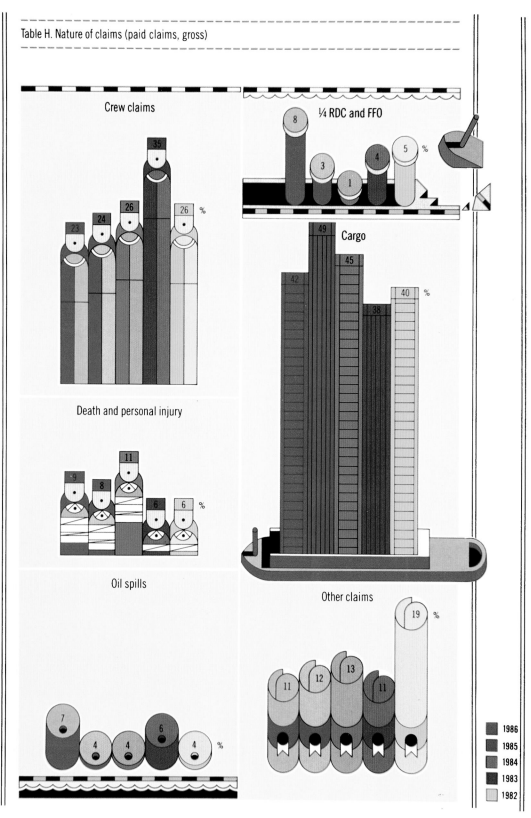

Crew claims

Death and personal injury

Oil spills

¼ RDC and FFO

Cargo

Other claims

1986	
1985	
1984	
1983	
1982	

Table F. Balances available to meet outstanding

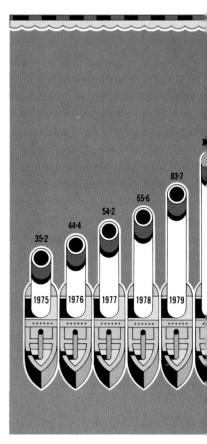

to USD 10.4 million (USD 12.2 million). The increas
in funds since 1975 is illustrated in Table F.

As indicated in Note 7 to the Accounts, the funds
available contain a prudent reserve in excess of t
funds needed to meet known and unreported
claims. Unlimited liability, which has been a
cornerstone of the International Group's policy,
places potentially enormous burdens on clubs an
individual shipowners. The Association, therefore,
considers it appropriate that a significant reserve
should be retained against the possibility of the
Association being called upon to meet its share of
major catastrophe, as well as to meet other
potential liabilities outlined in Note 7.

CHARTS & SCORES

MAPS

ARCHITECTURAL
PLANS & DRAWINGS

INSTRUCTIONAL DIAGRAMS
FOR PRODUCTS

SCIENTIFIC
ILLUSTRATIONS

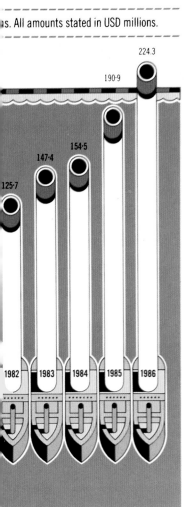

s. All amounts stated in USD millions.

224.3

190·9

154·5

147·4

125·7

1982 1983 1984 1985 1986

...ropriateness of the level of this reserve is
...der constant review. Given the lack of any
...e in general premium ratings for the last five
...nd the recent low or zero rate of contribution,
...kely that, unless investment returns remain
...t levels, this reserve will continue to
...e.

CHANGES IN COVER

...were two significant Rule changes at the
...t of the 1987 policy year and two further
...nges in cover, which did not require a change
...ules.

Table E. Estimated cost of notified Pool claims, as
estimated at the following numbers of years after
the start of each policy year (in USD millions).

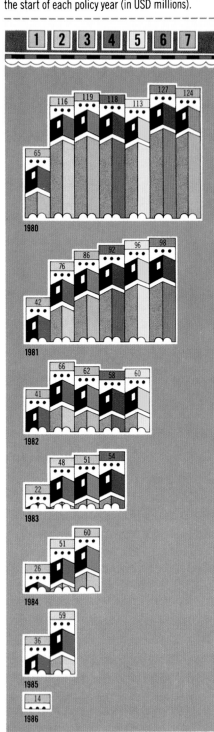

1 2 3 4 5 6 7

1980 — 65, 116, 119, 118, 113, 127, 124

1981 — 42, 76, 86, 92, 96, 98

1982 — 41, 66, 62, 58, 60

1983 — 22, 48, 51, 54

1984 — 26, 51, 60

1985 — 36, 59

1986 — 14

Table B. Age of entered vessels
20th February, 1987.

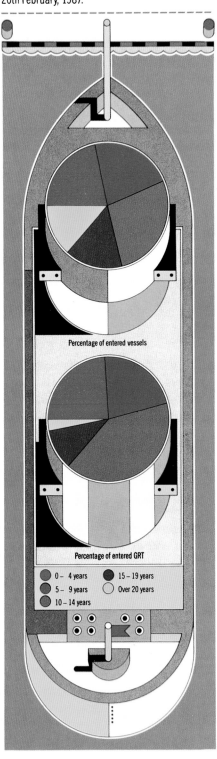

Percentage of entered vessels

Percentage of entered GRT

0 – 4 years
5 – 9 years
10 – 14 years
15 – 19 years
Over 20 years

Diagrams for the review section of Assuranceforeningen Gard's Report & Accounts illustrating statistical information relevant to the company and industry.
アシュランスフォレニンゲン・ガード社のアニュアルリポートより、同社の決算報告と関連業界の統計データを表したグラフ。

STATISTICAL
TABLES & GRAPHS

CHARTS & SCORES

MAPS

ARCHITECTURAL
PLANS & DRAWINGS

INSTRUCTIONAL DIAGRAMS
FOR PRODUCTS

SCIENTIFIC
ILLUSTRATIONS

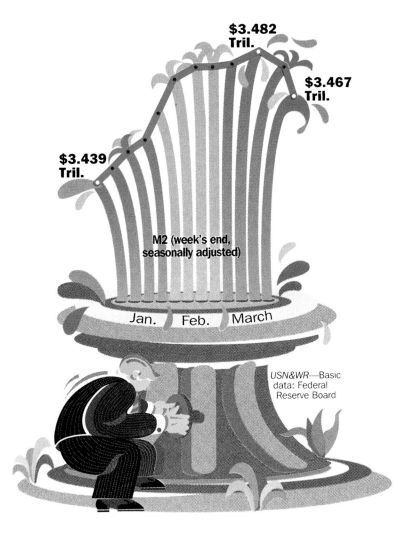

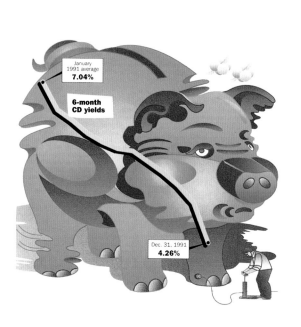

National revenue graph and economic index graph. From U.S. News & World Report magazine.
「USニュース&ワールド・リポートマガジン」より、国家財源および経済指標を表す2つのグラフ。

STATISTICAL TABLES & GRAPHS

CHARTS & SCORES

MAPS

ARCHITECTURAL PLANS & DRAWINGS

INSTRUCTIONAL DIAGRAMS FOR PRODUCTS

SCIENTIFIC ILLUSTRATIONS

TREE TOP, INC.

USA 1987

AD,D:John Hornall

D:Luann Bice

I:Bruce Hale

DF:Hornall Anderson Design Works

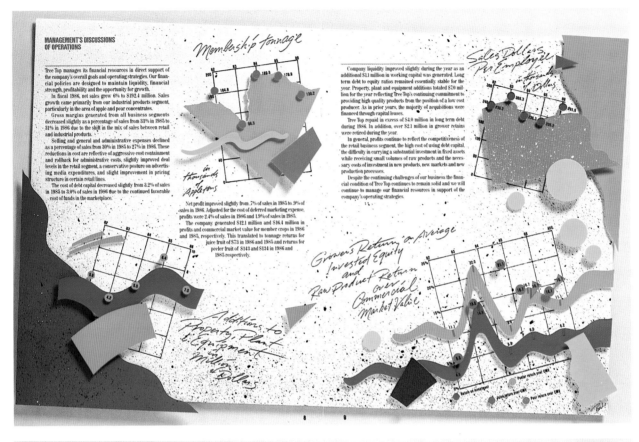

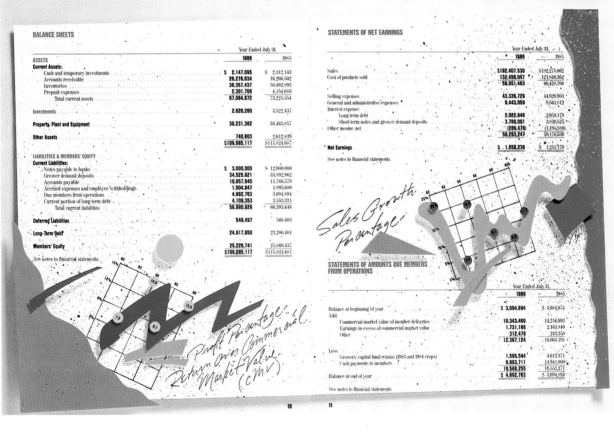

Graphs illustrating performance of an apple growers' co-op. From a Tree Top, Inc. annual report.

ツリートップ社のアニュアルリポートより、リンゴ共同農家組合の業務成績を表したグラフ。

CAMPAIGN MAGAZINE
ENGLAND 1986,1987
D,I:Peter Grundy/Tilly Northedge
DF:Grundy & Northedge

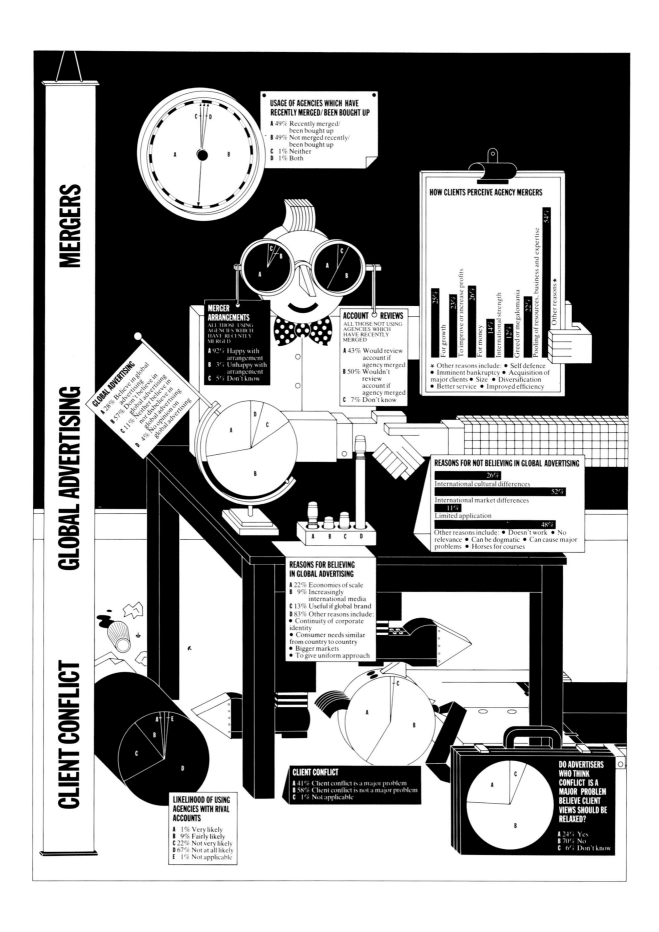

Statistical diagram from the London ad agency magazine, Campaign.
広告会社向けの専門誌「キャンペーン」に掲載された統計図。

COMMERCIAL BANK OF KUWAIT
ENGLAND 1979
CD,AD,D:Alan Fletcher
D:Paul Anthony
I:Michael Foreman
DF:Pentagram Design Ltd.

STATISTICAL
TABLES & GRAPHS

CHARTS & SCORES

MAPS

ARCHITECTURAL
PLANS & DRAWINGS

INSTRUCTIONAL DIAGRAMS
FOR PRODUCTS

SCIENTIFIC
ILLUSTRATIONS

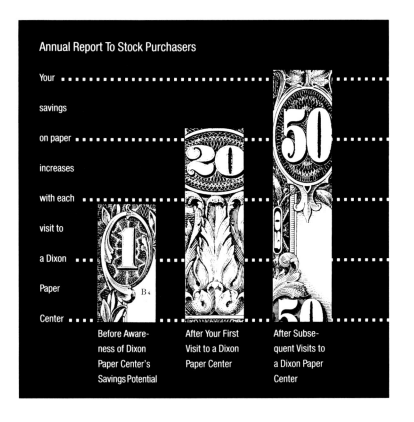

Graph showing financial advantage of purchasing Dixon Paper Centers stocks.
From an advertisement carried in the "Colorado Creative" directory.
名簿録「コロラド・クリエイティブ」に掲載された広告より、
ディクソン・ペーパーセンター社の株を購入した際の利点を伝えるグラフ。

Statistical diagram from a Commercial Bank of Kuwait annual report.
クウェート商業銀行のアニュアルリポートより、統計図表。

STATISTICAL
TABLES & GRAPHS

CHARTS & SCORES

MAPS

ARCHITECTURAL
PLANS & DRAWINGS

INSTRUCTIONAL DIAGRAMS
FOR PRODUCTS

SCIENTIFIC
ILLUSTRATIONS

COLLAGEN CORPORATION
USA 1991
CD,AD,D:Earl Gee
D:Fani Chung
P:Geoffrey Nelson
DF:Earl Gee Design

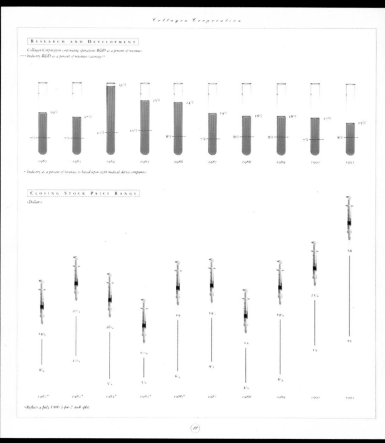

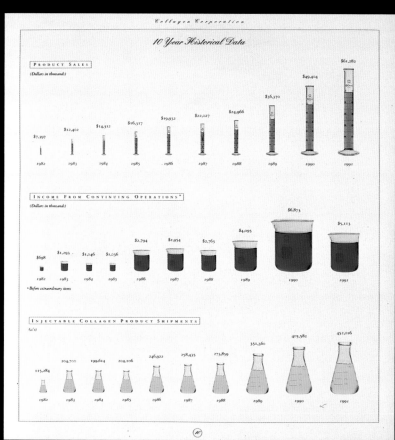

Graphs of the biomedical company's ten-year financial milestones using common scientific measuring devices as picture elements. From a Collagen Corporation annual report.

生物医学を扱う企業「コラーゲン社」のアニュアルリポートより、研究用の測定用器具をモチーフに同社の過去10年間における財政上重要な出来事を表したグラフ。

STATISTICAL
TABLES & GRAPHS

CHARTS & SCORES

MAPS

ARCHITECTURAL
PLANS & DRAWINGS

INSTRUCTIONAL DIAGRAMS
FOR PRODUCTS

SCIENTIFIC
ILLUSTRATIONS

AIRBORNE EXPRESS
USA 1992
AD,D:Julia LaPine
D:John Hornall/Heidi Hatlestad
P:Tom Collicott
I,DF:Hornall Anderson Design Works

ACTIVE
CUSTOMER
BASE

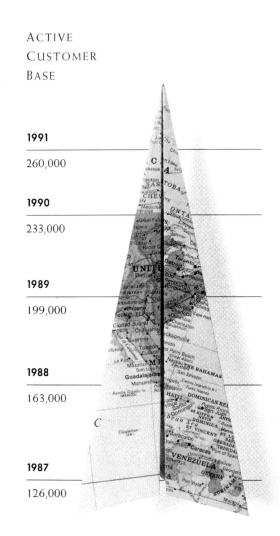

1991
260,000

1990
233,000

1989
199,000

1988
163,000

1987
126,000

TOTAL SHIPMENTS
(*Thousands*)

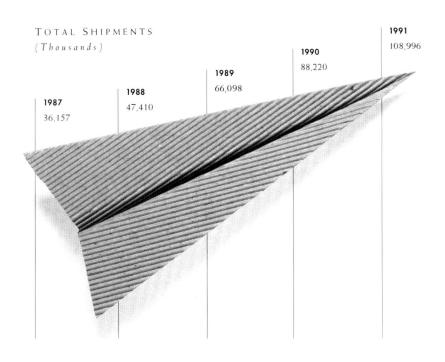

1987
36,157

1988
47,410

1989
66,098

1990
88,220

1991
108,996

In these graphs the paper airplanes are symbolic of Airborne Express' worldwide customer base and total shipments. From an Airborne Express annual report.
エアボーン・エクスプレス社を象徴する紙飛行機をモチーフに同社の全世界における顧客数、及び年間輸送量を表したグラフ。

Sauce (and Application) of Funds

From Shareholder's, share premium
and undistributed profits.
HK$458,534.80

We owe
HK$22,679.47

Profits from share dealings,
dividends, usury and currency
manipulations.
HK$118,976.07

Godown charges etc.
(HK$11,219.90)

We are owed
(HK$531.69)

Tax Man's slice.
(HK$15,183.00)

Meat by-products derived from
animals, potato starch, sodium
caseinate, polyphosphates,
sodium ascorbate, sodium
nitrite and colouring matters.
Inspected and passed by the
Argentine Secretariate of State
for Agriculture and Live-stock.

Investments in paper, bullion,
land and the negotiable contents
of the Cough Pastille Tin.
(HK$573,255.75)

Pie graph of source and application of funds. From a TGIF Investments Ltd. annual report.
TGIFインベストメンツ社のアニュアルリポートより、資産の源泉、及び使途や運用の割合を表す円グラフ。

SIZZLER RESTAURANTS INTERNATIONAL INC.
USA 1988
CD,AD:Don Kano
D:Adam Shanosky
P:Art Montes de Oca
DF:Kano Design Group

STATISTICAL TABLES & GRAPHS

CHARTS & SCORES

MAPS

ARCHITECTURAL PLANS & DRAWINGS

INSTRUCTIONAL DIAGRAMS FOR PRODUCTS

SCIENTIFIC ILLUSTRATIONS

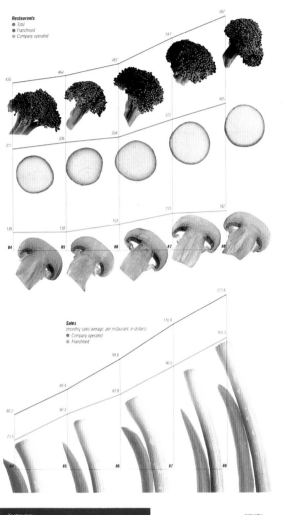

Restaurants
- Total
- Franchised
- Company operated

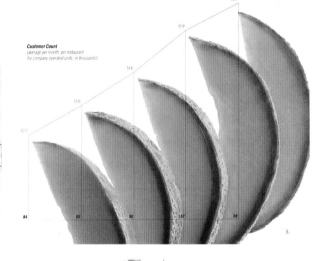

Customer Count
(average per month, per restaurant for company operated units, in thousands)

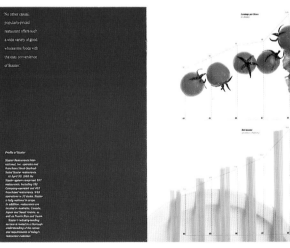

Sales
(monthly sales average, per restaurant, in dollars)
- Company operated
- Franchised

buging and retiring approximately 700,000 shares at an average price of $15.10. Employing the same rationale, in March 1988 our Board authorized a third repurchase of up to 1.7 million shares.

Looking forward, our continuing growth will largely reflect our thorough understanding of the casual dining category — the fastest growing dining segment. We have positioned Sizzler to match America's mood for lighter, fresher tastes as we continue to address the evolving needs of our consumer. The depth of this understanding is perhaps best illustrated by our solid uptrend in customer counts, which rose 6% per store over prior year. In contrast, average industry customer counts, at best, remain flat.

In today's marketplace, the restaurant offering the highest quality products, facilities and services, while presenting the right imagery and best perception of value, will emerge the industry winner. We think Sizzler is that concept.

During fiscal 1988 Sizzler Executive Vice President Michael M. Minchin, Jr. was elected to the Company's Board. His contributions in the areas of marketing, product development and advertising have been significant.

The contributions of our employees and franchisees for the year were no less stellar, as success in the face of a somewhat sluggish industry is not easy to achieve. Extraordinary success under the same conditions is even harder!

Finally, we thank our stockholders, whose support we consider invaluable.

We are anxious to sustain — and improve on — Sizzler's performance in the years ahead. Employing our time-honed success formula, we feel confident of achieving nothing less.

James A. Collins
Chairman of the Board

Richard P. Bermingham
Vice Chairman of the Board

Thomas L. Gregory
President and Chief Executive Officer

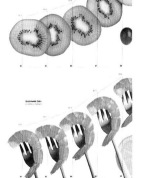

Graphs using food as a picture element. From the Sizzler Restaurants International Inc. annual report.
シズラーレストランのアニュアルリポートより、食品をモチーフにデザインされたグラフ。

STATISTICAL
TABLES & GRAPHS

CHARTS & SCORES

MAPS

ARCHITECTURAL
PLANS & DRAWINGS

INSTRUCTIONAL DIAGRAMS
FOR PRODUCTS

SCIENTIFIC
ILLUSTRATIONS

**DEUTSCHE
GENOSSENSCHAFTS-HYPOTHEKENBANK**
GERMANY 1989
AD,I:Achim Kiel
P:Uwe Brandes
DF:Pencil Corporate Art

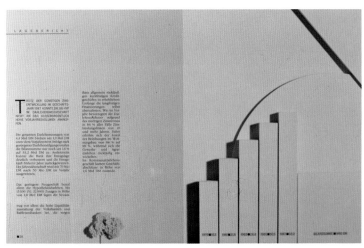

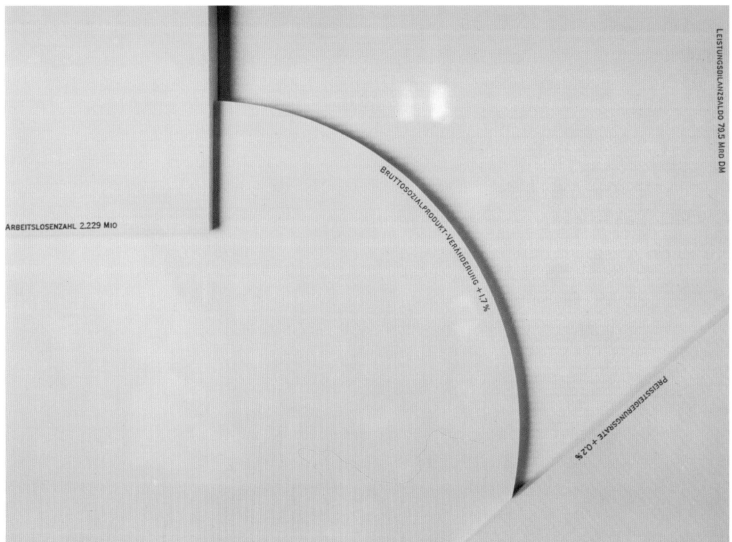

Series of banking diagrams showing financial data. From a Deutsche Genossenschafts-Hypothekenbank business report.
ドイツ組合銀行のビジネスリポートより、財務データを表すグラフシリーズ。

SULLIVAN DENTAL PRODUCTS INC.
USA 1992
CD,AD,D:Gary Haas
P:John Niehuis
DF:Professional Marketing Services

STATISTICAL
TABLES & GRAPHS

CHARTS & SCORES

MAPS

ARCHITECTURAL
PLANS & DRAWINGS

INSTRUCTIONAL DIAGRAMS
FOR PRODUCTS

SCIENTIFIC
ILLUSTRATIONS

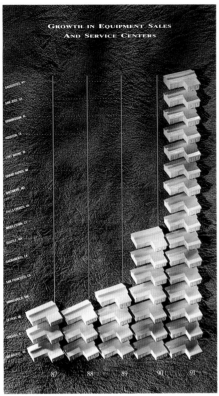

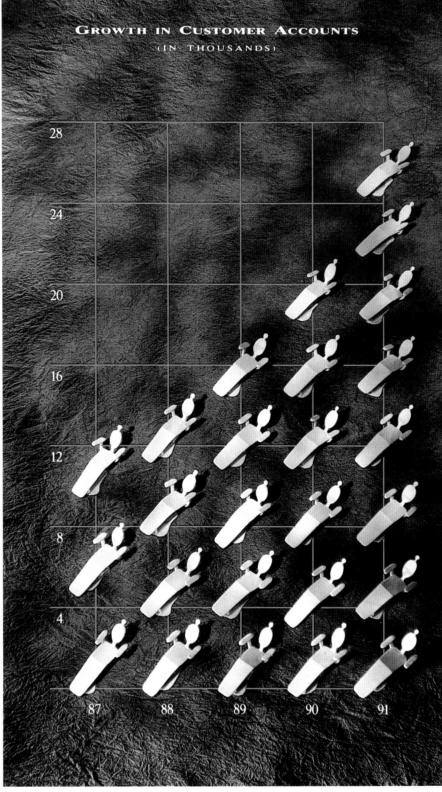

Graphs showing growth in equipment sales & service centers, customer accounts and sales force of a distributor of dental supplies and equipment.
From a Sullivan Dental Products, Inc. annual report.
サリバン・デンタルプロダクツ社のアニュアルリポートより、歯科治療機器や補給品を取り扱う販売会社の売上高・サービスセンター数、得意先数、販売力などを表すグラフ。

1. BBC
ENGLAND 1991
CD:Helen Alexiou
AD,D:Philip Kruger
P:Dave Denham

2. REED BUSINESS CALL
ENGLAND 1989
CD:Helen Alexiou
D:Philip Kruger
P:Jerome Zimmerman

**3. INTERNATIONAL
DISTILLERS & VINTNERS**
ENGLAND 1991
CD,AD,D,I:Philip Kruger
P:Dave Denham

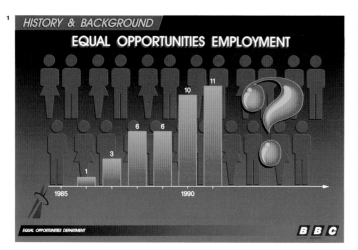

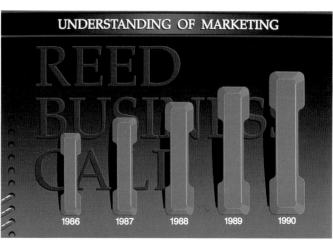

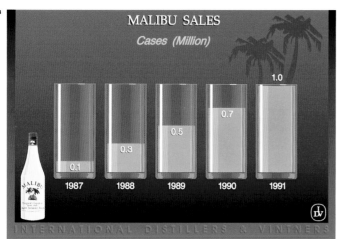

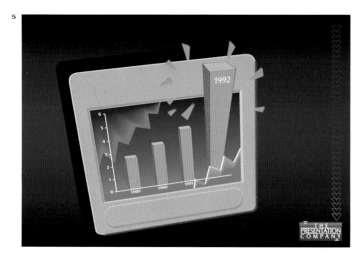

**4. 6. BBC TELEVISION, NEWS
AND CURRENT AFFAIRS**
ENGLAND 1992
D:Robert Shergold/Jean Cramond
DF:N/CA Graphic Design Department

5. THE PRESENTATION COMPANY
ENGLAND 1991
CD,AD,D,I:Philip Kruger
P:Dave Denham

STATISTICAL
TABLES & GRAPHS

CHARTS & SCORES

MAPS

ARCHITECTURAL
PLANS & DRAWINGS

INSTRUCTIONAL DIAGRAMS
FOR PRODUCTS

SCIENTIFIC
ILLUSTRATIONS

1. CHANNEL 4 TELEVISION
ENGLAND 1991
CD,AD,D,I:Richard Schedler
P:Dave Denham

2. 3. 4. 5. BBC TELEVISION, NEWS
AND CURRENT AFFAIRS
ENGLAND 1992
D:Steve Aspinall/Kate Finding/
Bill Calder/Kaye Huddy
DF:News & Current Affairs
Graphic Design Dept.

6. INHOUSE
ENGLAND 1992
CD,AD,D,I:Philip Kruger
P:Dave Denham

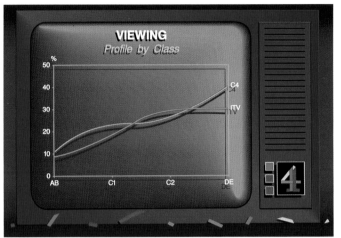

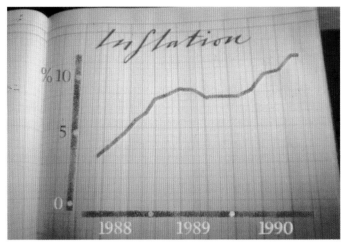

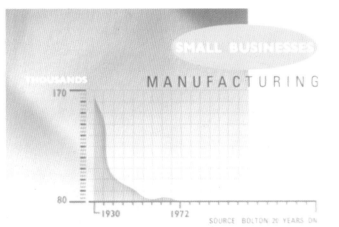

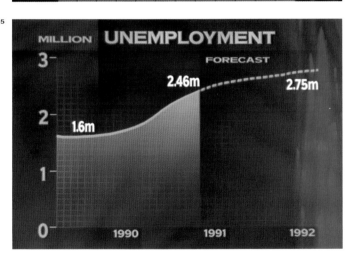

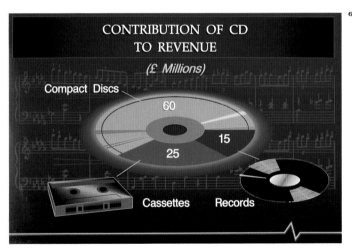

Visualized graphs produced for corporate or TV presentation.
テレビ番組や企業のプレゼンテーションの映像用に制作されたグラフ。

STATISTICAL
TABLES &
GRAPHS

CHARTS & SCORES

MAPS

ARCHITECTURAL
PLANS & DRAWINGS

INSTRUCTIONAL DIAGRAMS
FOR PRODUCTS

SCIENTIFIC
ILLUSTRATIONS

BRITISH GAS PLC
ENGLAND 1990
CD:Geoff Aldridge
AD,D,I:Duncan Wilson
I:Barry Brocklebank
DF:Communication by Design

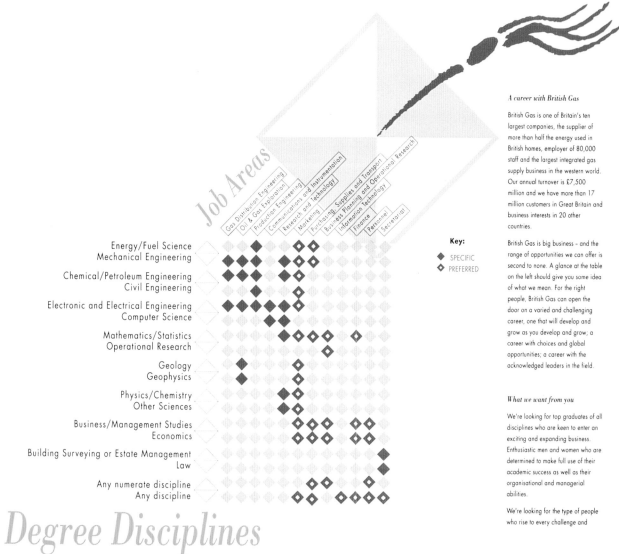

Job Areas

Degree Disciplines

Key:
◆ SPECIFIC
◇ PREFERRED

A career with British Gas

British Gas is one of Britain's ten largest companies, the supplier of more than half the energy used in British homes, employer of 80,000 staff and the largest integrated gas supply business in the western world. Our annual turnover is £7,500 million and we have more than 17 million customers in Great Britain and business interests in 20 other countries.

British Gas is big business – and the range of opportunities we can offer is second to none. A glance at the table on the left should give you some idea of what we mean. For the right people, British Gas can open the door on a varied and challenging career, one that will develop and grow as you develop and grow; a career with choices and global opportunities; a career with the acknowledged leaders in the field.

What we want from you

We're looking for top graduates of all disciplines who are keen to enter an exciting and expanding business. Enthusiastic men and women who are determined to make full use of their academic success as well as their organisational and managerial abilities.

We're looking for the type of people who rise to every challenge and follow up each new opening – the type of people who'll keep British Gas at the top well into the next century.

What we offer you

At British Gas we know that your future is our future and if it's important for us to get the best people, it's just as important for you to get the best employment package.

The extent of our involvement in every aspect of gas means that we can offer the widest range of jobs in the energy business. And our commitment to exploration and production, and to our global gas business, means that this range is constantly increasing.

But on top of the best jobs we also offer:

● complete financial support for further education

● extensive management and skills training

● competitive salaries and benefits

● generous holiday allowances

● career-break/skills-retention scheme

● profit sharing and share option schemes

● relocation assistance.

Whatever your degree discipline and whichever area you start out in, you'll step straight into our Graduate Development Programme. It'll teach you a lot about the business – and a lot about yourself.

You can decide how far you want to go – then it's up to you...

Degree/discipline matrix table showing graduates the job areas appropriate to their particular qualifications. From a British Gas PLC. recruitment guide.

ブリティッシュ・ガス社の就職案内より、卒業生の取得資格に見合った職業分野を知らせるための学位・専門科目行列表。

STATISTICAL
TABLES & GRAPHS

CHARTS & SCORES

MAPS

ARCHITECTURAL
PLANS & DRAWINGS

INSTRUCTIONAL DIAGRAMS
FOR PRODUCTS

SCIENTIFIC
ILLUSTRATIONS

[RIG RENTSCH]
TRIMBACH, SWITZERLAND
SWITZERLAND 1988
CD,AD,D,I:Michael Baviera
DF:BBV Michael Baviera

[RIG RENTSCH]

Anteile am konsolidierten Umsatz.

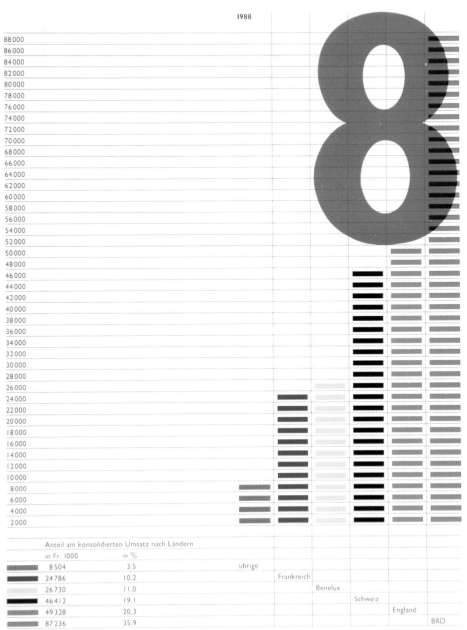

	Anteil am konsolidierten Umsatz nach Ländern		
	in Fr. 1000	in %	
	8 504	3,5	übrige
	24 786	10,2	Frankreich
	26 730	11,0	Benelux
	46 412	19,1	Schweiz
	49 328	20,3	England
	87 236	35,9	BRD

13

Graph showing break down of consolidated turnover. From a Rig Rentsch annual report.
リグレンチ社のアニュアルリポートより、複合出来高の内訳を表したグラフ。

STATISTICAL
TABLES & GRAPHS

CHARTS & SCORES

MAPS

ARCHITECTURAL
PLANS & DRAWINGS

INSTRUCTIONAL DIAGRAMS
FOR PRODUCTS

SCIENTIFIC
ILLUSTRATIONS

IBM DIRECTIONS
USA 1989
CD,AD,D:Wynn Medinger
I:Diane Peterson
DF:Jones Medinger Kindschi Bushko,Inc.

人類の情報伝達手段の発展を歴史的に表すチャート。

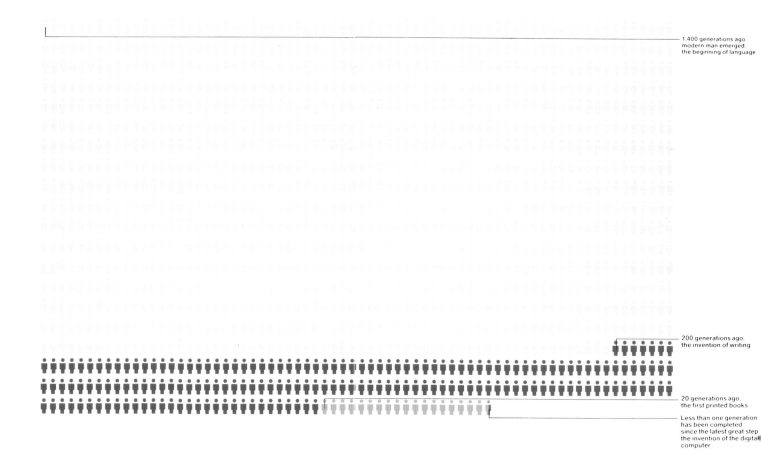

1,400 generations ago,
modern man emerged,
the beginning of language

200 generations ago,
the invention of writing

20 generations ago,
the first printed books

Less than one generation
has been completed
since the latest great step
the invention of the digital
computer

Chart illustrating the history of the development of human communication.
人類の情報伝達手段の発展を歴史的に表すチャート。

JIYU KOKUMIN-SHA
JAPAN 1988
AD:Tokihiro Okuda
D:Mitsuko Kato/Kumiko Yamagami
I:Fumiyo Kojima

STATISTICAL
TABLES & GRAPHS

CHARTS & SCORES

MAPS

ARCHITECTURAL
PLANS & DRAWINGS

INSTRUCTIONAL DIAGRAMS
FOR PRODUCTS

SCIENTIFIC
ILLUSTRATIONS

実質GNP成長率(%)

失業率(%)

経常収支(億ドル)

資料 大蔵省
[見通しの主な前提条件]
● 実施済あるいは発表済の政策不変
● 為替レートは、1988年4月14日水準で一定($1=¥126.0、DM1.69)
● 原油価格、1バーレル=$15(88年上半期)、$16(88年下半期以降)
[注]イギリス、フランス、イタリアについては実質GDP成長率である

(1988年6月)

経済協力開発機構/OECD(Economic Outlook)による経済見通し

Graph showing economic conditions in various countries based on data provided by the OECD.
From an article in the terminology dictionary, "Basic Knowledge of Contemporary Terminology".
用語辞典「現代用語の基礎知識」の記事より、経済協力機構(OECD)による世界各国の経済状況見通しを表すグラフ。

CENTOCOR, INC.
USA 1991
CD:Stephen Ferrari
D:John Ball
I:Michael Crumpton/
Martin Haggland/Micro Color
DF:The Graphic Expression, Inc.

STATISTICAL
TABLES & GRAPHS

CHARTS & SCORES

MAPS

ARCHITECTURAL
PLANS & DRAWINGS

INSTRUCTIONAL DIAGRAMS
FOR PRODUCTS

SCIENTIFIC
ILLUSTRATIONS

Centocor Pharmaceuticals

	Preclinical testing	Phase I testing	Phase II testing	Phase III testing	Product license application	European approval and launch	U.S. approval and launch
Centoxin (Treatment for gram negative septic shock)					●		
CenTNF (Treatment for bacterial infections)	●						
CentoRx (Treatment for blood clot-related disorders)		●					
Centara (Treatment for rheumatoid arthritis)		●					
Panorex (Treatment for gastrointestinal cancer)			●				
Myoscint (Cardiac imaging agent)						●	
Fibriscint (Blood clot imaging agent)				●			
Capiscint (Atherosclerotic plaque imaging agent)		●					

Centocor Diagnostics

	Development	Release for research use	First commercial sale
CA 125 (Ovarian cancer test)			●
CA 19-9 (Pancreatic cancer test)			●
CA 15-3 (Breast cancer test)			●
CA 72-4 (Gastric cancer test)			●
P-glycoCHEK (Multidrug resistance test)		●	

This chart is a representation of the company's drug "Pipeline" showing the product line and where in the process each product is currently. From a Centocor Inc. annual report.

セントコア社のアニュアルリポートより、同社の医薬製品「パイプライン」の製造過程を表した図。

STATISTICAL TABLES & GRAPHS

CHARTS & SCORES

MAPS

ARCHITECTURAL PLANS & DRAWINGS

INSTRUCTIONAL DIAGRAMS FOR PRODUCTS

TECHNICAL ILLUSTRATIONS

BNN CO.

JAPAN 1992

AD,D:Sonoe Takigami

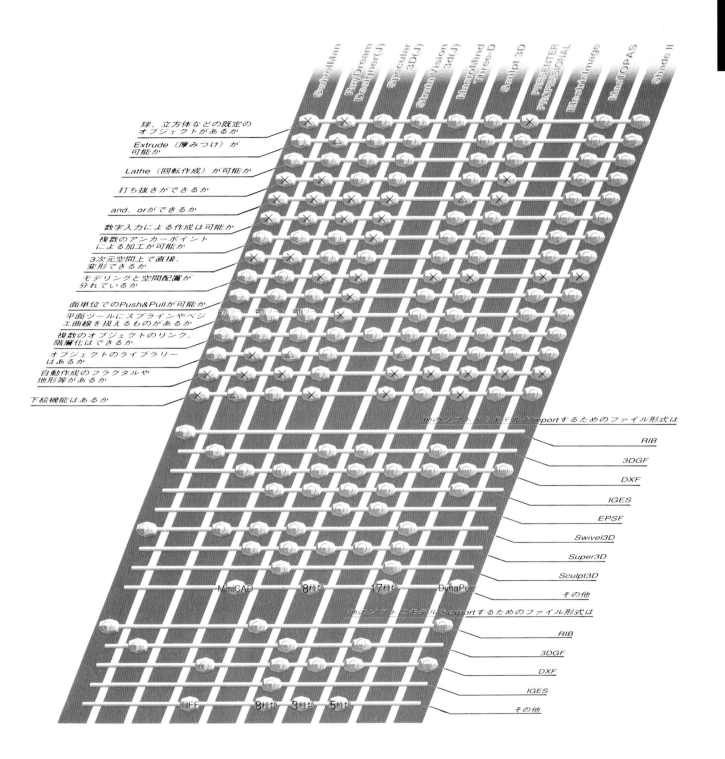

Comparison table of 3-D modelling functions in graphics software programs for the Macintosh computer. From Maclife magazine.

月刊誌「マックライフ」より、マッキントッシュ・コンピューターの3Dグラフィックソフト・モデリング機能比較表。

STATISTICAL TABLES & GRAPHS

CHARTS & SCORES

MAPS

ARCHITECTURAL PLANS & DRAWINGS

INSTRUCTIONAL DIAGRAMS FOR PRODUCTS

SCIENTIFIC ILLUSTRATIONS

IBM JAPAN, LTD.
JAPAN 1990,1991
CD:Haruo Yoshida
AD:Jun Tabohashi
D:Seijo Kawaguchi/
Nobukuni Takada
P:Yutaka Sakano
PR:Hideo Wakana

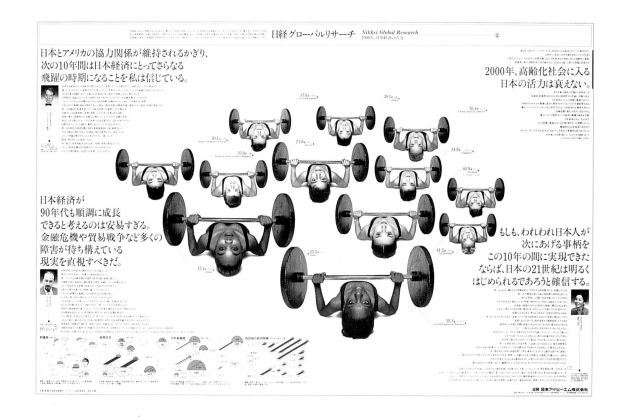

Graphs based upon a photo for forecasting the emissions of CO2 and the average age in various countries in the year 2000.

日本IBM社の企業広告より、2000年における各国の二酸化炭素の排出量、及び平均年齢の予測を写真で表現したグラフ。

STATISTICAL
TABLES & GRAPHS

CHARTS & SCORES

MAPS

ARCHITECTURAL
PLANS & DRAWINGS

INSTRUCTIONAL DIAGRAMS
FOR PRODUCTS

SCIENTIFIC
ILLUSTRATIONS

BLUEPRINT MAGAZINE
ENGLAND 1992
D.I:Peter Grundy/
Tilly Northedge
DF:Grundy & Northedge
Information Designers

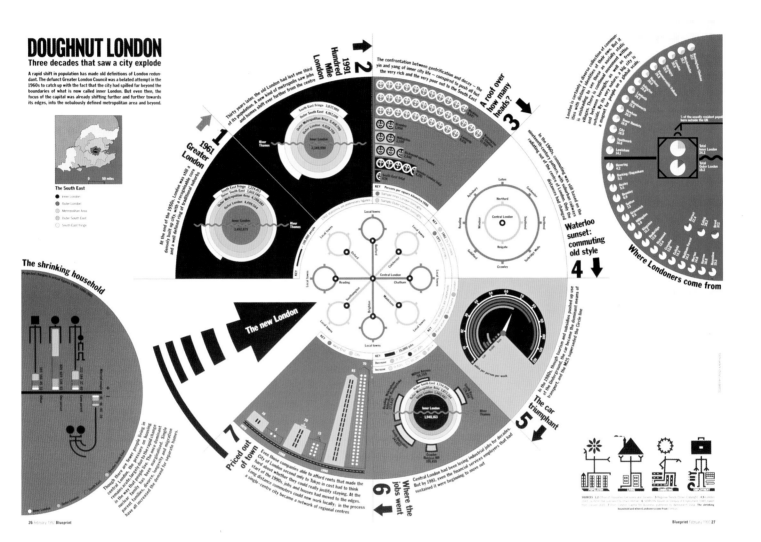

DOUGHNUT LONDON
Three decades that saw a city explode

A rapid shift in population has made old definitions of London redundant. The defunct Greater London Council was a belated attempt in the 1960s to catch up with the fact that the city had spilled far beyond the boundaries of what is now called inner London. But even then, the focus of the capital was already shifting further and further towards its edges, into the nebulously defined metropolitan area and beyond.

The South East

The shrinking household

Visual magazine "Blueprint" article detailing social changes in London over the last 30 years.
ビジュアル雑誌「ブルー・プリント」の記事より、過去30年におけるロンドンの社会変化を詳細に表しているダイアグラム。

STATISTICAL
TABLES &
GRAPHS

CHARTS & SCORES

MAPS

ARCHITECTURAL
PLANS &
DRAWINGS

INSTRUCTIONAL DIAGRAMS
FOR PRODUCTS

SCIENTIFIC
ILLUSTRATIONS

ELECTRICAL & ELECTRONIC
INSULATION ASSOCIATION - (EEIA)
ENGLAND 1992
D:Ian Moore

INTERNATIONAL PLANNED
PARENTHOOD FEDERATION
ENGLAND 1990
CD,AD,D,I:Tilly Northedge
DF:Grundy & Northedge

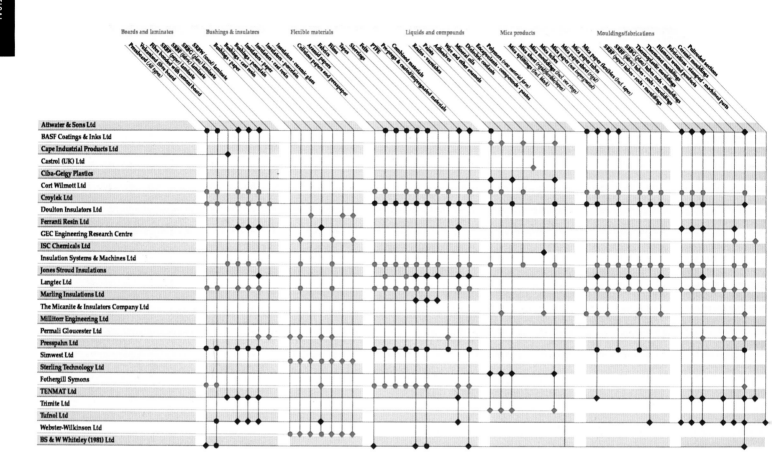

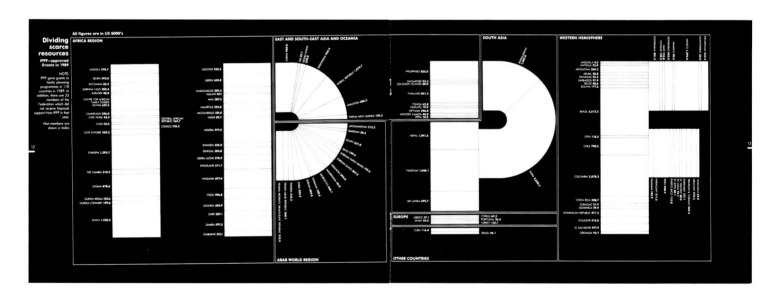

A comprehensive guide to the members of the
"Electrical & Electronic Insulation Association" (EEIA, London) and their range of products.
ロンドンのエレクトリカル＆エレクトロニック・インシュレイション協会（EEIA）のメンバー、
及び製品群についての総合案内図。

Financial graph for International Planned Parenthood Federation (IPPF)
from an annual report.
国際家族計画連盟（IPPF）のアニュアルリポートより、財務に関するグラフ。

SATELLITE DIGITAL AUDIO
BROADCASTING CO., LTD.
JAPAN 1991
CD:Ryozo Tada/Sho Akiyama
AD:Gan Hosoya
D:Haruto Takanashi
P:Kazuyoshi Miyoshi

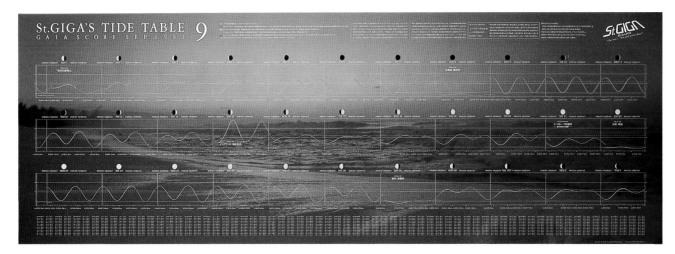

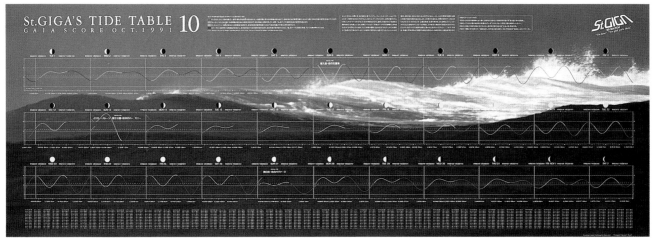

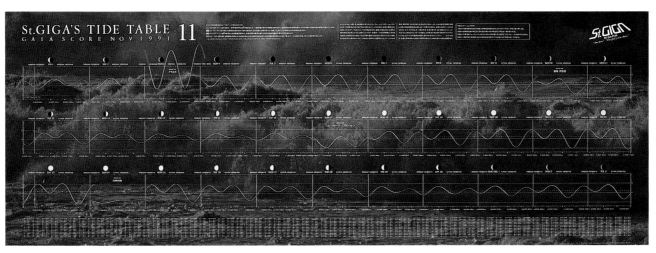

Program table (tide table at the satellite TV station St. Giga) which schedules its programming according to the tides.

潮の満ち引き（タイド）にあわせて時間帯を設定し番組を放送する衛星TV局St. GIGAの番組表（タイドテーブル）。

STATISTICAL
TABLES & GRAPHS

CHARTS & SCORES

MAPS

ARCHITECTURAL
PLANS & DRAWINGS

INSTRUCTIONAL DIAGRAMS
FOR PRODUCTS

SCIENTIFIC
ILLUSTRATIONS

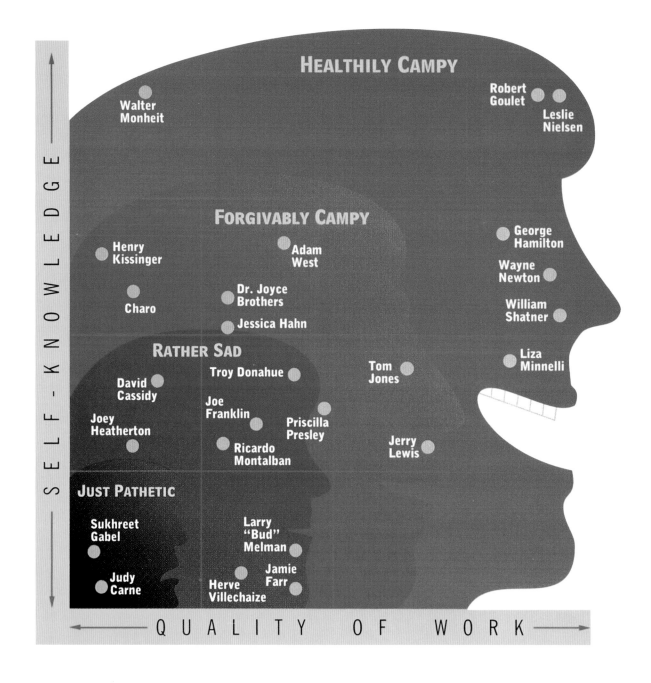

Celebrity-delusion index. Who's "in" and knows it, and who's "out" but does not know it! From Spy magazine.
「スパイマガジン」より、有名人の勘違い指数を表したグラフ。

チャート & スコア

データ相互の関係や流れを、グラフに較べて、より自由な形式で視覚化したダイアグラムが、チャートとスコアである。

チャートの基本は、図による式、すなわち図式にある。時間的に一方向にしか流れない文章表現に対して、空間的に多方向に展開する視覚表現がチャートである、ともいえる。

その応用範囲は、概念や論理の構造を示す図式からはじまって、それをモデル化する模式図、相互関係を示す関係図、変化の様相を示す過程図から、組織的な構造を示す組織図、系図や進化系統樹のような系統図に至るまで、きわめて広範囲に及んでいる。ともかく、文字づらだけを追っていたのでは内容を把握しにくいデータの相互関係や構造を、視覚的なイメージとして解説するのがチャートの目的である。

チャートには、表やグラフのような、データの配置上の明確なルールがないケースも多い。したがって、デザイナーの仕事も、ダイアグラムの視覚的な面白さとデータの読み取りやすさを両立させるための、デザイン上のルール作りから始まることになる。

画面が複雑になりがちなのが、このダイアグラムの特徴でもあるので、ある程度以上の数の記号を使用する際などには、地図の凡例にあたる、「読み方のルール一覧」をどこかで明示する親切さも忘れないようにしたい。

スコアは、楽譜や年譜のように、時間などの流れと、その流れに沿ったデータの変化を視覚的に記述したもののことである。

変化を表わすということでは、既に紹介したグラフなども有力な手段ではあったが、同じ「変化」の図解であっても、グラフがその「量」の変化を表示しているのに対して、スコアは、楽譜の例からもわかる通り、その「質」の変化の方を表示するものである。

したがって、スコアでは、グラフのように、視覚的に数量化された線や面のデザイン要素と、「質」を記述するための文字や記号の複合的な表現が見られ、内容的にも広がりの大きな画面が形成されることも多い。

チャートやグラフのようには多くの作例は見られないダイアグラムながら、スコアというものには視覚表現としてのダイアグラムの大きな可能性が秘められているといえよう。

チャート & スコア

CHARTS & SCORES

CHARTS

& SCORES

A diagram that needs to visualize the interrelations of data and the flow of changing data requires a somewhat more free-form approach. These diagrams are called charts or scores. Basically, a chart is a formula that has been schematized graphically. In other words, a chart is a visual expression that evolves in many directions at once. The chart uses space for this purpose, as opposed to written notation because writing flows in only one direction in time and space, and so has difficulty in expressing the dynamics required.

The range of application for charts and scores is, not surprisingly, very wide. It may be a simple schematic to indicate a basic concept and its logical structure. Where a generalization is drawn from a model, it may be charted so that the relationships are indicated. Flow-charts in which the sequence and vectors of change are tracked graphically. Organizational charts that indicate the structure of organizations through systematic spatial arrangements, such as family trees, evolutionary charts etc. The purpose of the chart is to describe correspondences in the structure of data which would otherwise be quite difficult to grasp. The complex interplay of forces that can be easily demonstrated in a chart may be virtually impossible to convey with a narrative of written text or numerical expression. The designer's task starts with establishing a set of graphic design rules so that both visual appeal and readability can be achieved. The problem inherent to this type of diagram is that it can easily become too complicated and crowded. If the designer is going to use more than a certain minimum number of symbols, then he must remember to provide the viewer with "list of symbols" such as the legends seen in maps.

スチャート&
コャ
アート
&

A score is a visual description of the flow of changes in data, often along a time line. This includes musical scores, chronological records and so forth. Speaking of describing changes, a graph is also an effective means to do this, but there is a difference. Both graphs and scores illustrate "change" but while the graph indicates a quantitative change, the score as you can clearly see in the example of a musical score, indicates changes in quality. In a score, therefore, one sees a combination of expressive devices and design elements such as lines and surfaces which provide visual quality as well as characters and symbols which are used to describe the "quantities". Thus, a score can represent a vast range of content. A score is a type of diagram which, although not seen so often, still represents enormous possibilities for the visual expression of complex data.

STATISTICAL
TABLES & GRAPHS

CHARTS & SCORES

MAPS

ARCHITECTURAL
PLANS & DRAWINGS

INSTRUCTIONAL DIAGRAMS
FOR PRODUCTS

SCIENTIFIC
ILLUSTRATIONS

HORNALL ANDERSON DESIGN WORKS
USA 1990
AD,D:Jack Anderson
DF:Hornall Anderson Design Works

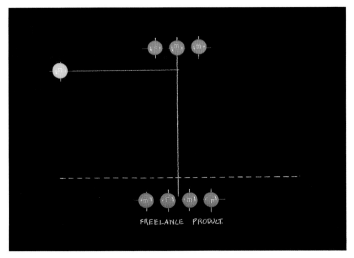

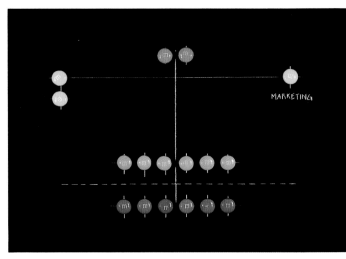

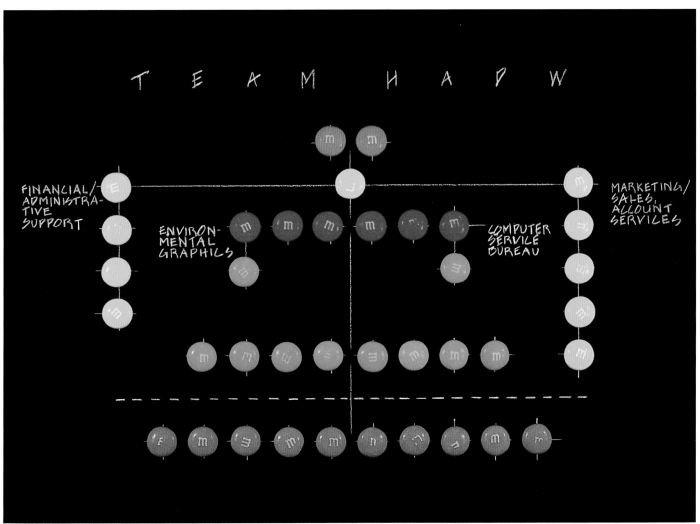

Company organization charts by Hornall Anderson Design Works.
ホーネルアンダーソン・デザインワークスによる会社組織図。

AGOURON PHARMACEUTICALS, INC.

USA 1991

AD,D,I:Rik Besser

AD:Douglas Joseph

I:Koji Takei

DF:Besser Joseph Partners, Inc.

STATISTICAL
TABLES & GRAPHS

CHARTS & SCORES

MAPS

ARCHITECTURAL
PLANS & DRAWINGS

INSTRUCTIONAL DIAGRAMS
FOR PRODUCTS

SCIENTIFIC
ILLUSTRATIONS

1. Investigational New Drug
Application (IND)

2. Clinical Trials

3. New Drug Application (NDA)

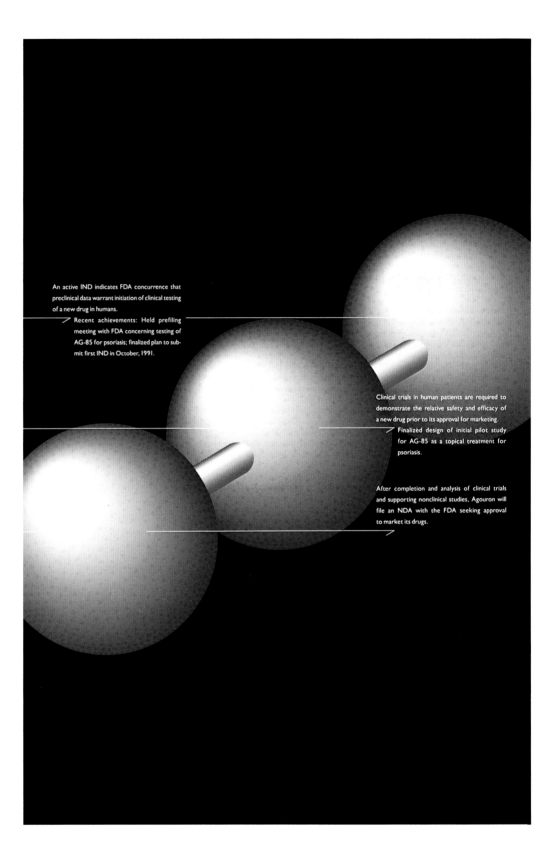

STATISTICAL
TABLES & GRAPHS

CHARTS & SCORES

MAPS

ARCHITECTURAL
PLANS & DRAWINGS

INSTRUCTIONAL DIAGRAMS
FOR PRODUCTS

SCIENTIFIC
ILLUSTRATIONS

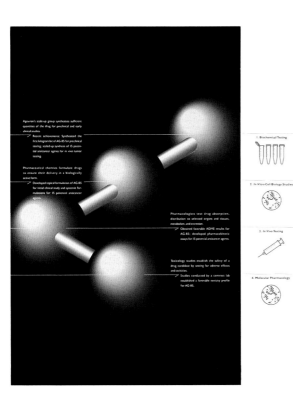

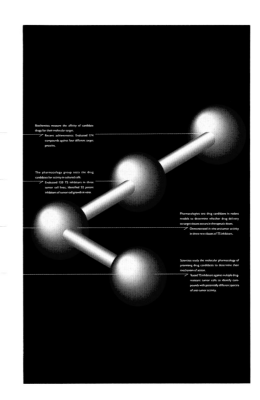

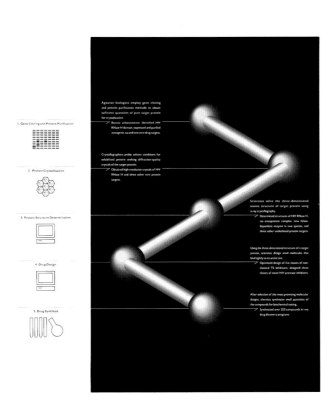

Chart based on molecular models designed to represent the company's drug development process. From an Agouron Pharmaceuticals Inc. annual report.
アグーロン製薬会社のアニュアルリポートより、薬品開発のプロセスを分子モデルをモチーフにして表したチャート。

STATISTICAL
TABLES & GRAPHS

CHARTS & SCORES

MAPS

ARCHITECTURAL
PLANS & DRAWINGS

INSTRUCTIONAL DIAGRAMS
FOR PRODUCTS

SCIENTIFIC
ILLUSTRATIONS

WESTMARK INTERNATIONAL
USA 1992
AD,D:John Hornall
D:Julia LaPine/Mary Hermes/Brian O'Neill
I,DF:Hornall Anderson Design Works

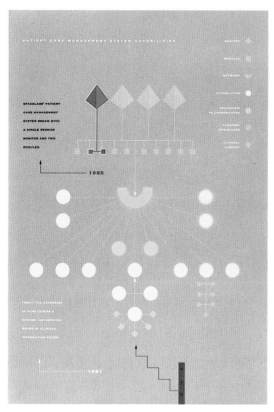

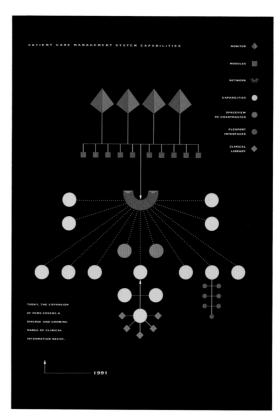

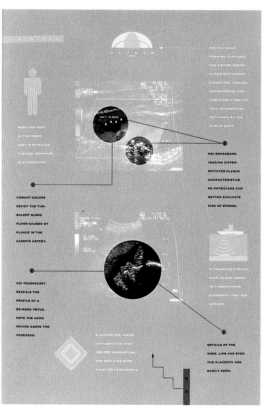

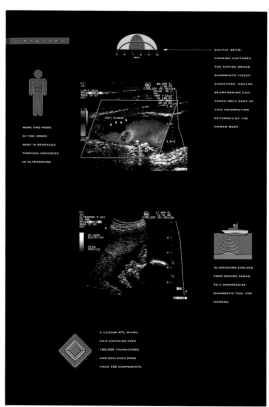

Chart delineating SpaceLabs patient care management system capabilities past (the overlay) and present.
Chart and accompanying overlay capture a variety of significant points in the development of high definition imaging created by Advanced Technology Laboratories.
From a Westmark International annual report.
ウエストマーク・インターナショナル社のアニュアルリポートより、「スペースラブ」の過去から現在までの看護管理システムの能力を表したチャート、
及びアドバンスドテクノロジー・ラボラトリーズ社が制作した高品位映像の開発説明図。

STATISTICAL
TABLES & GRAPHS

CHARTS & SCORES

MAPS

ARCHITECTURAL
PLANS & DRAWINGS

INSTRUCTIONAL DIAGRAMS
FOR PRODUCTS

SCIENTIFIC
ILLUSTRATIONS

NATIONAL MEDICAL ENTERPRISES, INC.
USA 1991
CD:Ron Jefferies
D,I:Claudia Jefferies
DF:The Jefferies Association

Discharge Planning Phase
As the end of the hospital
stay approaches, a plan for
continuing outpatient care
may be formulated, and a
final regimen of medication
is determined. Then, the
patient leaves the hospital,
prepared to return to a pro-
ductive life with new skills
and renewed self-confidence.

Skills Development Phase
There are two goals in the
skills development phase,
one is to educate the patient
to the biochemical nature
of depression and establish
therapeutic levels of medication. The other is to develop
new behavior skills. A variety of individual and group
therapies is employed, up to
six hours a day, seven days a
week.

Treatment Planning
The multidisciplinary treatment team is assembled.
With the patient's participation, specific goals are
established for addressing
behavioral problems and
correcting biochemical
imbalances.

Diagnostic Phase
After a patient is admitted
to the hospital by a psychi-
atrist, a comprehensive
battery of biological and
psychological tests is
administered. A case man-
ager is assigned to monitor
treatment progress.

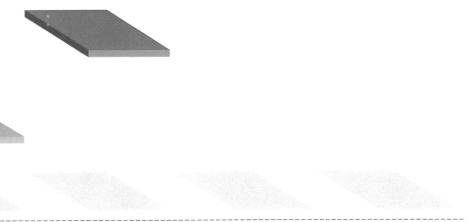

Diagram visualizing the idea of a four step program to restore a patient from acute depression to normalcy. From a National Medical Enterprises Inc. annual report.
ナショナルメディカル・エンタープライズ社のアニュアルリポートより、患者を急性鬱状態から正常な状態へと回復させる4段階のプログラム概念を視覚化したチャート。

STATISTICAL
TABLES & GRAPHS

CHARTS & SCORES

MAPS

ARCHITECTURAL
PLANS & DRAWINGS

INSTRUCTIONAL DIAGRAMS
FOR PRODUCTS

SCIENTIFIC
ILLUSTRATIONS

ROCHE PRODUCTS LIMITED
ENGLAND 1971
CD,AD,D:Mervyn Kurlansky
D:Maddy Bennet
DF:Pentagram Design Ltd.

ERICSSON INFORMATION SYSTEMS
ENGLAND 1983
CD,AD,D:David Hillman
D:Bruce Mau/Sarah Pyne
DF:Pentagram Design Ltd.

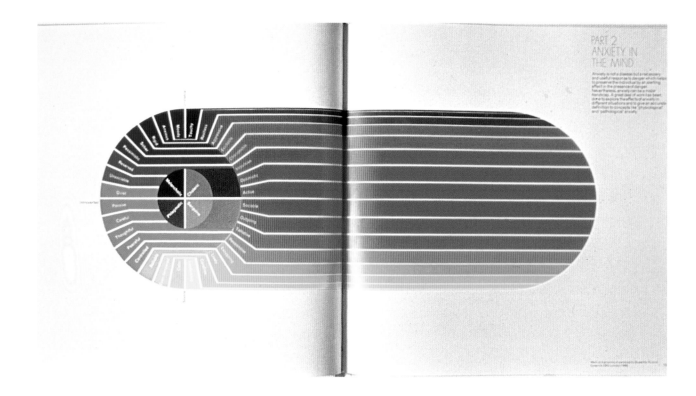

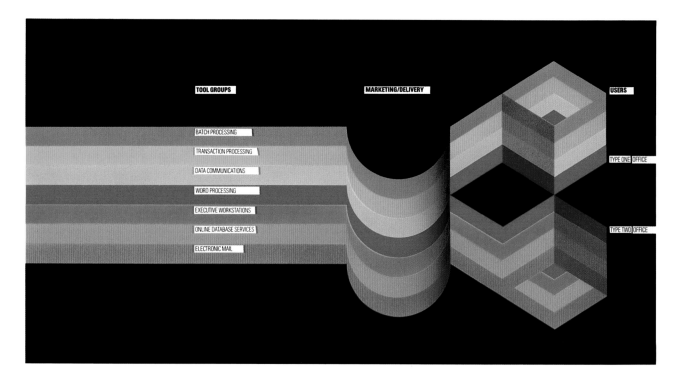

Illustration showing the main dimensions of personality.
From a Roche Products Limited promotional
brochure for a new tranquillizer.
ロッシュ・プロダクツ社の新精神安定剤のプロモーション用パンフレットより、人格の主な種類を示すチャート。

Color-coded chart showing the specific requirements of two types of offices.
From Information Resource Management magazine.
「インフォメーション・リソース・マネージメントマガジン」より、
オフィスが必要とする2タイプの特定の要素を色分けで示すチャート。

STATISTICAL
TABLES & GRAPHS

CHARTS & SCORES

MAPS

ARCHITECTURAL
PLANS & DRAWINGS

INSTRUCTIONAL DIAGRAMS
FOR PRODUCTS

SCIENTIFIC
ILLUSTRATIONS

ERICSSON INFORMATION SYSTEMS
ENGLAND 1983
CD,AD,D:David Hillman
D:Bruce Mau/Sarah Pyne
DF:Pentagram Design Ltd.

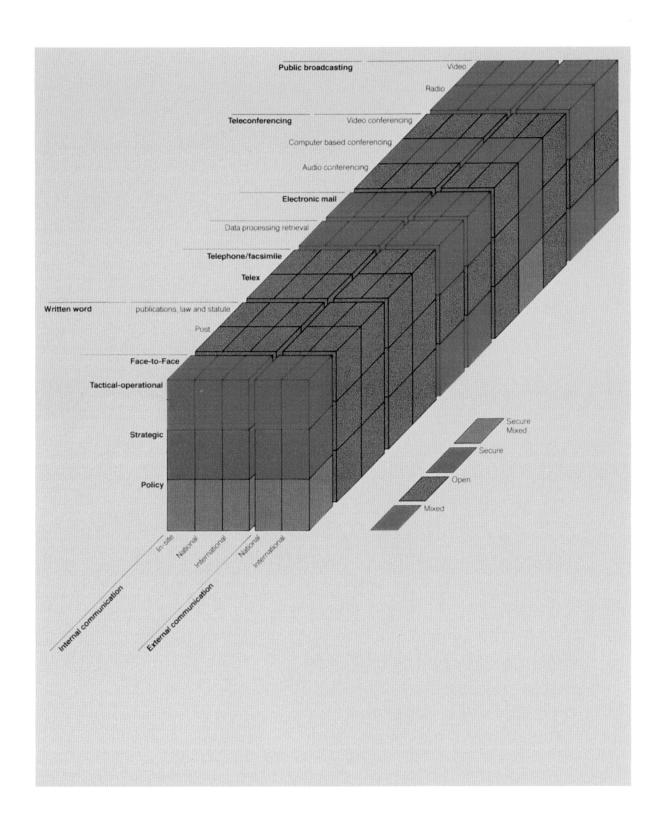

Chart showing communication within the company. From Information Resource Management magazine.
「インフォメーション・リソース・マネージメントマガジン」より、会社内でのコミュニケーションの様子を表すチャート。

STATISTICAL
TABLES & GRAPHS

CHARTS & SCORES

MAPS

ARCHITECTURAL
PLANS & DRAWINGS

INSTRUCTIONAL DIAGRAMS
FOR PRODUCTS

SCIENTIFIC
ILLUSTRATIONS

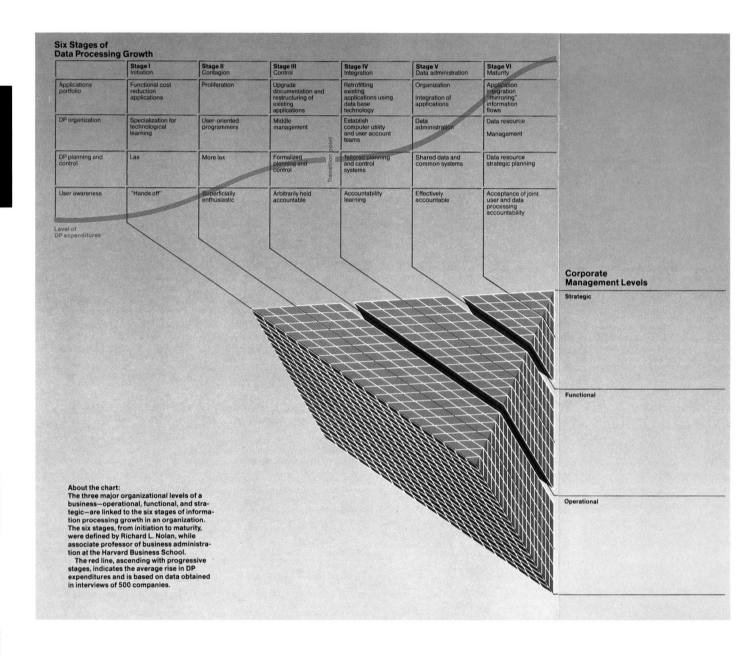

Six Stages of Data Processing Growth

	Stage I Initiation	Stage II Contagion	Stage III Control	Stage IV Integration	Stage V Data administration	Stage VI Maturity
Applications portfolio	Functional cost reduction applications	Proliferation	Upgrade documentation and restructuring of existing applications	Retrofitting existing applications using data base technology	Organization Integration of applications	Application integration "mirroring" information flows
DP organization	Specialization for technological learning	User-oriented programmers	Middle management	Establish computer utility and user account teams	Data administration	Data resource Management
DP planning and control	Lax	More lax	Formalized planning and control	Tailored planning and control systems	Shared data and common systems	Data resource strategic planning
User awareness	"Hands off"	Superficially enthusiastic	Arbitrarily held accountable	Accountability learning	Effectively accountable	Acceptance of joint user and data processing accountability

Transition point

Level of DP expenditures

Corporate Management Levels

Strategic

Functional

Operational

About the chart:
The three major organizational levels of a business—operational, functional, and strategic—are linked to the six stages of information processing growth in an organization. The six stages, from initiation to maturity, were defined by Richard L. Nolan, while associate professor of business administration at the Harvard Business School.

The red line, ascending with progressive stages, indicates the average rise in DP expenditures and is based on data obtained in interviews of 500 companies.

Chart demonstrating the vertical pathways of computing in a contemporary corporation.
今日の会社組織におけるコンピューターの役割を表すチャート。

STATISTICAL
TABLES & GRAPHS

CHARTS & SCORES

MAPS

ARCHITECTURAL
PLANS & DRAWINGS

INSTRUCTIONAL DIAGRAMS
FOR PRODUCTS

SCIENTIFIC
ILLUSTRATIONS

ERICSSON INFORMATION SYSTEMS
ENGLAND 1983
CD,AD,D:David Hillman
D:Bruce Mau/Sarah Pyne
DF:Pentagram Design Ltd.

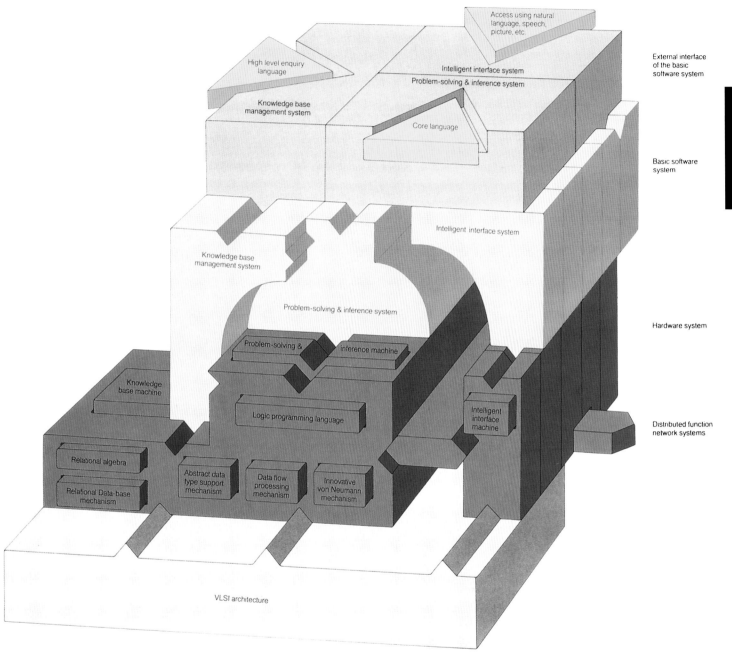

Basic configuration of the fifth generation computer systems. From Information Resource Management magazine.
「インフォメーション・リソース・マネージメントマガジン」より、第5世代コンピューターシステムの基本配置図。

STATISTICAL
TABLES & GRAPHS

CHARTS & SCORES

MAPS

ARCHITECTURAL
PLANS & DRAWINGS

INSTRUCTIONAL DIAGRAMS
FOR PRODUCTS

SCIENTIFIC
ILLUSTRATIONS

SEQUOIA SYSTEMS, INC.

USA 1991
AD:Stephen Mignogna
D:Victoria Stamm
I:In House
DF:Belk Mignogna Associates Ltd.

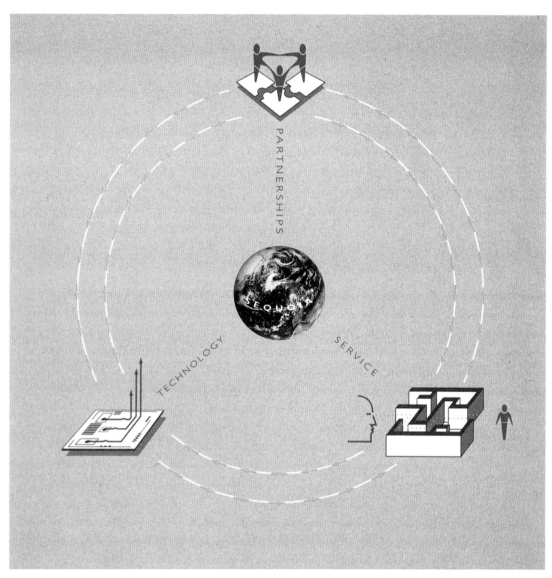

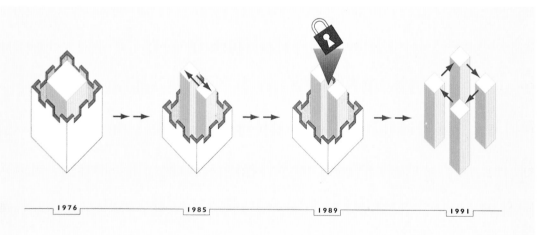

These charts illustrate Sequoia's dedication to serve its customer needs by focusing on technical strengths,
strategic alliances and service oriented capabilities. From a Sequoia Systems Inc. annual report.
セコイア・システムズ社のアニュアルリポートより、同社の技術力、戦略的提携、サービス能力を解説するチャート。

STATISTICAL
TABLES & GRAPHS

CHARTS & SCORES

MAPS

ARCHITECTURAL
PLANS & DRAWINGS

INSTRUCTIONAL DIAGRAMS
FOR PRODUCTS

SCIENTIFIC
ILLUSTRATIONS

JANNOCK LIMITED
CANADA 1992
AD,D:Roslyn Eskind
D:Sandi King
I:Gary Mansbridge
DF:Eskind Waddell

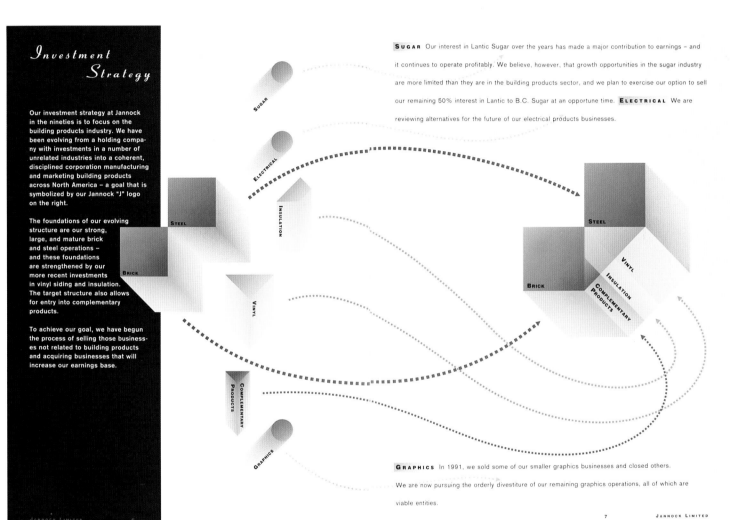

Investment
Strategy

Our investment strategy at Jannock in the nineties is to focus on the building products industry. We have been evolving from a holding company with investments in a number of unrelated industries into a coherent, disciplined corporation manufacturing and marketing building products across North America – a goal that is symbolized by our Jannock "J" logo on the right.

The foundations of our evolving structure are our strong, large, and mature brick and steel operations – and these foundations are strengthened by our more recent investments in vinyl siding and insulation. The target structure also allows for entry into complementary products.

To achieve our goal, we have begun the process of selling those businesses not related to building products and acquiring businesses that will increase our earnings base.

SUGAR Our interest in Lantic Sugar over the years has made a major contribution to earnings – and it continues to operate profitably. We believe, however, that growth opportunities in the sugar industry are more limited than they are in the building products sector, and we plan to exercise our option to sell our remaining 50% interest in Lantic to B.C. Sugar at an opportune time. **ELECTRICAL** We are reviewing alternatives for the future of our electrical products businesses.

GRAPHICS In 1991, we sold some of our smaller graphics businesses and closed others. We are now pursuing the orderly divestiture of our remaining graphics operations, all of which are viable entities.

JANNOCK LIMITED

Chart illustrating strategic divestiture of unrelated businesses, with the corporate symbol as a matrix. From a Jannock Limited annual report.
ジャノック社のアニュアルリポートより、企業のシンボルをモチーフに非関連事業の戦略的な獲得のしくみを表すチャート。

STATISTICAL
TABLES & GRAPHS

CHARTS & SCORES

MAPS

ARCHITECTURAL
PLANS & DRAWINGS

INSTRUCTIONAL DIAGRAMS
FOR PRODUCTS

SCIENTIFIC
ILLUSTRATIONS

AGOURON PHARMACEUTICALS, INC.
USA 1989
AD,D:Rik Besser
AD:Douglas Joseph
P:Jeff Zaruba
DF:Besser Joseph Partners, Inc.

A crystallographer monitors
experiments within multiple-well
dishes. Each well contains a drop of
the target protein in different solvents,
which may produce protein crystals to
be used in x-ray diffraction studies.

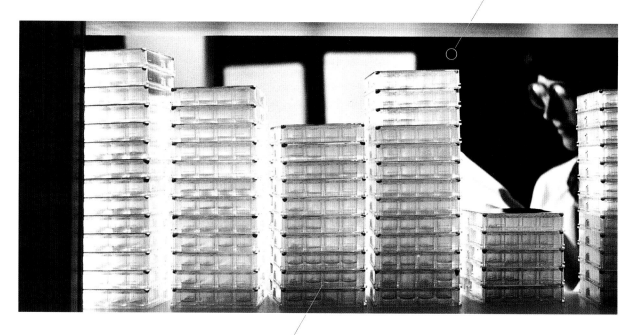

CLONING

CRYSTALLIZATION

STRUCTURE DETERMINATION

Scientists experiment with solubilized
target protein under a variety of conditions to obtain diffraction quality
crystals of the target protein.

DRUG DESIGN

SYNTHESIS

BIOEVALUATION

Chart displaying all steps necessary for protein structure-based drug design. From an Agouron Pharmaceuticals Inc. annual report.
アグーロン製薬会社のアニュアルリポートより、蛋白質構造をモチーフに薬品開発に必要なすべての段階を表したチャート。

APPLIED BIOSYSTEMS INC.
USA 1991
CD,AD:Michael J. Zinke
D,I:Lesley Gasparetti
DF:Bay Graphics Design, Inc.

STATISTICAL
TABLES & GRAPHS

CHARTS & SCORES

MAPS

ARCHITECTURAL
PLANS & DRAWINGS

INSTRUCTIONAL DIAGRAMS
FOR PRODUCTS

SCIENTIFIC
ILLUSTRATIONS

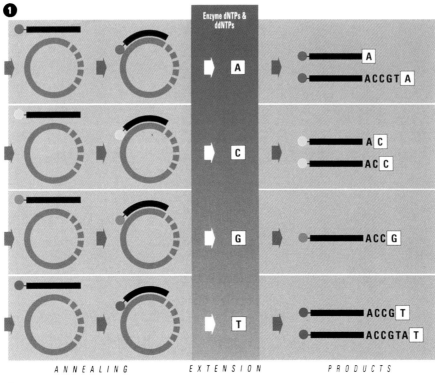

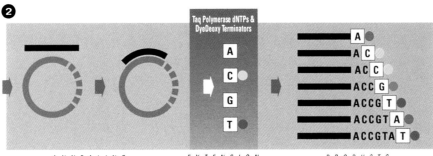

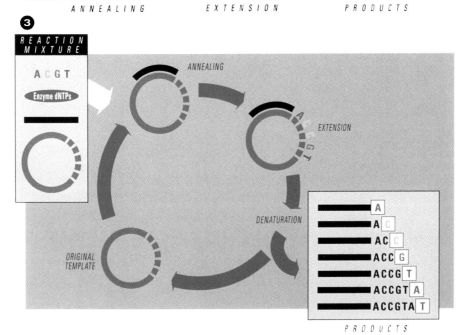

Charts showing steps in preparing DNA sample for one-lane sequencing by pairing four primers, labeled with flourescent dyes, with specific dideoxynucleotide reactions. From an Applied Biosystems Inc. sales brochure.

アプライド・バイオシステムズ社の製品パンフレットより、ディオキシヌクレオチド反応のある4つの核分子を組み合わせてワンレーンシーケンス用のDNAサンプルを作成する段階図。

STATISTICAL
TABLES & GRAPHS

CHARTS & SCORES

MAPS

ARCHITECTURAL
PLANS & DRAWINGS

INSTRUCTIONAL DIAGRAMS
FOR PRODUCTS

SCIENTIFIC
ILLUSTRATIONS

UNA
NETHERLANDS 1988
AD:Hans Bockting/
Will de l'Ecluse
AD,D,P:Henk Hoebë
P:Pieter Vandermeer
DF:UNA Amsterdam

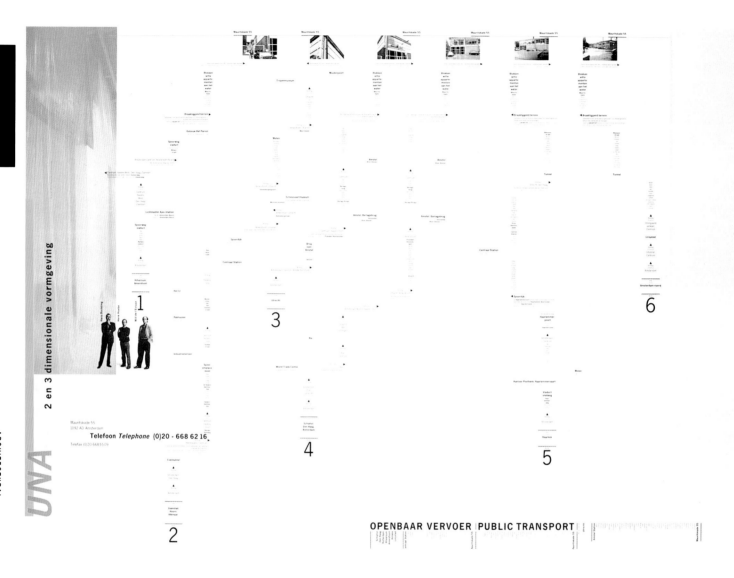

Chart of directions for reaching UNA Amsterdam's new offices (from six different starting points).
Each set of instructions is laid out in the direction of travel across a fold-out sheet.
デザイン会社「UNAアムステルダム」の新オフィスへの行き方を示すチャート。6つの異なった出発地点からそれぞれの行き方が説明されている。

STATISTICAL
TABLES & GRAPHS

CHARTS & SCORES

MAPS

ARCHITECTURAL
PLANS & DRAWINGS

INSTRUCTIONAL DIAGRAMS
FOR PRODUCTS

SCIENTIFIC
ILLUSTRATIONS

NIPPON ELECTRIC GLASS CO., LTD.
JAPAN 1990
CD,AD,D:Tetsuya Ohta

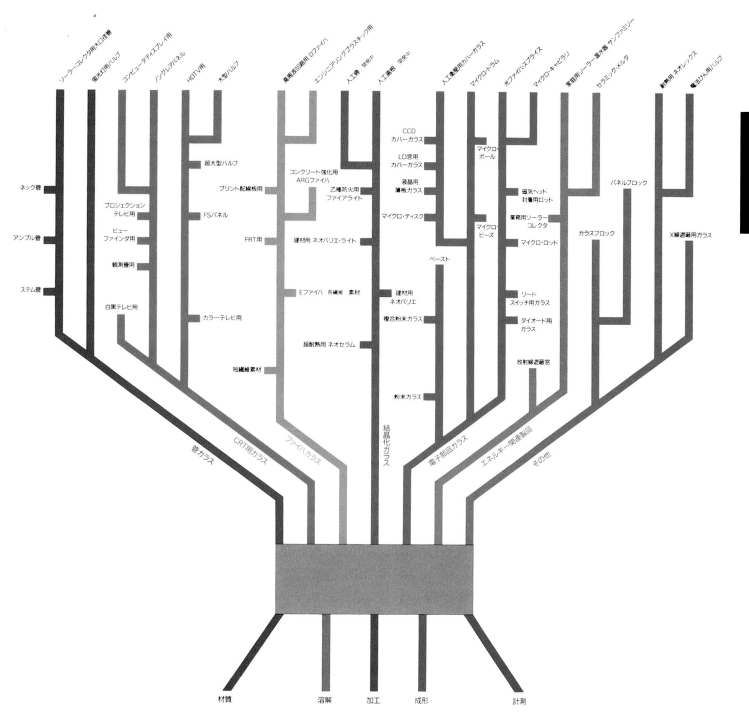

System tree for Nippon Electric Glass' high-tech glass products.
日本電気硝子社のハイテクガラス製品の系統樹。

CHARTS & SCORES

MAPS

ARCHITECTURAL
PLANS & DRAWINGS

INSTRUCTIONAL DIAGRAMS
FOR PRODUCTS

SCIENTIFIC
ILLUSTRATIONS

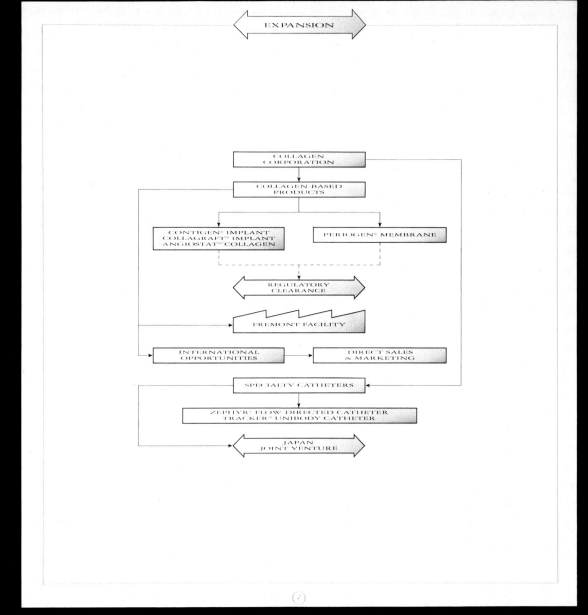

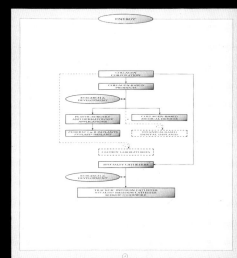

Symbolic flowchart highlighting the company's objectives and direction. The gradated boxes symbolize the company's transition. From a Collagen Corporation annual
コラーゲン社のアニュアルリポートより、会社の目標、及び方向性に焦点を当てたフローチャート。四角の中のグラデーションは会社の変遷を象徴している。

Concept Behind The Building

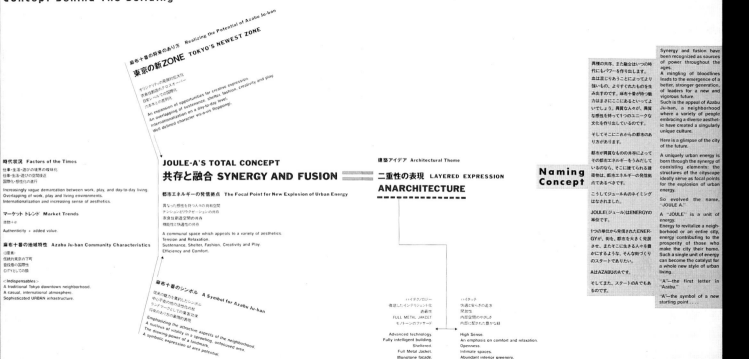

麻布十番の将来のあり方　Realizing the Potential of Azabu Ju-ban

東京の新ZONE　TOKYO'S NEWEST ZONE

オリジナリティの発揮的拡大化
衣食住創造のクロスオーバー
日常レベルでの国際化
六本木との差別化

An expansion of opportunities for creative expression.
An overlapping of sustenance shelter, fashion, creativity and play.
Internationalization on a day-to-day level.
Well defined character vis-a-vis Roppongi.

時代状況　Factors of the Times

仕事・生活・遊びの境界の曖昧化
仕事・生活・遊びの空間接近
国際化・感性化の進行

Increasingly vague demarcation between work, play, and day-to-day living.
Overlapping of work, play and living environments.
Internationalization and increasing sense of aesthetics.

マーケット トレンド　Market Trends

本物+α

Authenticity + added value.

麻布十番の地域特性　Azabu Ju-ban Community Characteristics

〈3要素〉
伝統的東京の下町
普段着の国際性
CITYとしての器

〈Indispensables〉
A traditional Tokyo downtown neighborhood.
A casual, international atmosphere.
Sophisticated URBAN infrastructure.

JOULE-A'S TOTAL CONCEPT

共存と融合　SYNERGY AND FUSION

都市エネルギーの発信拠点　The Focal Point for New Explosion of Urban Energy

異なった感性を持つ人々の共有空間
テンションとリラクゼーションの共有
衣食住創造空間の共有
機能性と快適性の共有

A communal space which appeals to a variety of aesthetics.
Tension and Relaxation.
Sustenance, Shelter, Fashion, Creativity and Play.
Efficiency and Comfort.

麻布十番のシンボル　A Symbol for Azabu Ju-ban

従来の魅力を集約したシンボル
中心不在の街の活性化の核
ランドマークとしての集客効果
将来のあり方の象徴的表現

Emphasizing the attractive aspects of the neighborhood.
A nucleus of vitality in a sprawling, unfocused area.
The drawing power of a landmark.
A symbolic expression of area potential.

建築アイデア　Architectural Theme

二重性の表現　LAYERED EXPRESSION

ANARCHITECTURE

ハイテクノロジー
徹底したインテリジェント化
遮蔽性
FULL METAL JAKCET
モノトーンのフサード

Advanced technology.
Fully intelligent building.
Sheltered.
Full Metal Jacket.
Monotone facade.

ハイタッチ
快適と安らぎの追求
開放性
内部空間のやさしさ
内部に配された豊かな緑

High Sense.
An emphasis on comfort and relaxation.
Openness.
Intimate spaces.
Abundant interior greenery.

Naming Concept

異種の共存、また融合はいつの時代にもパワーを作り出します。
血は混じりあうことによってより強いもの、よりすぐれたものを生み出すのです。麻布十番が持つ魅力はまさにここにあるといってよいでしょう。異質な人々が、異質な感性を持って1つのユニークな文化を作り出しているのです。

そしてそこにこれからの都市のあり方があります。

都市が異質なものの共存によってその都市エネルギーをうみだしているのなら、そこに建てられる建築物は、都市エネルギーの発信拠点であるべきです。

こうしてジュール-Aのネイミングはなされました。

JOULE(ジュール)はENERGYの単位です。

1つの単位から発信されたENERGYが、街を、都市を大きく発展させ、またそこに生きる人々を豊かにするような、そんな街づくりのスタートでありたい。

AはAZABUのAです。

そしてまた、スタートのAでもあるのです。

Synergy and fusion have been recognized as sources of power throughout the ages.
A mingling of bloodlines leads to the emergence of a better, stronger generation, of leaders for a new and vigorous future.
Such is the appeal of Azabu Ju-ban, a neighborhood where a variety of people embracing a diverse aesthetic have created a singularly unique culture.

Here is a glimpse of the city of the future.

A uniquely urban energy is born through the synergy of coexisting elements: the structures of the cityscape ideally serve as focal points for the explosion of urban energy.

So evolved the name, "JOULE A."

A "JOULE" is a unit of energy.
Energy to revitalize a neighborhood or an entire city, energy contributing to the prosperity of those who make the city their home. Such a single unit of energy can become the catalyst for a whole new style of urban living.

"A"—the first letter in "Azabu."

"A"—the symbol of a new starting point . . . .

STATISTICAL
TABLES & GRAPHS

CHARTS & SCORES

MAPS

ARCHITECTURAL
PLANS & DRAWINGS

INSTRUCTIONAL DIAGRAMS
FOR PRODUCTS

SCIENTIFIC
ILLUSTRATIONS

A single modular element is the basis for at least nine different table layouts for meetings. The dots represent the clients and executives of the advertising agency.

少なくとも9通りはある会議用のテーブル・レイアウト図。一つのモジュールが基本の構成要素となり、点はクライアントと広告代理店の幹部を表す。

VISCOM LTD.
ENGLAND 1979
CD,AD,D:David Hillman
D:Nancy Williams/Liz James
I:Dan Fern
DF:Pentagram Design Ltd.

STATISTICAL
TABLES & GRAPHS

CHARTS & SCORES

MAPS

ARCHITECTURAL
PLANS & DRAWINGS

INSTRUCTIONAL DIAGRAMS
FOR PRODUCTS

SCIENTIFIC
ILLUSTRATIONS

A symbol for a visual communications company involved in film-making
- the basic semaphore figure is used to spell out the name of film trailers in both animation and print forms.
映画制作に関わるビジュアル・コミュニケーション会社のシンボル。基本的な手旗信号はアニメーションや印刷物において、映画予告を表すために使用されている。

STATISTICAL
TABLES & GRAPHS

CHARTS & SCORES

MAPS

ARCHITECTURAL
PLANS & DRAWINGS

INSTRUCTIONAL DIAGRAMS
FOR PRODUCTS

SCIENTIFIC
ILLUSTRATIONS

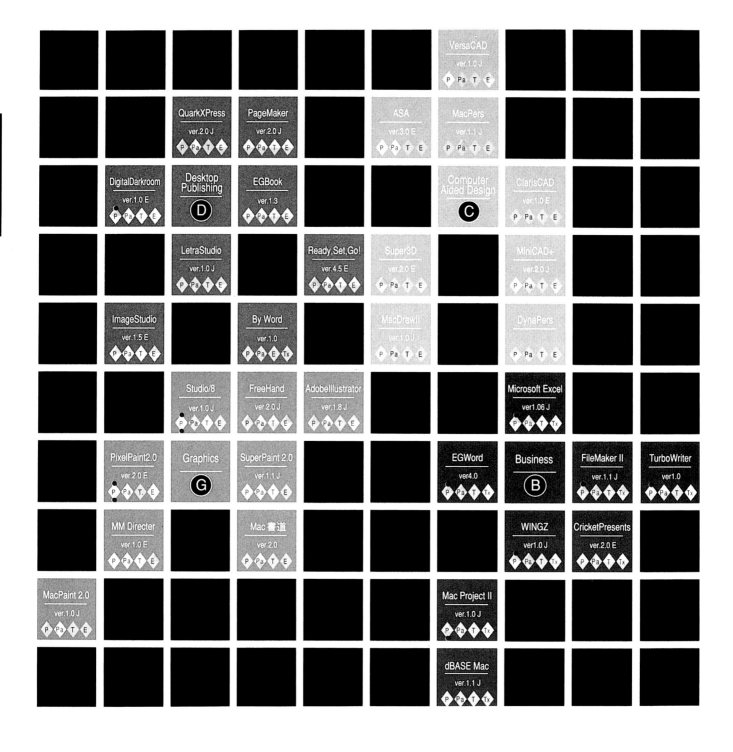

Pictograph indicating the functions of various software programs for the Macintosh computer.
マッキントッシュ・コンピューターの各ソフトの機能をピクトグラムで表したチャート。

STATISTICAL
TABLES & GRAPHS

CHARTS & SCORES

MAPS

ARCHITECTURAL
PLANS & DRAWINGS

INSTRUCTIONAL DIAGRAMS
FOR PRODUCTS

SCIENTIFIC
ILLUSTRATIONS

YAMATO INTERNATIONAL INC.
JAPAN 1991
CD:Junichi Itoh
AD,D:Mari Sasaki

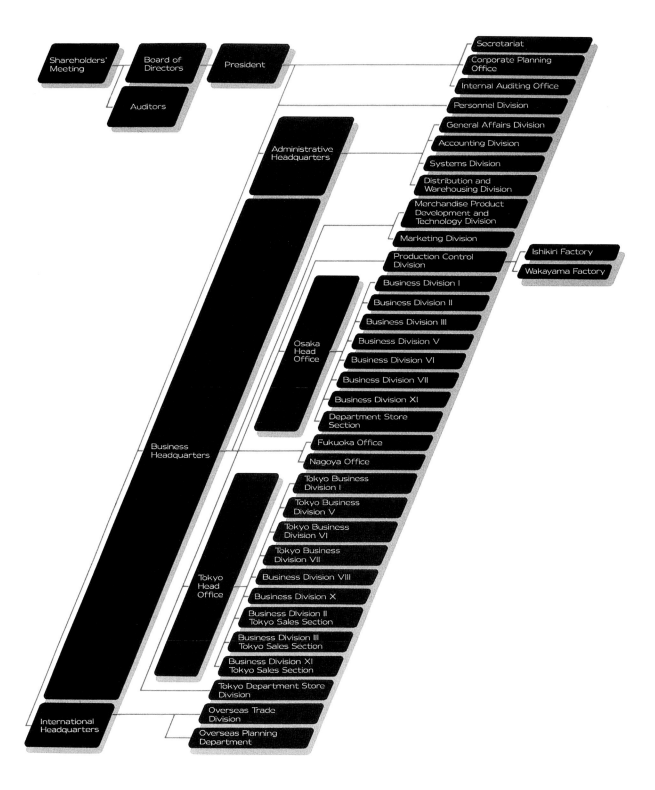

Corporate organizational diagram. From a Yamato International Inc. annual report.
ヤマト・インターナショナル社のアニュアルリポートより、会社組織図。

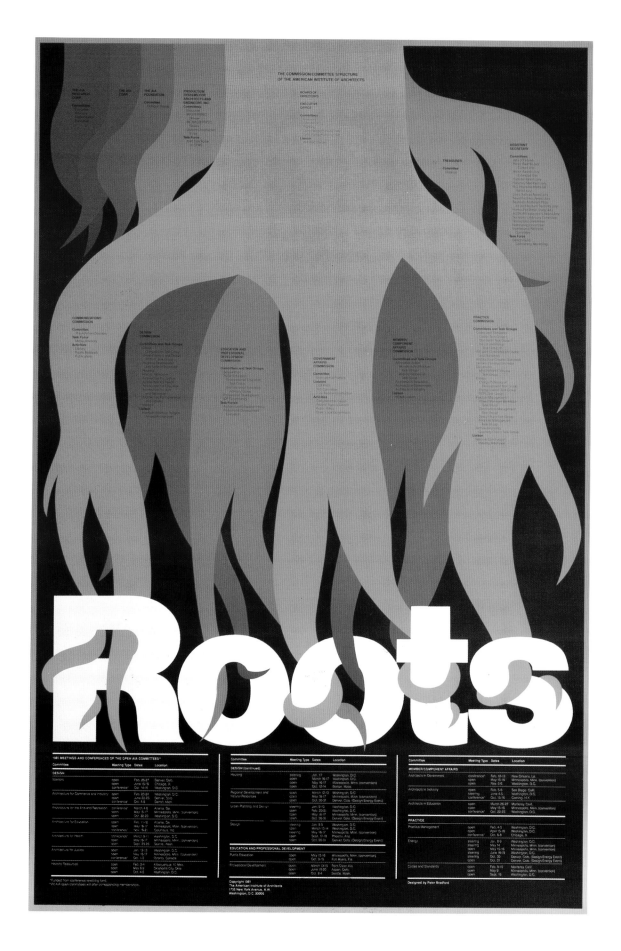

Chart of AIA's organizational structure and schedule of regional events.
AIA（アメリカ建築家協会）の組織の構造を表した図と諸地域で開催されるイベントのスケジュール表。

STATISTICAL
TABLES & GRAPHS

CHARTS & SCORES

MAPS

ARCHITECTURAL
PLANS & DRAWINGS

INSTRUCTIONAL DIAGRAMS
FOR PRODUCTS

SCIENTIFIC
ILLUSTRATIONS

ASPEN DESIGN CONFERENCE
USA
AD,D,I:Peter Bradford
AD:Richard Saul Wurman
DF:Peter Bradford & Associates

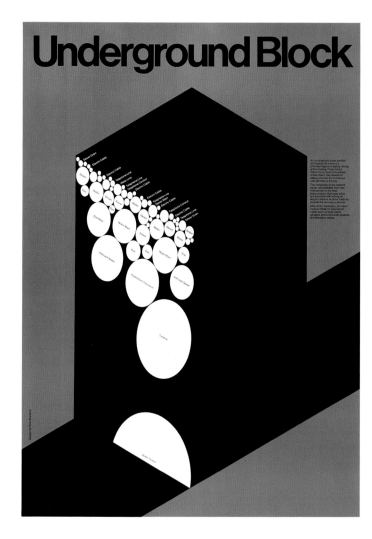

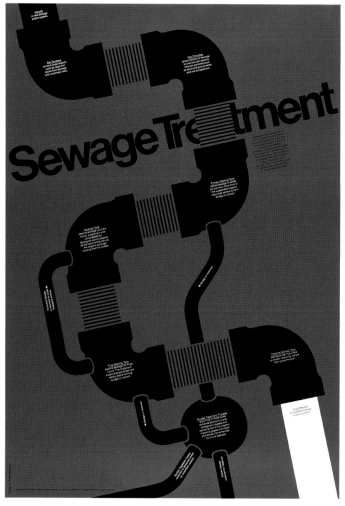

Diagrams of an underground utility system and typical city sewage treatment system.
地下を利用する公共事業設備、及び典型的な都市の下水処理システムを表したダイアグラム。

STATISTICAL
TABLES & GRAPHS

CHARTS & SCORES

MAPS

ARCHITECTURAL
PLANS & DRAWINGS

INSTRUCTIONAL DIAGRAMS
FOR PRODUCTS

SCIENTIFIC
ILLUSTRATIONS

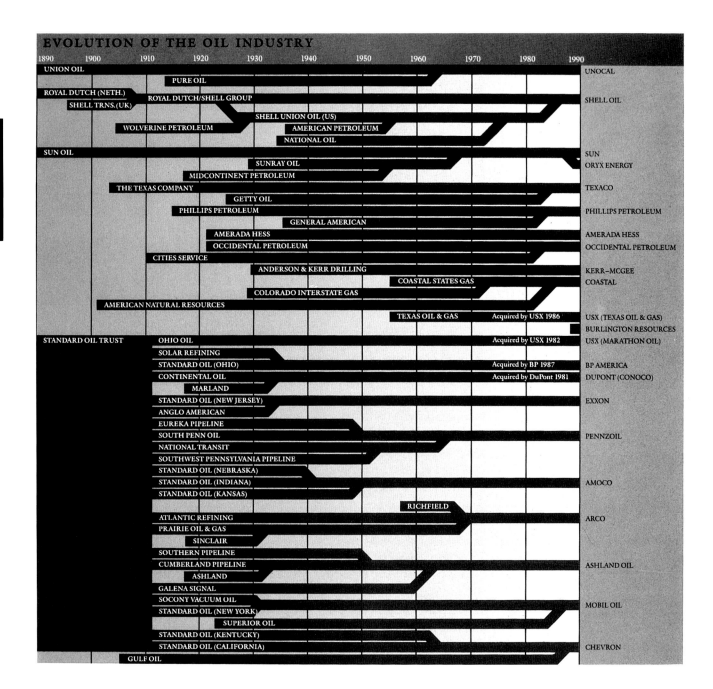

Chart describing how oil is produced. From a Unocal Corporation history book.
ユノカル社の社史より、石油の生産方法を解説したチャート。

STATISTICAL
TABLES & GRAPHS

CHARTS & SCORES

MAPS

ARCHITECTURAL
PLANS & DRAWINGS

INSTRUCTIONAL DIAGRAMS
FOR PRODUCTS

SCIENTIFIC
ILLUSTRATIONS

PFU LTD.
JAPAN 1991
D:Yukimasa Matsuda

SEARS ROEBUCK & CO.
USA 1989
AD:Robert Gersin
D:David Au
I:Alan Kikuchi
DF:Robert P. Gersin Assoc. Inc.

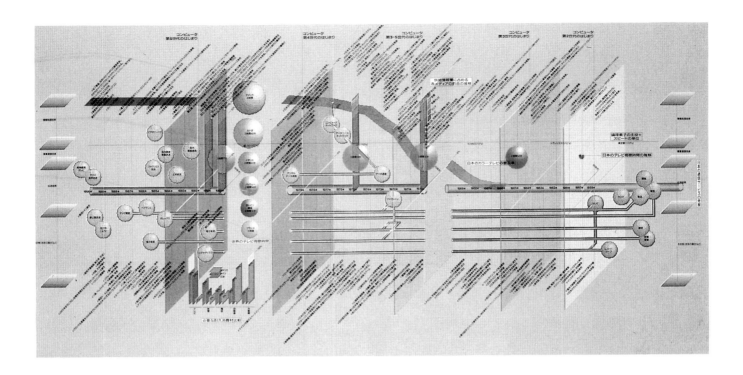

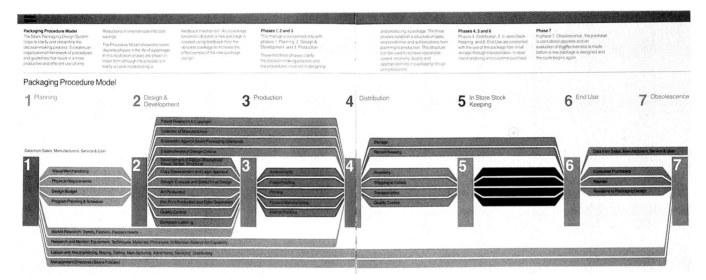

Diagram of the history of information and communication over the past 30 years.
過去30年間の情報とコミュニケーションの歴史を解説したチャート。

Chart illustrating package lifetime
from identification of need through design and production to obsolescence.
需要を確認し、デザイン、生産、やがては使用廃止に至るまでのパッケージの終生を解説するチャート。

STATISTICAL
TABLES & GRAPHS

CHARTS & SCORES

MAPS

ARCHITECTURAL
PLANS & DRAWINGS

INSTRUCTIONAL DIAGRAMS
FOR PRODUCTS

SCIENTIFIC
ILLUSTRATIONS

1. N.I STAFF CORPORATION
JAPAN 1988
AD,D:Osamu Sato

2. THE KOMATSU STORE CO., LTD.
JAPAN 1988
AD,D:Ichiro Higashiizumi
D:Kazuhiro Kishi
DF:Huia Media Design Co., Ltd.

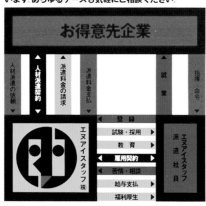

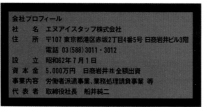

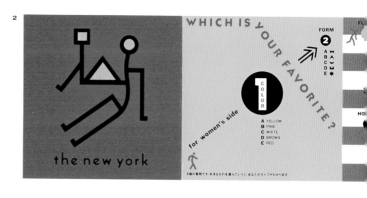

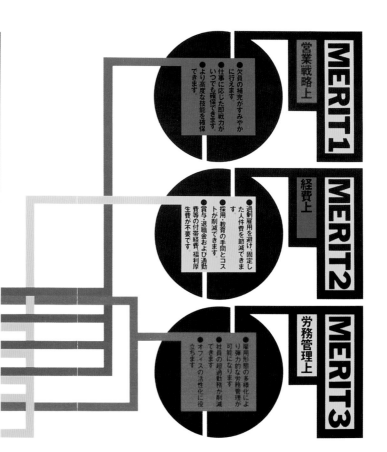

1. Chart explaining the operations system of a personnel dispatching company.
From N.I Staff Corporation corporate introductions.
エヌアイ・スタッフ社の企業案内より、人材派遣会社の業務システムを説明するチャート。

2. Flow-chart type self analysis test for the Komatsu Store Co., Ltd. promotional brochure.
コマツ・ストアーのプロモーション用パンフレットより、自己診断テストのためのフローチャート。

3. XYPLEX, INC.

USA 1992
AD:Kathleen Forsythe
D:Renate Gokl
DF:Forsythe Design

STATISTICAL
TABLES & GRAPHS

CHARTS & SCORES

MAPS

ARCHITECTURAL
PLANS & DRAWINGS

INSTRUCTIONAL DIAGRAMS
FOR PRODUCTS

SCIENTIFIC
ILLUSTRATIONS

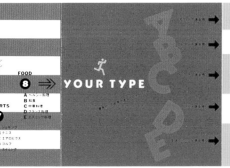

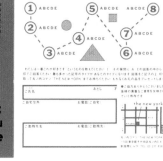

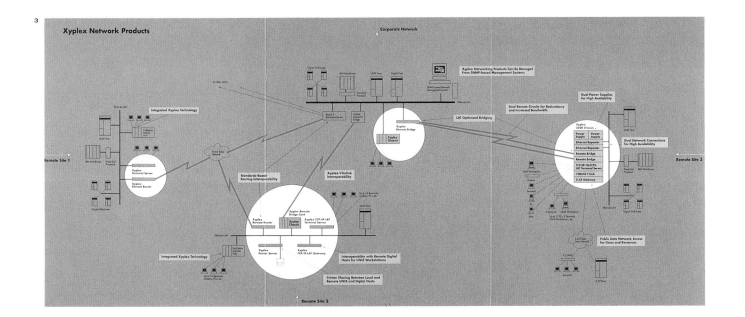

3. Diagram of various local and remote office computer connectivity solutions provided by Xyplex equipment. From a Xyplex Inc. brochure.
サイプレックス社のパンフレットより、遠距離・近距離オフィス間のコンピュータ接続における問題に対し、同社が提供する各種の解決策を表すチャート。

STATISTICAL
TABLES & GRAPHS

CHARTS & SCORES

MAPS

ARCHITECTURAL
PLANS & DRAWINGS

INSTRUCTIONAL DIAGRAMS
FOR PRODUCTS

SCIENTIFIC
ILLUSTRATIONS

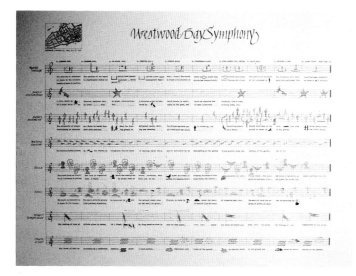

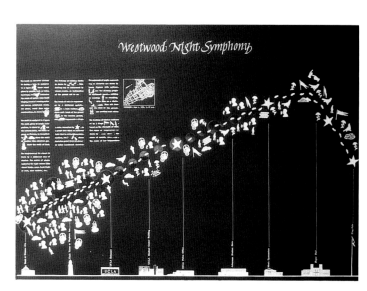

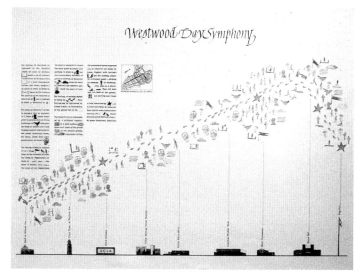

A score representing the activity on Westwood St., L.A. done separately for day and night.
ロサンジェルス/ウェストウッド通りの様子を昼夜別に記録、表現したスコア。

STATISTICAL
TABLES & GRAPHS

CHARTS & SCORES

MAPS

ARCHITECTURAL
PLANS & DRAWINGS

INSTRUCTIONAL DIAGRAMS
FOR PRODUCTS

SCIENTIFIC
ILLUSTRATIONS

INTERLEAF, INC.
USA 1988
AD,D,I:Karin Fickett/plus design inc.
DF:Interleaf Creative Group

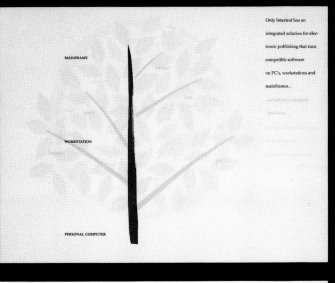

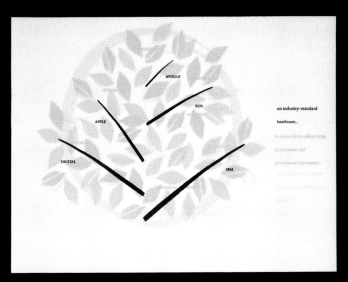

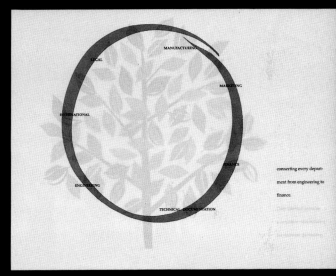

Illustration showing a corporate-wide solution for electronic publishing. It runs on a range of computing hardware, connects every department and produces a variety of documents. From an Interleaf Inc. annual report.

インターリーフ社のアニュアルリポートより、コンピューター・ネットワークの利用により、各部署が様々な文書を同時に出力することが可能な電子出版システムの利点を示すチャート。

STATISTICAL TABLES & GRAPHS

CHARTS & SCORES

MAPS

ARCHITECTURAL PLANS & DRAWINGS

INSTRUCTIONAL DIAGRAMS FOR PRODUCTS

SCIENTIFIC ILLUSTRATIONS

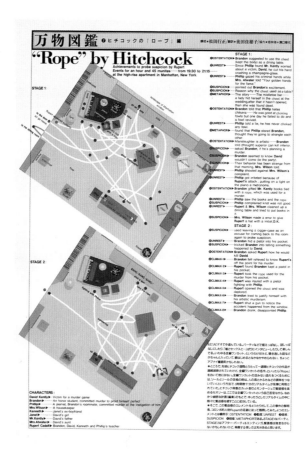

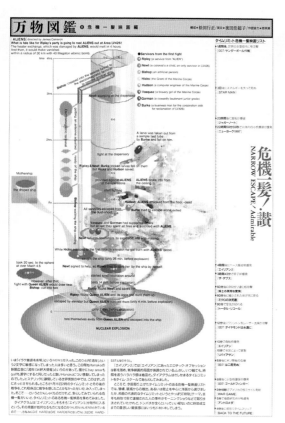

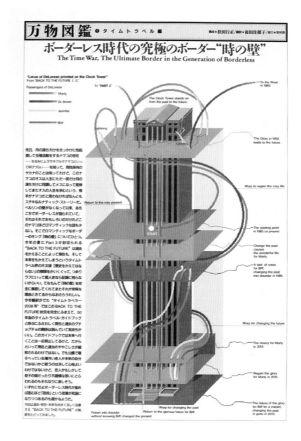

Storyline-scores of the movies, "Hitchcock's Rope", "Alien" and "Back to the Future". From the PFU Ltd. promotional brochure "Banbutsuzukan".
PFU社のプロモーション用パンフレット「万物図鑑」より、映画「ヒチコックのロープ」「エイリアン」「バックトゥザフューチャー」のストーリーをグラフィックで説明したスコア。

STATISTICAL TABLES & GRAPHS

CHARTS & SCORES

MAPS

ARCHITECTURAL PLANS & DRAWINGS

INSTRUCTIONAL DIAGRAMS FOR PRODUCTS

SCIENTIFIC ILLUSTRATIONS

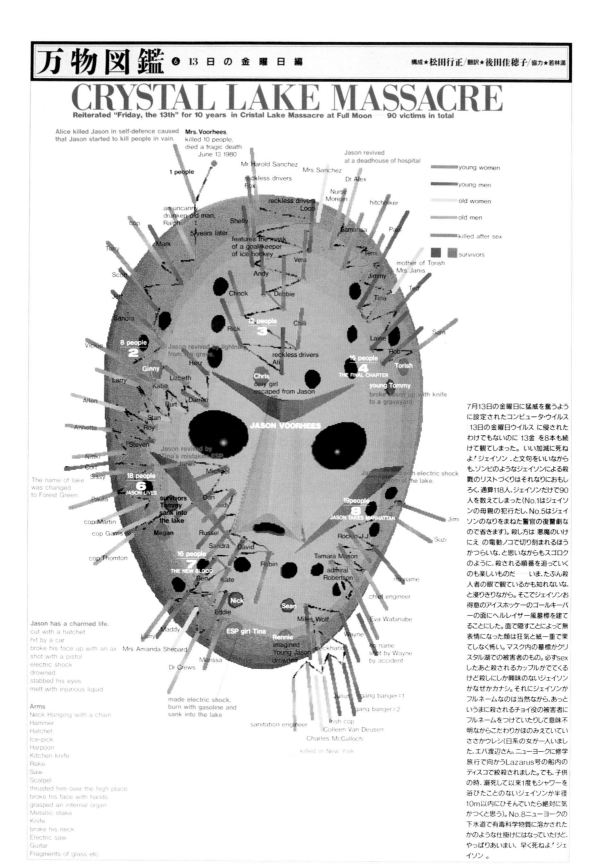

Chart of the victims in the movie, "Friday the 13th". From the PFU Ltd. promotional brochure "Banbutsuzukan".

PFU社のプロモーション用パンフレット「万物図鑑」より、映画「13日の金曜日」の犠牲者たちの状況をグラフィックで表現したチャート。

STATISTICAL
TABLES & GRAPHS

CHARTS & SCORES

MAPS

ARCHITECTURAL
PLANS & DRAWINGS

INSTRUCTIONAL DIAGRAMS
FOR PRODUCTS

SCIENTIFIC
ILLUSTRATIONS

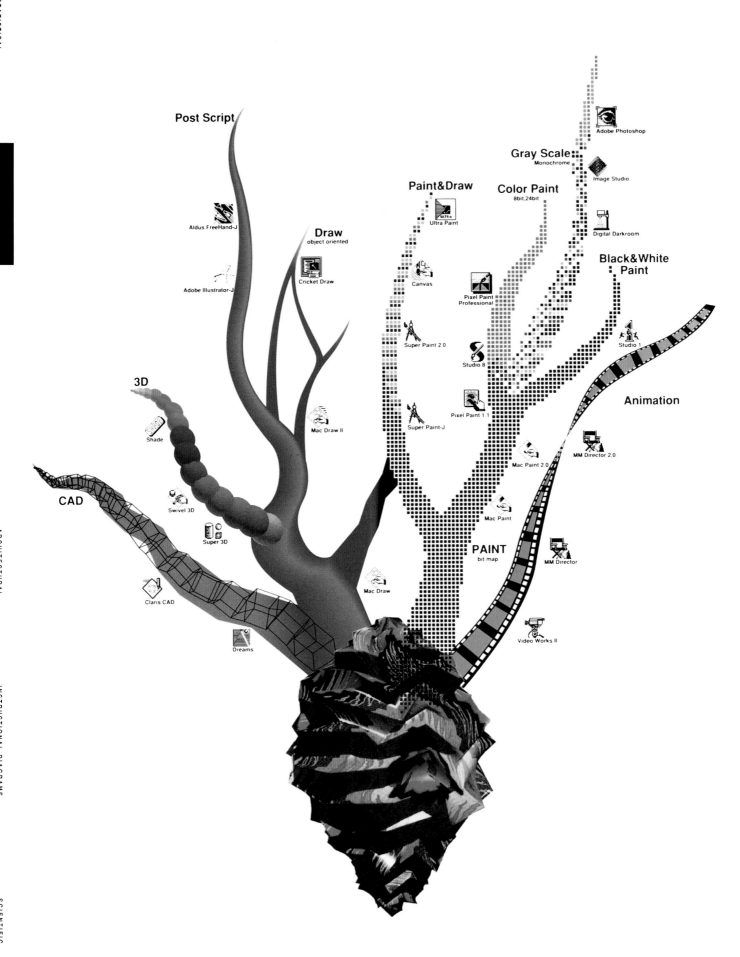

BNN CO.
JAPAN 1990
CD:Shoji Otsuki
AD,D,I:Mitsunobu Murakami

System diagram for software programs for the Macintosh computer. From Maclife magazine.
月刊誌「マックライフ」より、マッキントッシュ・コンピューターのソフト系統図。

BNN CO.
JAPAN 1991
AD,D:Sonoe Takigami

STATISTICAL
TABLES & GRAPHS

CHARTS & SCORES

MAPS

ARCHITECTURAL
PLANS & DRAWINGS

INSTRUCTIONAL DIAGRAMS
FOR PRODUCTS

SCIENTIFIC
ILLUSTRATIONS

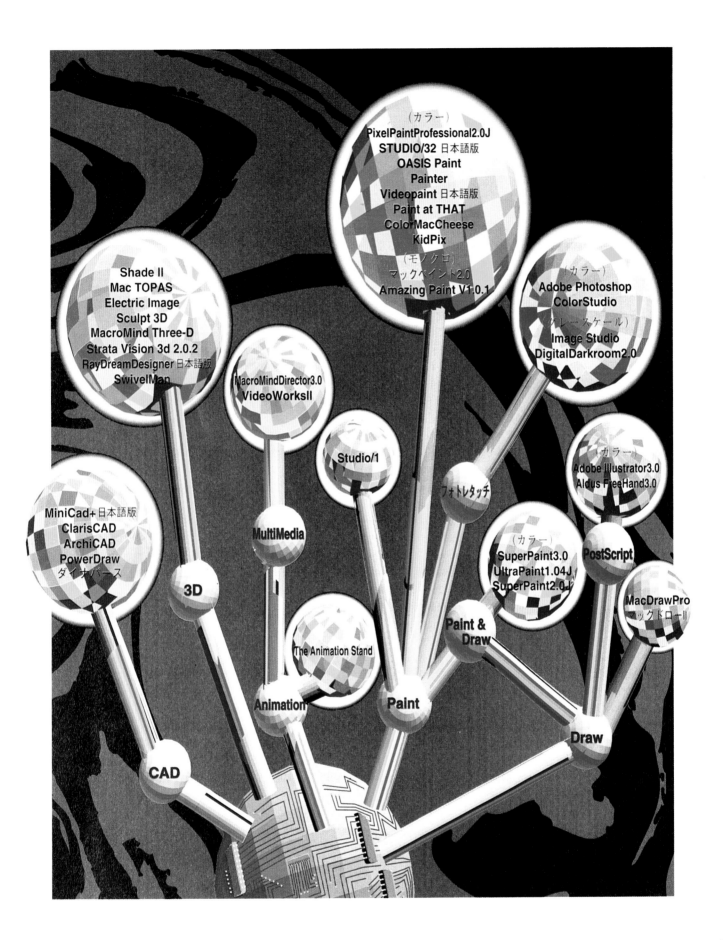

Genealogical tree of graphics software programs for the Macintosh computer. From Maclife magazine.
月刊誌「マックライフ」より、マッキントッシュ・コンピューターのグラフィックソフト系譜図。

BOEHRINGER MANNHEIM CORPORATION
USA 1991
AD:Chris Gilbert
AD,D,I:Rebecca Simms
DF:Henry Dreyfuss Associates

STATISTICAL
TABLES & GRAPHS

CHARTS & SCORES

MAPS

ARCHITECTURAL
PLANS & DRAWINGS

INSTRUCTIONAL DIAGRAMS
FOR PRODUCTS

SCIENTIFIC
ILLUSTRATIONS

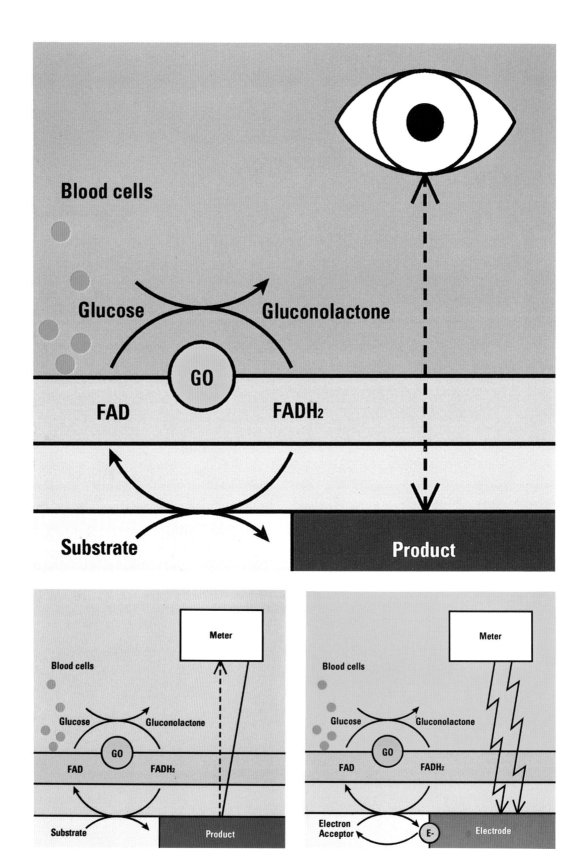

Graphic representations of the technology of three different methods of glucose self-monitoring for diabetic patients.
糖尿病患者が血糖を自己測定するための3つの方法における科学技術を解説するイラストレーション。

STATISTICAL
TABLES & GRAPHS

CHARTS & SCORES

MAPS

ARCHITECTURAL
PLANS & DRAWINGS

INSTRUCTIONAL DIAGRAMS
FOR PRODUCTS

SCIENTIFIC
ILLUSTRATIONS

BRITISH COUNCIL
ENGLAND 1986
CD:Richard Moon
D,I:Peter Grundy/Tilly Northedge
DF:Grundy & Northedge

MICHAEL PEHES LIHEAHVE
ENGLAND 1987
CD:Michael Peters
D,I:Peter Grundy/Tilly Northedge
DF:Grundy & Northedge

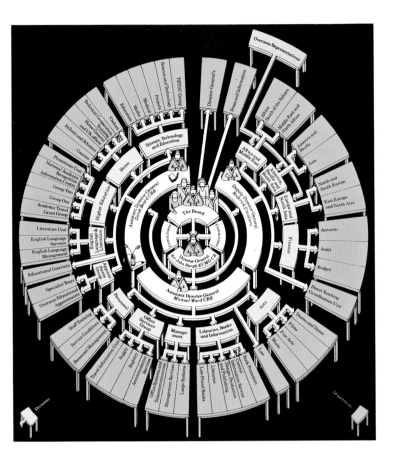

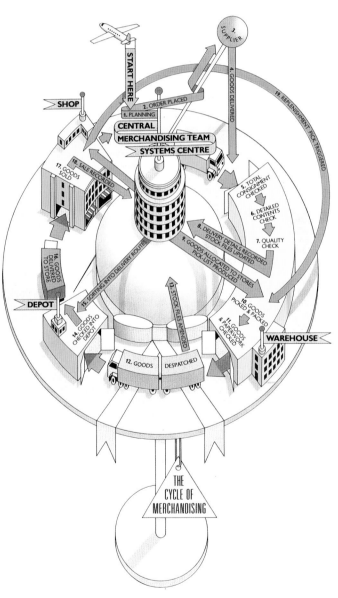

Structural diagram of the British Council's organization from an annual report.
ブリティッシュ・カウンシルのアニュアルリポートより、協会組織図。

Clothing distribution diagram for Burton. From an annual report.
バートン社のアニュアルリポートより、衣類流通経路図。

STATISTICAL
TABLES & GRAPHS

CHARTS & SCORES

MAPS

ARCHITECTURAL
PLANS & DRAWINGS

INSTRUCTIONAL DIAGRAMS
FOR PRODUCTS

SCIENTIFIC
ILLUSTRATIONS

Diagram showing how they work with clients. From a Grundy & Northedge design firm promotional brochure.
デザイン会社「グランディ ＆ ノースエッジ」の宣伝用パンフレットより、顧客への応対の仕方を表しているチャート。

STATISTICAL
TABLES & GRAPHS

CHARTS & SCORES

MAPS

ARCHITECTURAL
PLANS & DRAWINGS

INSTRUCTIONAL DIAGRAMS
FOR PRODUCTS

SCIENTIFIC
ILLUSTRATIONS

HILLHAVEN CORPORATION
USA 1991
AD,D:Jack Anderson
D:Mary Hermes
I:Jonathan Combs
DF:Hornall Anderson Design Works

ASDA
ENGLAND 1988,1989
AD,D:Amanda Tatham
I:Benoit Jacoues
DF:Tatham Pearce Ltd.

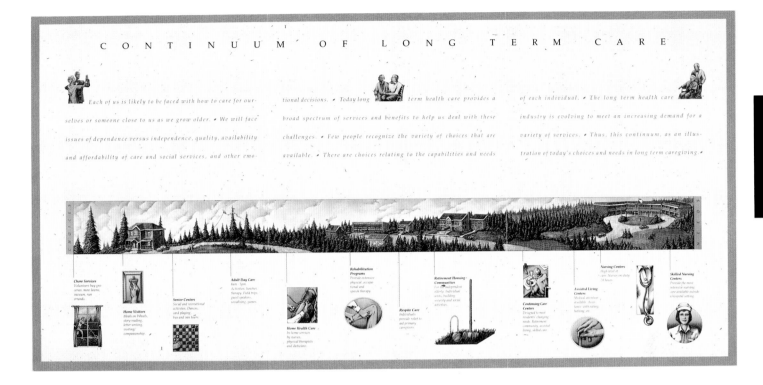

Chart dealing with long-term caregiving
from Hillhaven Corporation's brochure and poster.
ヒルヘイブン社のパンフレットやポスターより、長期ケアの様子を示すチャート。

Chart showing the performance of supermarket chain Asda
Group from a financial report to employees.
スーパーマーケット・チェーン「アスダグループ」の従業員への会計報告をイラストレーションで表したチャート。

GARBAGE MAGAZINE
USA 1992
AD:Patrick Mitchell
D,I:Scott A. MacNeill

STATISTICAL
TABLES & GRAPHS

CHARTS & SCORES

MAPS

ARCHITECTURAL
PLANS & DRAWINGS

INSTRUCTIONAL DIAGRAMS
FOR PRODUCTS

SCIENTIFIC
ILLUSTRATIONS

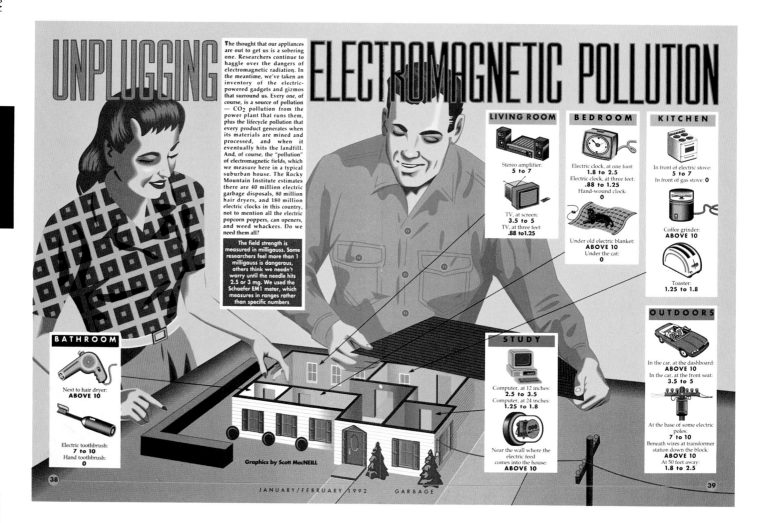

Illustration showing the EMF ratings of various household electrical devices and their locations in the home.
各家電製品のEMF（起電力）値、及び家庭内配置図。

STATISTICAL
TABLES & GRAPHS

CHARTS & SCORES

MAPS

ARCHITECTURAL
PLANS & DRAWINGS

INSTRUCTIONAL DIAGRAMS
FOR PRODUCTS

SCIENTIFIC
ILLUSTRATIONS

GROSSMONT HOSPITAL
USA 1992
CD:Monique Martineau
D,I:Tracy Sabin
DF:Sabin Design

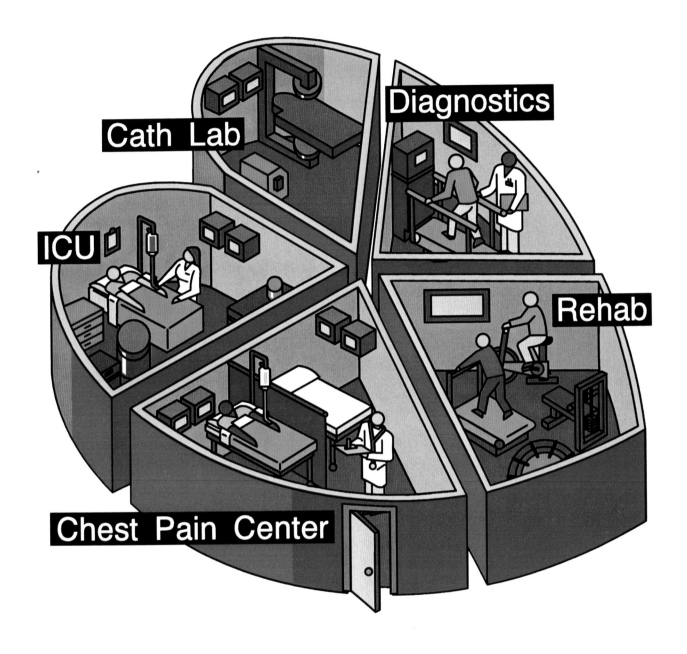

Chest Pain Center diagram used in newsletters and brochures.
ニュースレターやパンフレットに使用された「胸部ペインセンター」のチャート。

STATISTICAL
TABLES & GRAPHS

CHARTS & SCORES

MAPS

ARCHITECTURAL
PLANS & DRAWINGS

INSTRUCTIONAL DIAGRAMS
FOR PRODUCTS

SCIENTIFIC
ILLUSTRATIONS

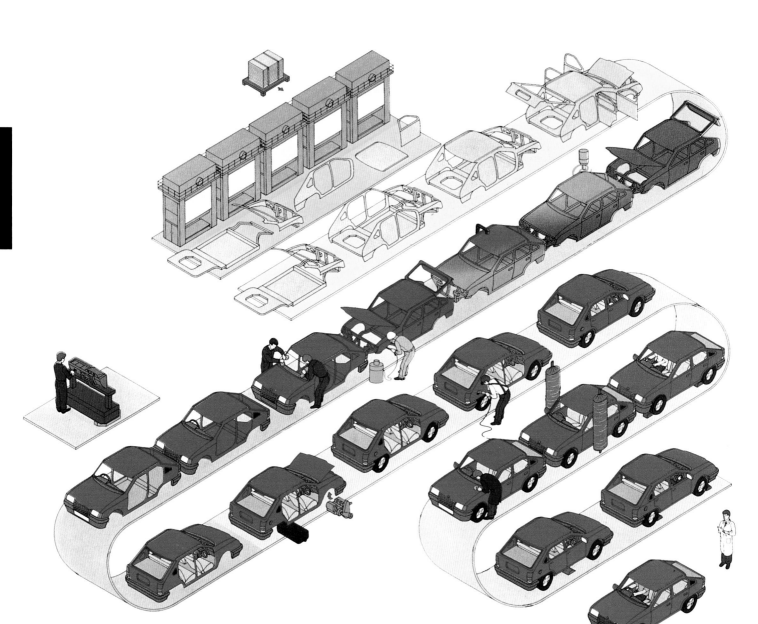

Diagram showing how a car is assembled on a production line in as simple a way as possible. From a Vauxhall Motors Ltd. brochure.
ヴォークソール・モーターズ社のパンフレットより、自動車が組み立てられる様子を表した生産ライン図。

STATISTICAL
TABLES & GRAPHS

CHARTS & SCORES

MAPS

ARCHITECTURAL
PLANS & DRAWINGS

INSTRUCTIONAL DIAGRAMS
FOR PRODUCTS

SCIENTIFIC
ILLUSTRATIONS

CENTOCOR, INC.
USA 1991
CD:Stephen Ferrari
D:John Ball
I:Michael Crumpton/
Martin Haggland/Micro Color
DF:The Graphic Expression, Inc.

DISCOVER
USA 1992
I:Andy Martin

Production of Centoxin

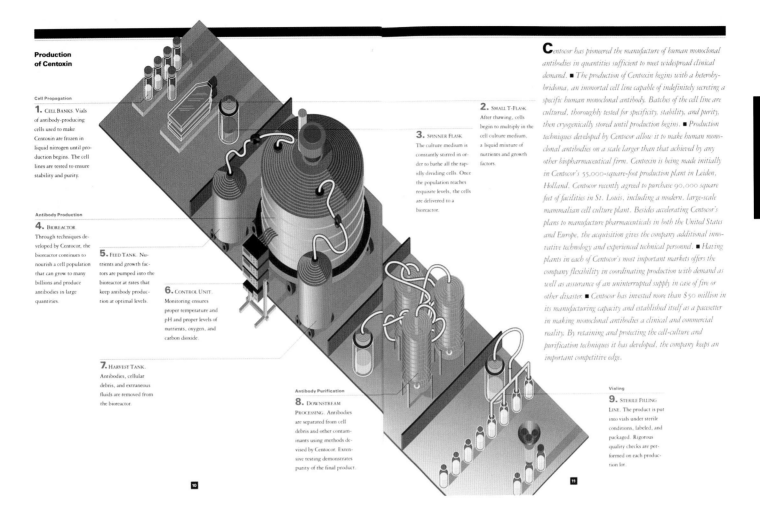

Cell Propagation

1. CELL BANKS. Vials of antibody-producing cells used to make Centoxin are frozen in liquid nitrogen until production begins. The cell lines are tested to ensure stability and purity.

Antibody Production

4. BIOREACTOR. Through techniques developed by Centocor, the bioreactor continues to nourish a cell population that can grow to many billions and produce antibodies in large quantities.

5. FEED TANK. Nutrients and growth factors are pumped into the bioreactor at rates that keep antibody production at optimal levels.

6. CONTROL UNIT. Monitoring ensures proper temperature and pH and proper levels of nutrients, oxygen, and carbon dioxide.

7. HARVEST TANK. Antibodies, cellular debris, and extraneous fluids are removed from the bioreactor.

2. SMALL T-FLASK. After thawing, cells begin to multiply in the cell culture medium, a liquid mixture of nutrients and growth factors.

3. SPINNER FLASK. The culture medium is constantly stirred in order to bathe all the rapidly dividing cells. Once the population reaches requisite levels, the cells are delivered to a bioreactor.

Antibody Purification

8. DOWNSTREAM PROCESSING. Antibodies are separated from cell debris and other contaminants using methods devised by Centocor. Extensive testing demonstrates purity of the final product.

Vialing

9. STERILE FILLING LINE. The product is put into vials under sterile conditions, labeled, and packaged. Rigorous quality checks are performed on each production lot.

*C*entocor has pioneered the manufacture of human monoclonal antibodies in quantities sufficient to meet widespread clinical demand. ■ The production of Centoxin begins with a heterohybridoma, an immortal cell line capable of indefinitely secreting a specific human monoclonal antibody. Batches of the cell line are cultured, thoroughly tested for specificity, stability, and purity, then cryogenically stored until production begins. ■ Production techniques developed by Centocor allow it to make human monoclonal antibodies on a scale larger than that achieved by any other biopharmaceutical firm. Centoxin is being made initially in Centocor's 55,000-square-foot production plant in Leiden, Holland. Centocor recently agreed to purchase 90,000 square feet of facilities in St. Louis, including a modern, large-scale mammalian cell culture plant. Besides accelerating Centocor's plans to manufacture pharmaceuticals in both the United States and Europe, the acquisition gives the company additional innovative technology and experienced technical personnel. ■ Having plants in each of Centocor's most important markets offers the company flexibility in coordinating production with demand as well as assurance of an uninterrupted supply in case of fire or other disaster. ■ Centocor has invested more than $50 million in its manufacturing capacity and established itself as a pacesetter in making monoclonal antibodies a clinical and commercial reality. By retaining and protecting the cell-culture and purification techniques it has developed, the company keeps an important competitive edge.

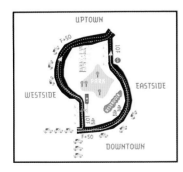
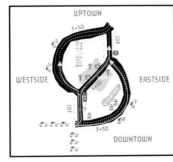
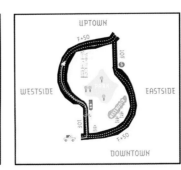
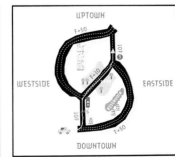

Illustration of the manufacturing process for a new drug called Centoxin.
From a Centocor Inc. annual report.
セントコア社のアニュアルリポートより、新薬「セントキシン」の製造プロセスを表すイラストレーション。

Charts showing the effect of added road capacity on traffic delays.
From an article in Discover magazine.
「ディスカバー・マガジン」より、道路交通量の増加と通行の遅れとの関係を表したチャート。

STATISTICAL
TABLES & GRAPHS

CHARTS & SCORES

MAPS

ARCHITECTURAL
PLANS & DRAWINGS

INSTRUCTIONAL DIAGRAMS
FOR PRODUCTS

SCIENTIFIC
ILLUSTRATIONS

FIRST BOSTON
ASSET MANAGEMENT CORPORATION
USA
CD:Stephen Ferrari
I,DF:The Graphic Expression, Inc.

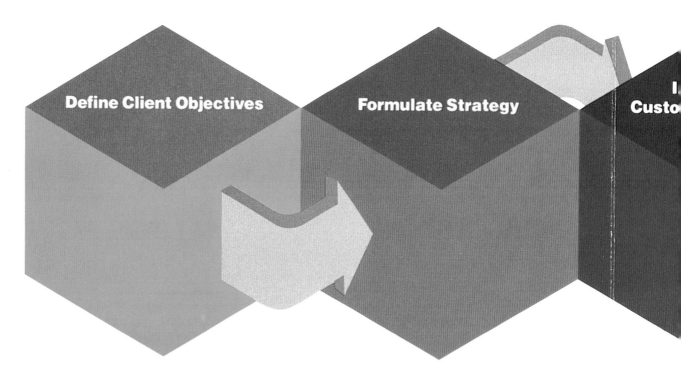

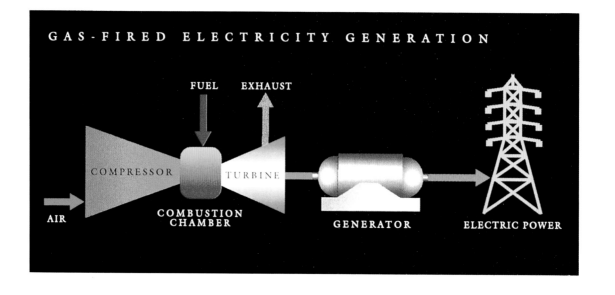

Chart showing the steps in customer/firm partnership used in
setting up an investment management program.
From a First Boston Asset Management Corporation brochure.
ファーストボストン・アセットマネージメント社のパンフレットより、
投資経営プログラムをたてるに際に使用される顧客と同社のパートナーシップの各段階を示すチャート。

UNOCAL CORPORATION
USA 1991
CD,AD,D,I:Ray Engle
DF:Ray Engle & Associates

STATISTICAL
TABLES & GRAPHS

CHARTS & SCORES

MAPS

ARCHITECTURAL
PLANS & DRAWINGS

INSTRUCTIONAL DIAGRAMS
FOR PRODUCTS

SCIENTIFIC
ILLUSTRATIONS

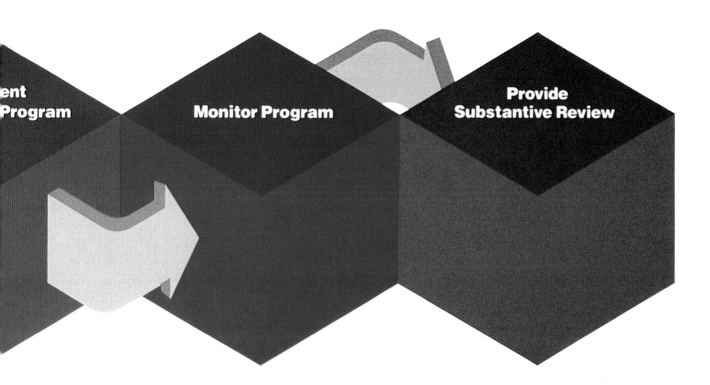

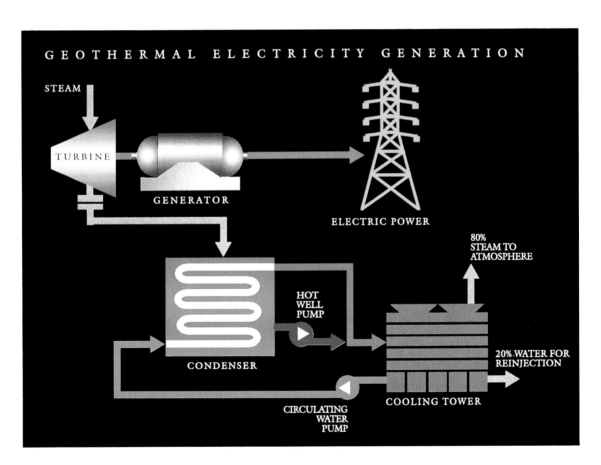

Chart of electricity generation for a magazine article on geothermal energy.
"地熱エネルギー"に関する雑誌記事より、発電のシステムを説明するチャート。

STATISTICAL
TABLES & GRAPHS

CHARTS & SCORES

MAPS

ARCHITECTURAL
PLANS & DRAWINGS

INSTRUCTIONAL DIAGRAMS
FOR PRODUCTS

SCIENTIFIC
ILLUSTRATIONS

ARCO
USA 1991
CD:Ron Jefferies
D:Scott Lambert
P:Keith Wood
I:Hank Fisher
DF:The Jefferies Association

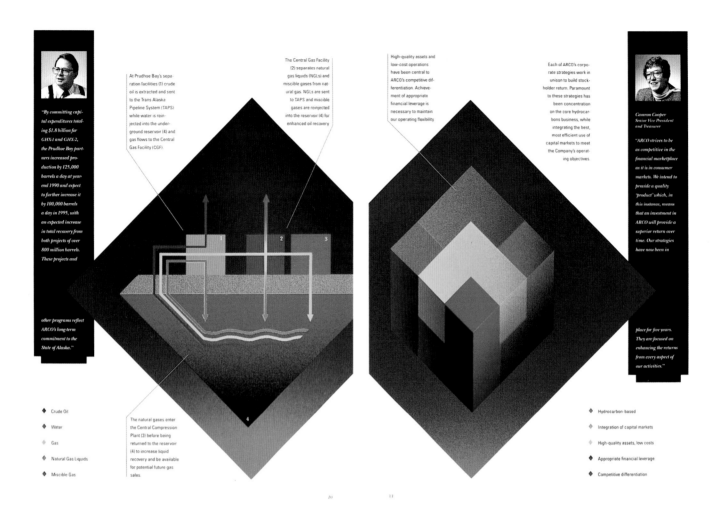

"By committing capital expenditures totaling $1.8 billion for GHX-1 and GHX-2, the Prudhoe Bay partners increased production by 125,000 barrels a day at year-end 1990 and expect to further increase it by 100,000 barrels a day in 1995, with an expected increase in total recovery from both projects of over 800 million barrels. These projects and

other programs reflect ARCO's long-term commitment to the State of Alaska."

At Prudhoe Bay's separation facilities (1) crude oil is extracted and sent to the Trans Alaska Pipeline System (TAPS) while water is reinjected into the underground reservoir (4) and gas flows to the Central Gas Facility (CGF).

The Central Gas Facility (2) separates natural gas liquids (NGLs) and miscible gases from natural gas. NGLs are sent to TAPS and miscible gases are reinjected into the reservoir (4) for enhanced oil recovery.

High-quality assets and low-cost operations have been central to ARCO's competitive differentiation. Achievement of appropriate financial leverage is necessary to maintain our operating flexibility.

Each of ARCO's corporate strategies work in unison to build stockholder return. Paramount to these strategies has been concentration on the core hydrocarbons business, while integrating the best, most efficient use of capital markets to meet the Company's operating objectives.

*Camron Cooper
Senior Vice President
and Treasurer*

"ARCO strives to be as competitive in the financial marketplace as it is in consumer markets. We intend to provide a quality 'product' which, in this instance, means that an investment in ARCO will provide a superior return over time. Our strategies have now been in

place for five years. They are focused on enhancing the returns from every aspect of our activities."

The natural gases enter the Central Compression Plant (3) before being returned to the reservoir (4) to increase liquid recovery and be available for potential future gas sales.

◆ Crude Oil
◆ Water
◆ Gas
◆ Natural Gas Liquids
◆ Miscible Gas

◆ Hydrocarbon-based
◆ Integration of capital markets
◆ High-quality assets, low costs
◆ Appropriate financial leverage
◆ Competitive differentiation

Diagram showing how crude oil is extracted from the reservoir and how miscible gases are reinjected and sent into the Trans Alaska Pipeline System (TAPS).
Diagram showing how five interconnecting strategies combine to build stockholder return. From an Arco annual report.
アルコ社のアニュアルリポートより、原油を貯蔵槽より引き出し、トランスアラスカ・パイプラインシステム（TAPS）に送る様子や混和性ガスを再注入する様子を表したチャート、
及び5つの相互に連結した戦略が株主の利益を築いていく様子を表したチャート。

SIGMA XI
USA 1991
AD:Linda Huff
D:Michael Szpir
D,I:Elyse Carter

STATISTICAL
TABLES & GRAPHS

CHARTS & SCORES

MAPS

ARCHITECTURAL
PLANS & DRAWINGS

INSTRUCTIONAL DIAGRAMS
FOR PRODUCTS

SCIENTIFIC
ILLUSTRATIONS

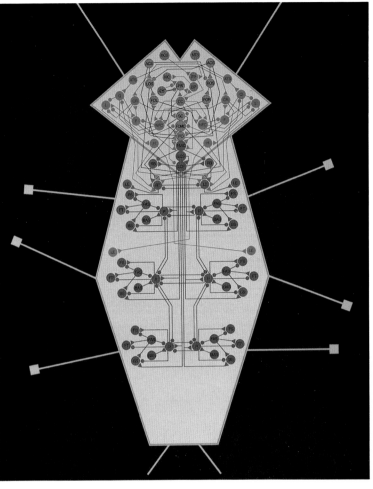

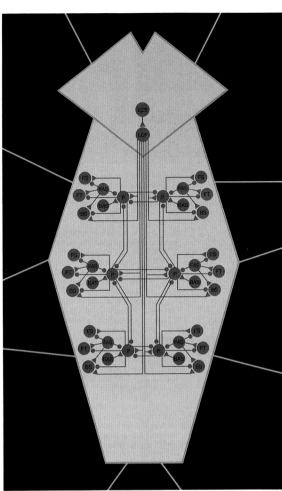

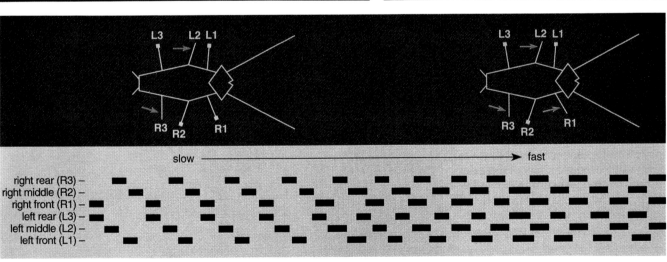

A computer-simulated insect reproduces some of the behaviors of the American cockroach.
The circuitry is color-coded for different aspects of the artificial insect's behavior. From American Scientist magazine.

「アメリカン・サイエンティストマガジン」より、人工昆虫を制作するためにコンピュータによりシミュレーションしたアメリカゴキブリの行動図。様々な行動の形態に従って回路が色分けされている。

STATISTICAL
TABLES & GRAPHS

CHARTS & SCORES

MAPS

ARCHITECTURAL
PLANS & DRAWINGS

INSTRUCTIONAL DIAGRAMS
FOR PRODUCTS

SCIENTIFIC
ILLUSTRATIONS

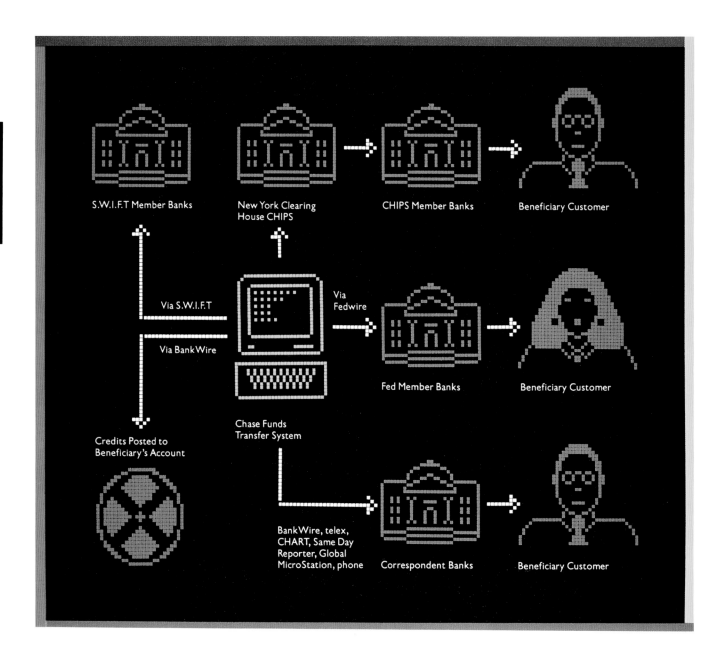

Chart explaining a marketing program for a bank.
銀行のマーケティングプログラムを説明したチャート。

マップ

マップすなわち地図は、私たちにとって最も身近なダイアグラムである。

基本的には、地域ないしは区域などの空間を表わすダイアグラムがマップである。私たちの生活は、空間を移動することによって成立しており、マップは、この空間の広がりと構造を図解することで、そこをいかに移動すれば目的の場所に着けるのかを私たちに教えてくれる。

言い換えるならば、空間と移動を結ぶダイアグラムがマップなのである。

ただし、たとえば「興味の範囲」、あるいは「業界の周辺」というように、私たちの日常の言葉の表現にも、厳密な意味では空間ではないものを空間的な比喩で表わす例も多く見られる。これがダイアグラムにも影響し、現実的な区域や空間ではないものを、比喩的に空間化してマップ化した作例も少なくはない。興味の地図、業界マップ・・・という具合いで、こうした作例においては、マップは単純に区域や地域と移動を結ぶダイアグラムではなく、むしろ、概念や現象の「空間」を探索するための教材として作用している。

こうした作例は、近年、特に増えており、ダイアグラム表現の一般化と成熟を反映すると共に、膨大な量の情報と多様なメディアに囲まれて生活する現代人が自然と身につけざるを得ない、柔軟かつ複合的な感受性をも裏書きしているといえよう。

自分の暮らす世界の中でのものの配置を記した「頭の中の地図」のことを、心理学では認知地図という。この認知地図は、言語の修得以前は幼児の頭の中でも成立しており、地図というものが、人間が世界を把握する上での最も基本的な感覚の図解であることが実感される。

それだけに、古来よりの作例も多く、手法的にも探求しつくされているのが、このマップというダイアグラムである。視覚的な機能をそこなわずに、なおかつ従来の伝統を超える新しいイメージは、マップにおいてはそう簡単に提示できるものではないだろう。

地球規模での情報ネットワークが完備し、世界が狭くなる分だけ、人間ひとりひとりの心が具体的に想起し得る空間が大きくなり続ける今日にあって、人々の空間イメージにどれだけ即応できるマップを作れるかは、デザイナーにとって大きな課題ではある。

MAPS

MAPS

マップ

Maps are the most familiar diagrams there are. Basically, a map is a diagram which indicates a region within boundaries. Since our lives proceed largely by moving from one place to another through space, a map, by illustrating the expanse and structure of that space, guides our movement so that we can reach our goals. In other words, a map is a diagram of the link between space and movement.

It is interesting to note the presence of such verbal expressions as "a wide range of interests" and "the peripheral areas of the industry " in our everyday speech. Here are things which are not, strictly speaking, spatial in nature, being expressed in language with spatial metaphors. A similar phenomenon can be seen in diagram making, where things which really have nothing to do with space are expressed metaphorically with space and are made into maps. In this case, a map is not merely a diagram that connects areas with vectors of movement. Here, it serves the usual function of text by operating as learning material. With such a map, one can explore the metaphorical space of concepts and phenomena. Examples of this sort of map have been increasing rapidly in recent years and this probably reflects the fact that diagrams, as a form of expression, have matured and become more generalized. It also reveals the flexible and complex sensitivity which modern people have had to acquire, surrounded as they are by vast quantities of information brought to them in a variety of media. In psychological terminology, "the map in your head," wherein the things of the outer world are arranged into the inner world in which you live, is called a cognitive map. This cognitive map is apparently present in the brain of even a very young child who has not yet acquired language. Thus, it is probably fair to conclude that a map is the most basic representation of the way in which human sensory data are organized in our attempts to understand the world around us.

It is not surprising to discover, then, that there exists a tremendous wealth of superb maps which date back to ancient times. In many cases, artistic techniques have reached their zenith in the production of maps. For the designer, of course, this means that it will not be easy to come up with a new approach or an original kind of image. It will be difficult to surpass what has already been done in mapping without downgrading its main purpose as a functional map.

Today, with global information networks being put in place, and the world getting smaller and smaller, the kind of space that can and must be contained in each person's mind is growing larger and larger. The map designer now has to tackle the considerable challenge of producing a map which corresponds closely to people's spatial images of the world.

**LONDON DOCKLANDS
DEVELOPMENT CORPORATION**
ENGLAND 1981
CD,AD,D:John McConnell
D:Kia Boon
DF:Pentagram Design Ltd.

STATISTICAL
TABLES & GRAPHS

CHARTS & SCORES

MAPS

ARCHITECTURAL
PLANS & DRAWINGS

FAWE STREET

EAST INDIA DOCK ROAD

NORTH QUAY

WEST FERRY
ROAD

CANARY WHARF

LIMEHOUSE

HERON WHARF

BOW ROAD

DEVONS STREET

FAWE STREET

Figure showing tracks of the Docklands Light Railway, featuring the rail company's multipurpose sign system.
多目的サインシステムを取り入れている、ドッグランズライト鉄道の路線図。

STATISTICAL
TABLES & GRAPHS

CHARTS & SCORES

MAPS

ARCHITECTURAL
PLANS & DRAWINGS

INSTRUCTIONAL DIAGRAMS
FOR PRODUCTS

SCIENTIFIC
ILLUSTRATIONS

**PENNSYLVANIA DEPARTMENT
OF TRANSPORTATION**
USA 1991
CD:Lois Morasco
AD,D,I:Joel Katz
DF:Katz Wheeler Design

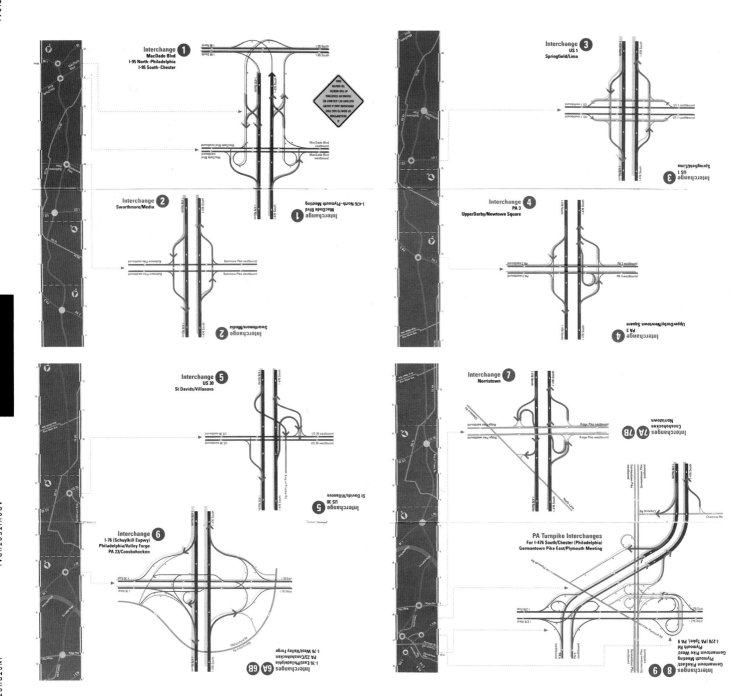

Guide to Interstate-476 providing information about the new expressway.
新しい高速道路「州間道路476号線」の情報ガイド。

CITY OF NIAGARA (NEW YORK)
USA
AD:Robert Gersin
D:James Goldschmidt
I:Unk
DF:Robert P. Gersin Assoc. Inc.

PENNSYLVANIA DEPARTMENT
OF TRANSPORTATION
USA 1990
CD:Lois Morasco
AD,D:Joel Katz
I:Tom Jackson
DF:Katz Wheeler Design

STATISTICAL
TABLES & GRAPHS

CHARTS & SCORES

MAPS

ARCHITECTURAL
PLANS & DRAWINGS

INSTRUCTIONAL DIAGRAMS
FOR PRODUCTS

SCIENTIFIC
ILLUSTRATIONS

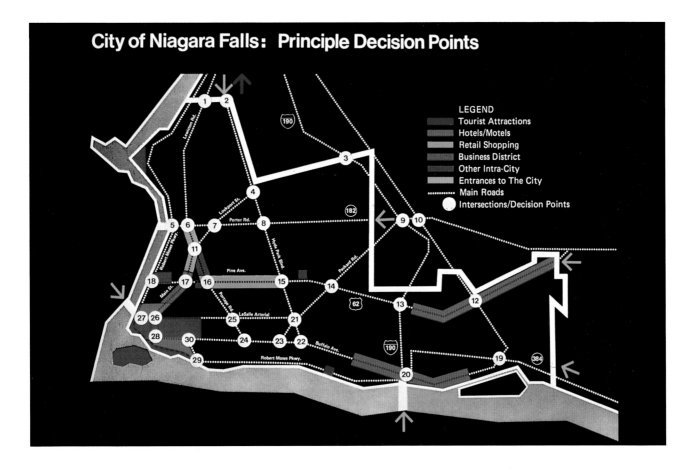

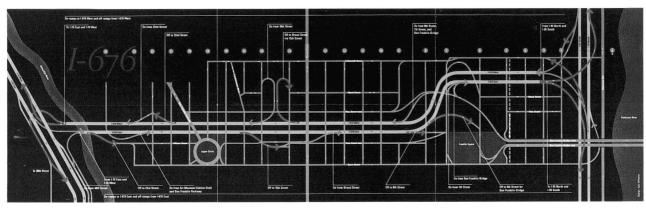

Map showing major decision points in the City of Niagara Falls, NY.
ニューヨーク州ナイアガラ・フォール市の観光プランの分岐ポイントを示した地図。

Guide to Interstate-676 providing information about the new expressway.
新しい高速道路「州間道路676号線」の情報ガイド。

STATISTICAL
TABLES & GRAPHS

CHARTS & SCORES

MAPS

ARCHITECTURAL
PLANS & DRAWINGS

INSTRUCTIONAL DIAGRAMS
FOR PRODUCTS

SCIENTIFIC
ILLUSTRATIONS

Street map of Houston, Texas where an AIA (American Institute of Architects) national convention was held. From a poster.

AIA（アメリカ建築家協会）国際会議ポスターより、会議の会場となったテキサス州ヒューストン市の街路図。

**STATISTICAL
TABLES & GRAPHS**

CHARTS & SCORES

MAPS

**ARCHITECTURAL
PLANS & DRAWINGS**

**INSTRUCTIONAL DIAGRAMS
FOR PRODUCTS**

**SCIENTIFIC
ILLUSTRATIONS**

THE NATIONAL GRID
ENGLAND 1990
CD,AD,D:John McConnell
D:Justus Oehler
DF:Pentagram Design Ltd.

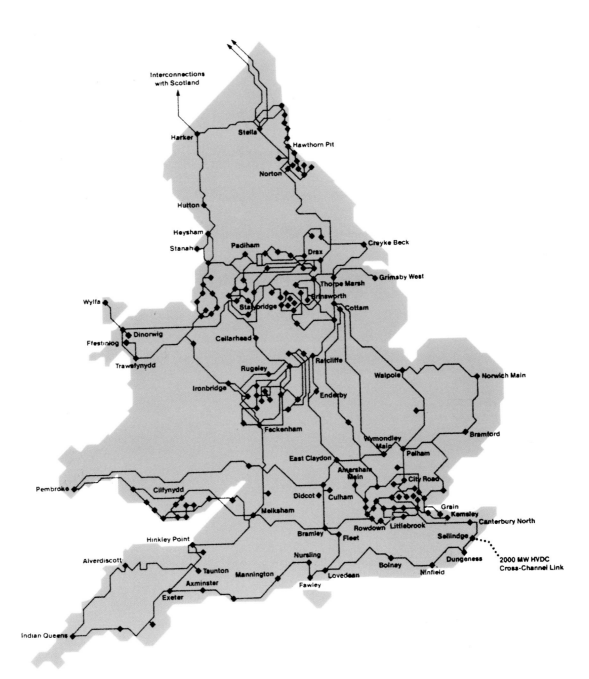

Map showing the locations of power stations. From a National Grid business report.
ナショナルグリッド社の業務報告書より、発電所の位置を示す地図。

STATISTICAL
TABLES & GRAPHS

CHARTS & SCORES

MAPS

ARCHITECTURAL
PLANS & DRAWINGS

INSTRUCTIONAL DIAGRAMS
FOR PRODUCTS

SCIENTIFIC
ILLUSTRATIONS

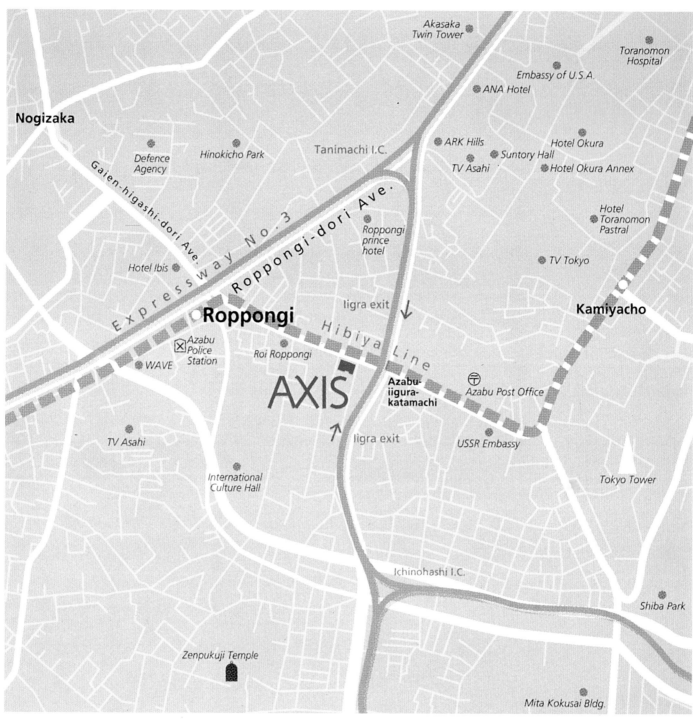

Location map of the commercial building Axis. From a promotional pamphlet.
プロモーション用パンフレットより、テナントビル「アクシス」の所在地図。

AZABU BUILDING CO., LTD.
JAPAN 1989
AD:Ichiro Higashiizumi
D:Kazuhiro Kishi/Yumiko Iizuka
DF:Huia Media Design Co., Ltd.

ASAHI SHIMBUN AERA DIVISION
JAPAN 1991
AD:Nobuko Edatsune
D:Nobuo Morishita

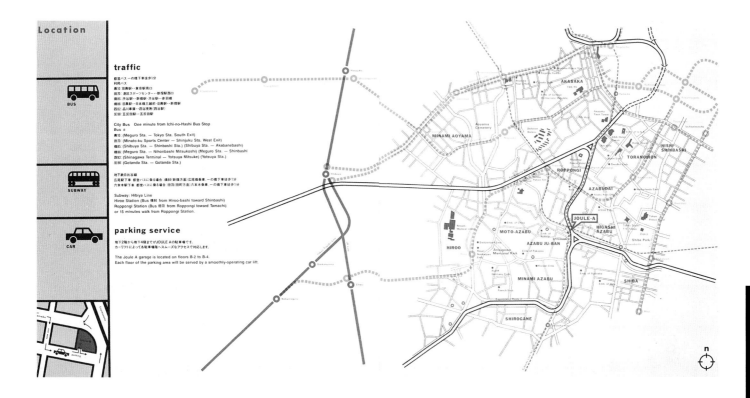

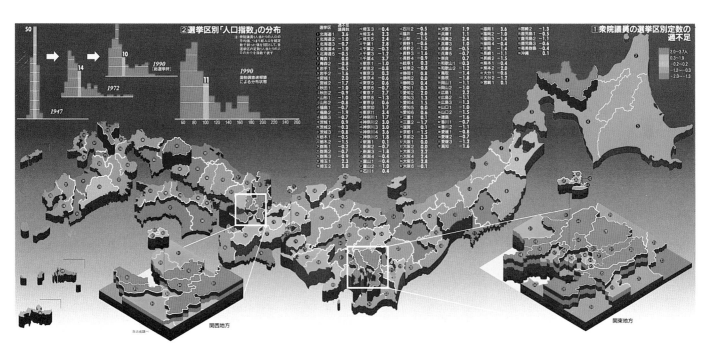

Map showing the location of the Joule-A Building.
Pictographs are used to explain public transportation routes to and from the building.
JOULE-Aビルの所在地図。交通機関の説明にピクトグラムが利用されている。

Graph for the article,
"Allotted number of representative seats for each constituency" in Aera magazine.
週刊誌「アエラ」より、"選挙区別定数"に関する記事に使用されたグラフ・マップ。

STATISTICAL
TABLES & GRAPHS

CHARTS & SCORES

MAPS

ARCHITECTURAL
PLANS & DRAWINGS

INSTRUCTIONAL DIAGRAMS
FOR PRODUCTS

SCIENTIFIC
ILLUSTRATIONS

MARATHON REALTY COMPANY LIMITED,
BUILDINGS GROUP
CANADA 1991
AD,D:Roslyn Eskind
D,I:Peter Scott
DF:Eskind Waddell

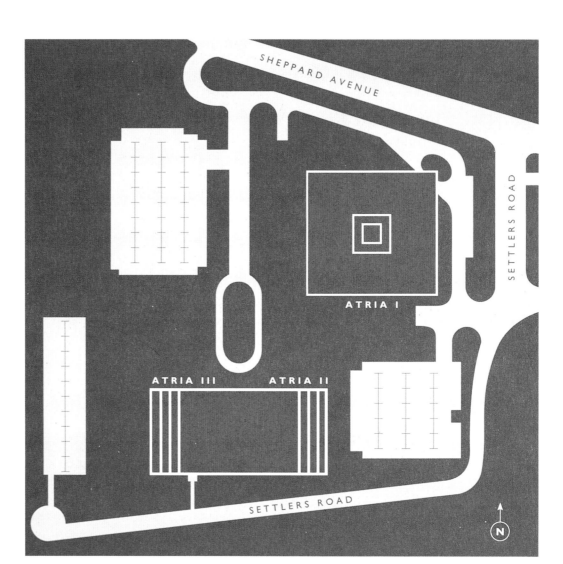

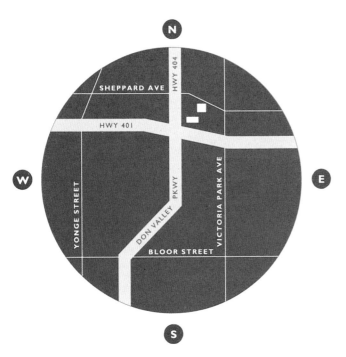

Site plan giving tenants of the commercial development a clear indication of building, parking and arterial road locations.
Map locating the development relative to major city access roads.
賃貸物件の便利性を示す、ビル・駐車場・幹線道路を含む商業開発区域平面図、及び都市につながる主要道路との位置関係地図。

STATISTICAL
TABLES & GRAPHS

CHARTS & SCORES

MAPS

ARCHITECTURAL
PLANS & DRAWINGS

INSTRUCTIONAL DIAGRAMS
FOR PRODUCTS

SCIENTIFIC
ILLUSTRATIONS

TOKYO DOME KORAKUEN PARK 91-92

LOVE LOVE LOVE

1 ウルトラツイスター
2 スカイフラワー
3 スカイサイクル
4 フライングキャビンUFO
5 フライングカーペット
6 後楽園タワー
7 トラバント
8 お化け屋敷
9 バルーン
10 ギディスウィング
11 サーカストレイン
12 ティーカップ
13 小メリーゴーランド
14 ラブエクスプレス
15 レインボー
16 キディランド
17 野外劇場
18 スーパーシャトル
19 スーパーテレコンバット
20 豆汽車
21 ジェットコースター
22 バイキング
23 大メリーゴーランド
24 ミラーワールド
25 大観覧車
26 チビッコ広場
27 カーニバル

Guide map of Korakuen Amusement Park in Tokyo. Printed on the admission ticket.
チケットに印刷された東京後楽園遊園地の案内地図。

STATISTICAL
TABLES & GRAPHS

CHARTS & SCORES

MAPS

ARCHITECTURAL
PLANS & DRAWINGS

INSTRUCTIONAL DIAGRAMS
FOR PRODUCTS

SCIENTIFIC
ILLUSTRATIONS

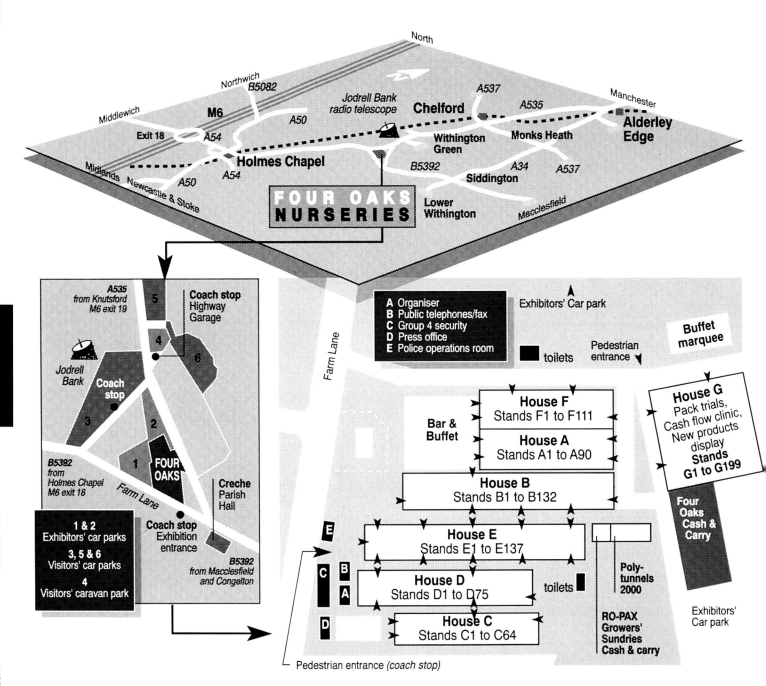

North

Northwich
B5082
Middlewich
M6
A50
Jodrell Bank
radio telescope
Chelford
A537
A535
Manchester
Alderley
Edge
Exit 18
A54
Withington
Green
Monks Heath
Holmes Chapel
B5392
A34
A537
Midlands
Newcastle & Stoke
A50
A54
Siddington
Macclesfield

FOUR OAKS
NURSERIES

Lower
Withington

A535
from Knutsford
M6 exit 19

Coach stop
Highway
Garage

Jodrell
Bank

Coach
stop

B5392
from
Holmes Chapel
M6 exit 18

Farm Lane

**FOUR
OAKS**

Creche
Parish
Hall

Coach stop
Exhibition
entrance

B5392
from Macclesfield
and Congelton

1 & 2
Exhibitors' car parks

3, 5 & 6
Visitors' car parks

4
Visitors' caravan park

A Organiser
B Public telephones/fax
C Group 4 security
D Press office
E Police operations room

Exhibitors' Car park

Pedestrian
entrance

**Buffet
marquee**

toilets

Farm Lane

House F
Stands F1 to F111

**Bar &
Buffet**

House A
Stands A1 to A90

House G
Pack trials,
Cash flow clinic,
New products
display
**Stands
G1 to G199**

House B
Stands B1 to B132

House E
Stands E1 to E137

**Four
Oaks
Cash &
Carry**

House D
Stands D1 to D75

toilets

Poly-
tunnels
2000

House C
Stands C1 to C64

**RO-PAX
Growers'
Sundries
Cash & carry**

Exhibitors'
Car park

Pedestrian entrance *(coach stop)*

Location stand guide for Four Oaks horticultural exhibition.
フォアオークス園芸展示会場の所在地を示すスタンド案内図。

STATISTICAL
TABLES & GRAPHS

CHARTS & SCORES

MAPS

ARCHITECTURAL
PLANS & DRAWINGS

INSTRUCTIONAL DIAGRAMS
FOR PRODUCTS

SCIENTIFIC
ILLUSTRATIONS

CITY OF LONDON POLICE
ENGLAND 1992
AD:Tom Griffin
D:Ian Moore
DF:Griffin Associates

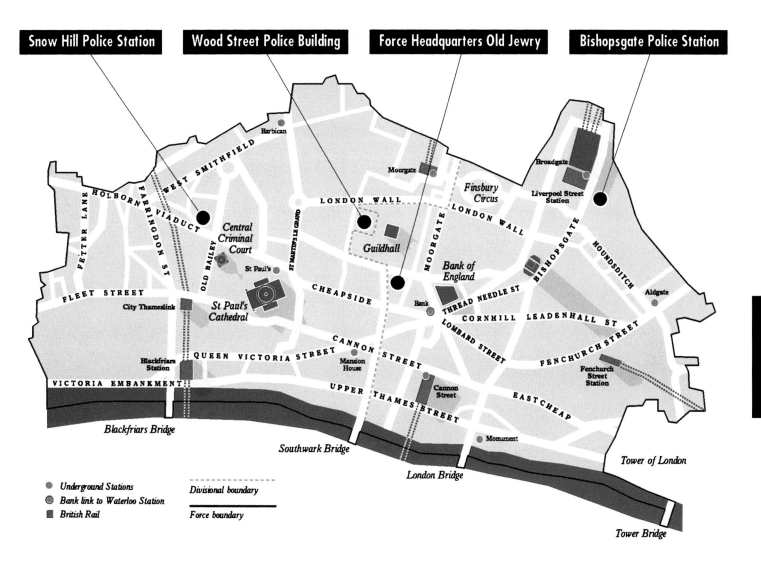

Snow Hill Police Station

Wood Street Police Building

Force Headquarters Old Jewry

Bishopsgate Police Station

● Underground Stations
◉ Bank link to Waterloo Station
■ British Rail

- - - Divisional boundary
——— Force boundary

City of London Police Force Boundaries Map
ロンドン市警察の管轄区域図。

LAMBTON PLACE
ENGLAND 1987
CD:David Pearce
AD,D:Amanda Tatham
DF:Lambton Place

STATISTICAL
TABLES & GRAPHS

CHARTS & SCORES

MAPS

ARCHITECTURAL
PLANS & DRAWINGS

INSTRUCTIONAL DIAGRAMS
FOR PRODUCTS

SCIENTIFIC
ILLUSTRATIONS

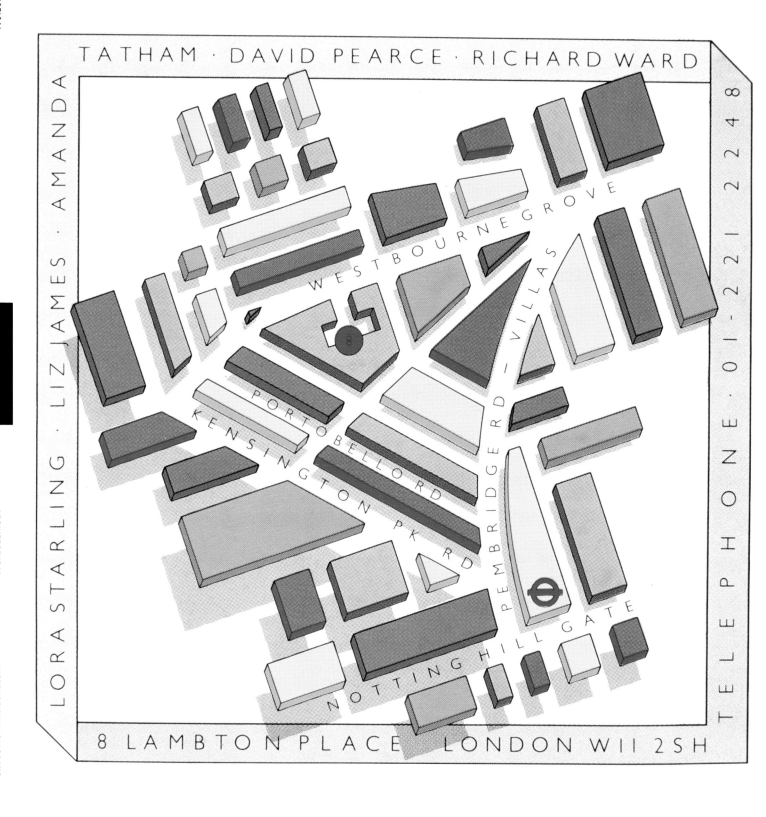

Location map of the design firm Lambton Place.
デザイン事務所「ラムトン・プレース」の所在地図。

STATISTICAL
TABLES & GRAPHS

CHARTS & SCORES

MAPS

ARCHITECTURAL
PLANS & DRAWINGS

INSTRUCTIONAL DIAGRAMS
FOR PRODUCTS

SCIENTIFIC
ILLUSTRATIONS

1. MCI
USA 1985
CD,AD,D:Susan Hochbaum
I:Steven Guarnaccia
DF:Pentagram Design Ltd.

2. SEAGRAM LONDON
ENGLAND 1990
CD,AD:Amanda Tatham
D:Paul Hannan
I:Michael Hill
DF:Tatham Pearce Ltd.

3. DEL MAR PLAZA
USA 1990
AD:Brenda Bodney
D,I:Tracy Sabin
DF:Bodney/Siedler Design

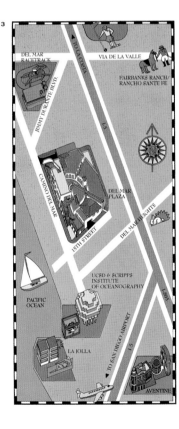

1. Stylized map of the world serviced by MCI, a telephone
communications company. From an annual report.
電信電話会社MCIのアニュアルリポートより、
同社によりサービスを受ける地域のイラストレーションマップ。

2. Seagram London's new building location map
ロンドン・シーグラム社の新ビル所在地図。

3. Del Mar Plaza location map used in brochures.
パンフレットに使用されたデルマルプラザ所在地図。

THE FUND FOR
THE BOROUGH OF BROOKLYN, INC.
USA 1984
CD,AD,D:Keith Godard
I:Cadre Graphics
DF:Studio Works

STATISTICAL TABLES & GRAPHS

CHARTS & SCORES

MAPS

ARCHITECTURAL PLANS & DRAWINGS

INSTRUCTIONAL DIAGRAMS FOR PRODUCTS

SCIENTIFIC ILLUSTRATIONS

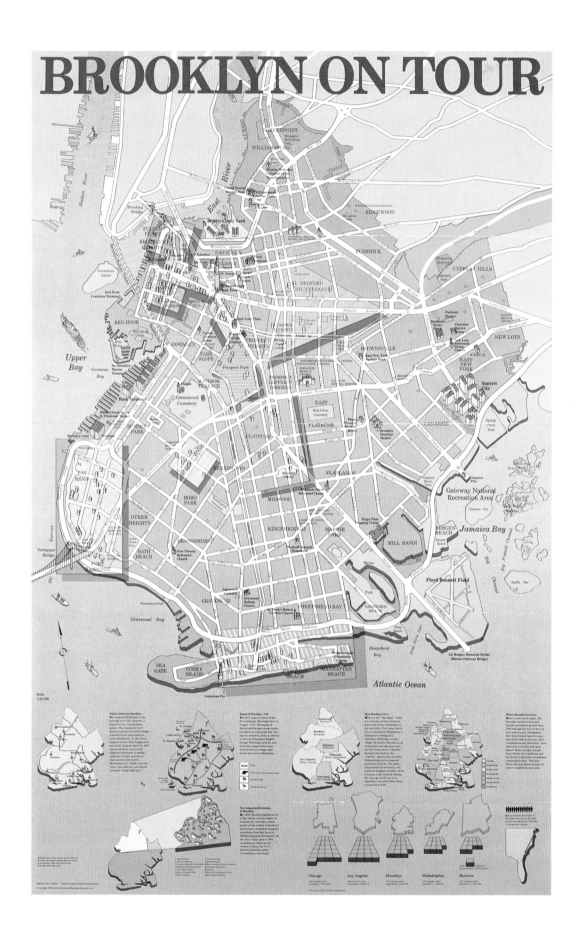

BROOKLYN ON TOUR

"Brooklyn On Tour" is an all-in-one map and guide to America's favorite hometown, Brooklyn.
「ブルックリン巡り」はアメリカで人気のホームタウン/ブルックリンの地図とガイドを一括で見ることができる。

STATISTICAL
TABLES & GRAPHS

CHARTS & SCORES

MAPS

ARCHITECTURAL
PLANS & DRAWINGS

INSTRUCTIONAL DIAGRAMS
FOR PRODUCTS

SCIENTIFIC
ILLUSTRATIONS

**APT · AZIENDA
PER LA PROMOZIONE TURISTICA
DELLA PROVINCIA DI FERRARA**
ITALY 1989,1990
AD:Craziano Uillani
D,I:Cinzia Calzolari

53RD STREET ASSOC.
USA
AD:Collin Forbes
D:Kaspar Schmid/Michael Gericke
I:Steven Guarnaccia

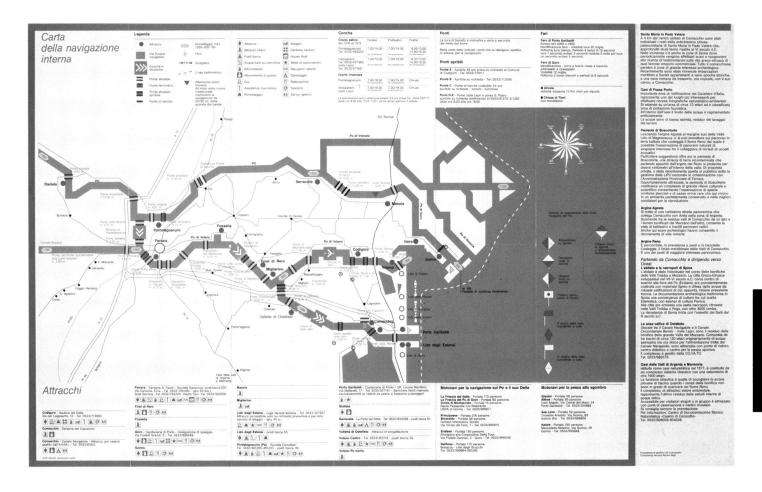

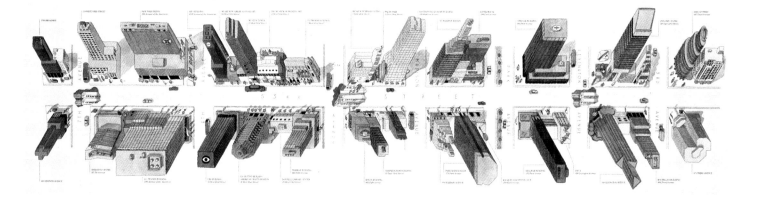

Tourist itinerary map for promotion of Ferrara city.
フェラーラ市のプロモーション用に制作された観光ルート地図。

Map showing important cultural institutions on 53rd Street, including the Museum of Modern Art, NY.
ニューヨーク近代美術館を含む重要な文化施設を表した53番街の地図。

STATISTICAL TABLES & GRAPHS

CHARTS & SCORES

MAPS

ARCHITECTURAL PLANS & DRAWINGS

INSTRUCTIONAL DIAGRAMS FOR PRODUCTS

SCIENTIFIC ILLUSTRATIONS

YAMANASHI PREFECTURE

JAPAN 1988

AD:Tokihiro Okuda

D:Mitsuko Kato

I:Fumiyo Kojima

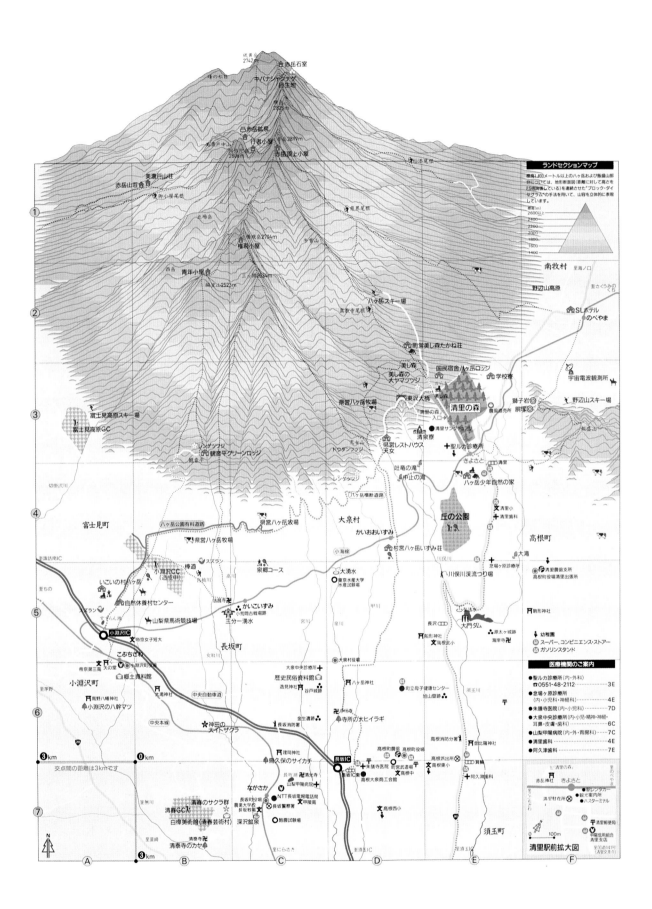

Map used in a leaflet advertising real estate in the Kiyosatonomori resort area.

別荘用分譲地のパンフレットより、リゾート地「清里の森」の地図。

NATIONAL GEOGRAPHIC MAGAZINE
USA 1991
CD:Allen Carroll
AD:John F. Dorr
D:Sally S. Summerall
I:John Dawson
DF:Carto Graphic Division of
National Geog. Magazine

STATISTICAL
TABLES & GRAPHS

CHARTS & SCORES

MAPS

ARCHITECTURAL
PLANS & DRAWINGS

INSTRUCTIONAL DIAGRAMS
FOR PRODUCTS

SCIENTIFIC
ILLUSTRATIONS

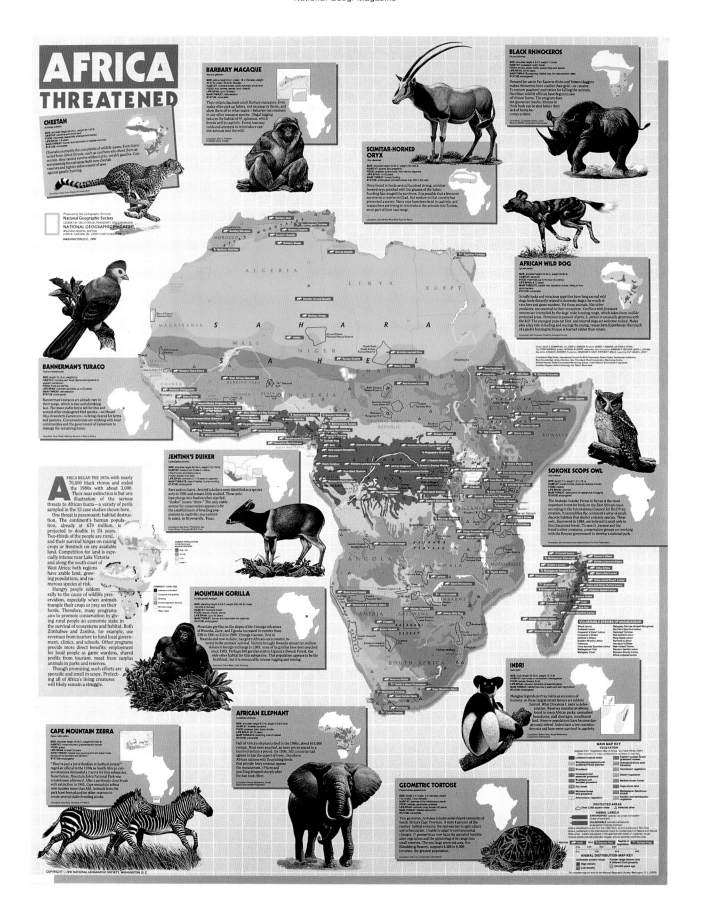

"Africa Threatened" map carried in the appendix of National Geographic Magazine reporting in detail on the current situation of various endangered species throughout Africa.

「ナショナル・ジオグラフィック・マガジン」の付録に使用された"アフリカへの脅威"地図。アフリカ各地で絶滅の危機に瀕している動物たちの現況を詳しく報告している。

STATISTICAL
TABLES & GRAPHS

CHARTS & SCORES

MAPS

ARCHITECTURAL
PLANS & DRAWINGS

INSTRUCTIONAL DIAGRAMS
FOR PRODUCTS

SCIENTIFIC
ILLUSTRATIONS

CLUB MED, INC.
USA 1991
CD,D,I:Stephen Ferrari
DF:The Graphic Expression, Inc.

**3,400
North American
GMs visited the
European zone**

**5,400
North American
GMs visited the
Asian zone**

**55,900
European and
South American
GMs visited the
American zone**

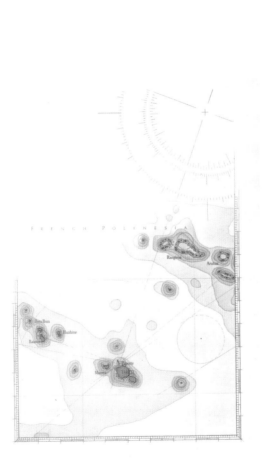

Map showing regional travel among Club Med Asian and American zones.
会員制クラブ「クラブ・メッド」のアジア・アメリカ旅行における地域施設案内図。

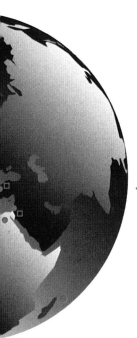

STATISTICAL
TABLES & GRAPHS

CHARTS & SCORES

MAPS

ARCHITECTURAL
PLANS & DRAWINGS

INSTRUCTIONAL DIAGRAMS
FOR PRODUCTS

SCIENTIFIC
ILLUSTRATIONS

WINDSTAR CRUISES
USA 1991
AD,D:Jack Anderson
D:Denise Weir/Paula Cox
I:Bruce Morser
DF:Hornall Anderson Design Works

21,000
European zone
GMs visited
the Asian zone

2,200
Asian GMs
visited the
European zone

2,400
Asian GMs
visited the
American zone

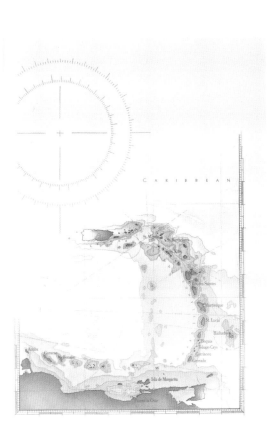

Maps showing the ports of call of Windstar Cruises. From a Windstar Cruises brochure.
ウィンドスター・クルージィーズ社のカタログより、クルーズ・ツアーの寄航地を示す地図。

STATISTICAL
TABLES & GRAPHS

CHARTS & SCORES

MAPS

ARCHITECTURAL
PLANS & DRAWINGS

INSTRUCTIONAL DIAGRAMS
FOR PRODUCTS

SCIENTIFIC
ILLUSTRATIONS

NORCEN ENERGY RESOURCES
USA 1990,1991
AD:Kit Hinrichs
D:Piper Murakami
I:Max Seabaugh
DF:Pentagram Design Ltd.

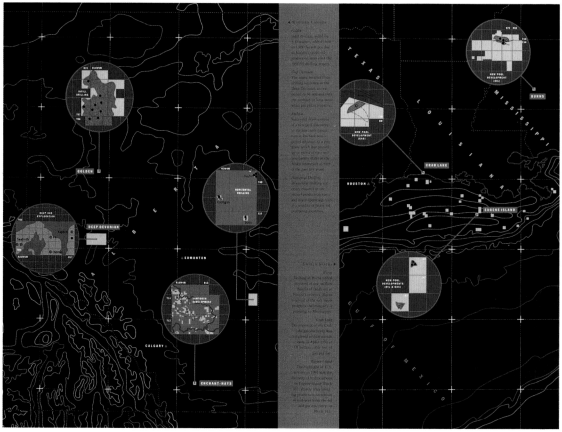

STATISTICAL
TABLES & GRAPHS

CHARTS & SCORES

MAPS

ARCHITECTURAL
PLANS & DRAWINGS

INSTRUCTIONAL DIAGRAMS
FOR PRODUCTS

SCIENTIFIC
ILLUSTRATIONS

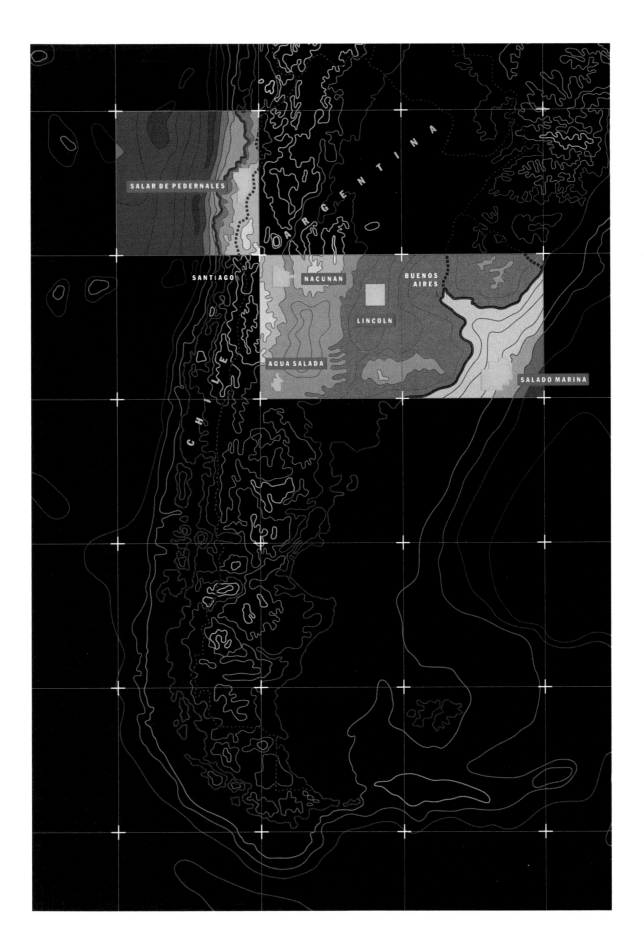

Maps showing areas developed and operated by Norcen Energy Resources. From an annual report.

ノーセン・エナジー・リゾース社のアニュアルリポートより、開発地域や業務地域を表した地図。

STATISTICAL
TABLES & GRAPHS

CHARTS & SCORES

MAPS

ARCHITECTURAL
PLANS & DRAWINGS

INSTRUCTIONAL DIAGRAMS
FOR PRODUCTS

SCIENTIFIC
ILLUSTRATIONS

ARCO

USA 1988

CD:Ron Jefferies

D,I:Ken Lotz

DF:The Jefferies Association

Simple line art maps showing very complicated exploration and production locations.
非常に複雑な実地探究や生産の立地を単純な線で示すアートマップ。

ARCO
USA 1991
CD:Ron Jefferies
D:Scott Lambert
P:Keith Wood
I:Hank Fisher
DF:The Jefferies Association

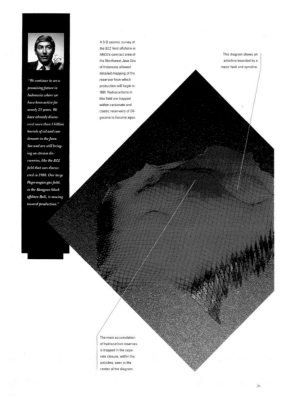

A 3-D seismic survey of the BZZ field offshore in ARCO's contract area of the Northwest Java Sea of Indonesia allowed detailed mapping of the reservoir from which production will begin in 1991. Hydrocarbons in this field are trapped within carbonate and clastic reservoirs of Oligocene to Eocene ages.

This diagram shows an anticline bounded by a major fault and syncline.

"We continue to see a promising future in Indonesia where we have been active for nearly 25 years. We have already discovered more than 1 billion barrels of oil and condensate in the Java Sea and are still bringing on stream discoveries, like the BZZ field that was discovered in 1988. Our large Pagerungan gas field, in the Kangean block offshore Bali, is moving toward production."

The main accumulation of hydrocarbon reserves is trapped in the separate closure, within the anticline, seen in the center of the diagram.

Washington has 209 branded outlets of which 100 are am/pm mini markets. Oregon has 89 outlets of which 29 are am/pm sites.

In Nevada, 50 of 76 branded outlets are am/pm sites, while in Arizona, ARCO has 75 outlets of which 63 are am/pm locations.

"We have continued to see demand growth for gasoline in our five-state marketing area, but economic conditions and improved public transportation could moderate this growth. Our formula is to maintain low price leadership while increasing marketing opportunities with am/pm mini markets and our new SMOGPROS service centers which have proved to be highly popular."

California has 1,098 branded outlets of which 510 are am/pm's and 112 are SMOGPROS. Six of the California am/pm's are mini markets only with no gasoline sales.

■ Refinery
● Distribution Terminal

ARCO is a participant in offshore drilling programs that are continuing in the Chukchi Sea, 350 miles from the State's large North Slope oil fields.

Prudhoe Bay and Kuparuk are situated on Alaska's North Slope. Lisburne underlies Prudhoe Bay and is adjacent to Point McIntyre. Additional development continues in these areas.

Exploration projects are active offshore in the Beaufort Sea where ARCO drilled two prospects in 1990 and plans more in 1991.

H.L. "Skip" Bilhartz
President
ARCO Alaska, Inc.

"Alaska is considered to hold significant potential for more large oil discoveries, and ARCO wants to be part of those. We are pursuing a balanced and well reasoned exploration program. We have already improved our competitive position using our exploration information, and we will be seeking new leases as they become available."

ARCO drilled one prospect in Cook Inlet in 1990 and expects to return for additional drilling during 1991.

■ ARCO exploration drilling 1990-1991
▲ Exploration drilling/ ARCO participation 1990-1991
● ARCO operational facilities

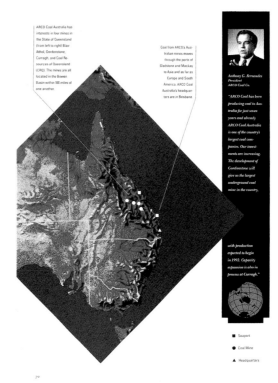

ARCO Coal Australia has interests in four mines in the State of Queensland (from left to right) Blair Athol, Gordonstone, Curragh, and Coal Resources of Queensland (CRQ). The mines are all located in the Bowen Basin within 100 miles of one another.

Coal from ARCO's Australian mines moves through the ports of Gladstone and Mackay to Asia and as far as Europe and South America. ARCO Coal Australia's headquarters are in Brisbane.

Anthony G. Fernandes
President
ARCO Coal Co.

"ARCO Coal has been producing coal in Australia for just seven years and already ARCO Coal Australia is one of the country's largest coal companies. Our investments are increasing. The development of Gordonstone will give us the largest underground coal mine in the country, with production expected to begin in 1992. Capacity expansion is also in process at Curragh."

■ Seaport
● Coal Mine
▲ Headquarters

ARCHITECTURAL
PLANS & DRAWINGS

INSTRUCTIONAL DIAGRAMS
FOR PRODUCTS

SCIENTIFIC
ILLUSTRATIONS

Maps designed to look like color-enhanced space photos, created on a Macintosh computer. From an Arco annual report.
アルコ社のアニュアルリポートより、色彩を強調し、宇宙写真をイメージしてマッキントッシュ・コンピューターでデザインされた地図。

STATISTICAL
TABLES & GRAPHS

CHARTS & SCORES

MAPS

ARCHITECTURAL
PLANS & DRAWINGS

INSTRUCTIONAL DIAGRAMS
FOR PRODUCTS

SCIENTIFIC
ILLUSTRATIONS

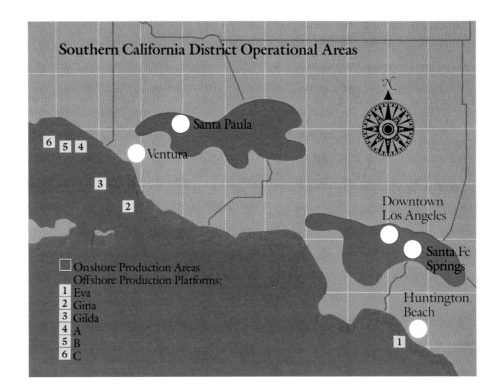

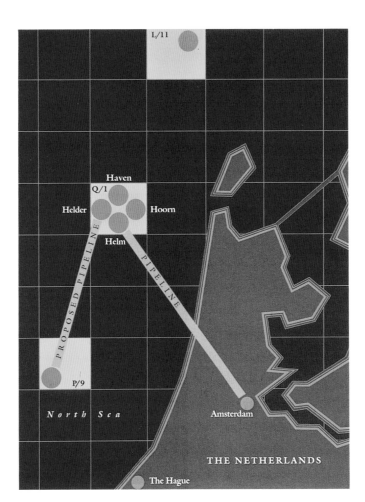

STATISTICAL
TABLES & GRAPHS

CHARTS & SCORES

MAPS

ARCHITECTURAL
PLANS & DRAWINGS

INSTRUCTIONAL DIAGRAMS
FOR PRODUCTS

SCIENTIFIC
ILLUSTRATIONS

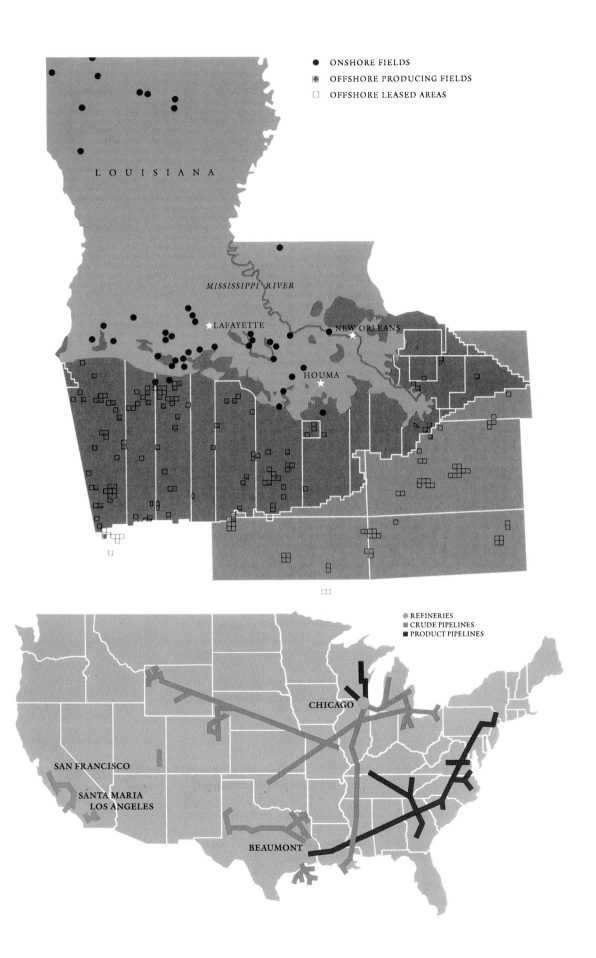

● ONSHORE FIELDS
▣ OFFSHORE PRODUCING FIELDS
☐ OFFSHORE LEASED AREAS

LOUISIANA

MISSISSIPPI RIVER

★LAFAYETTE   ★NEW ORLEANS

HOUMA

● REFINERIES
▮ CRUDE PIPELINES
▮ PRODUCT PIPELINES

CHICAGO

SAN FRANCISCO

SANTA MARIA
LOS ANGELES

BEAUMONT

Maps showing the development and production of petroleum resources in various parts of the world. From a magazine article.
雑誌記事より、世界各地における石油資源の開発、及び生産に関する地図。

GARBAGE MAGAZINE
USA 1991
AD,D:Rob George
D,I:Scott A. MacNeill

PHIBRO ENERGY, INC.
USA 1992
AD:Howard Belk
D:Dana Gonsalvez
I:In House
DF:Belk Mignogna Associates Ltd.

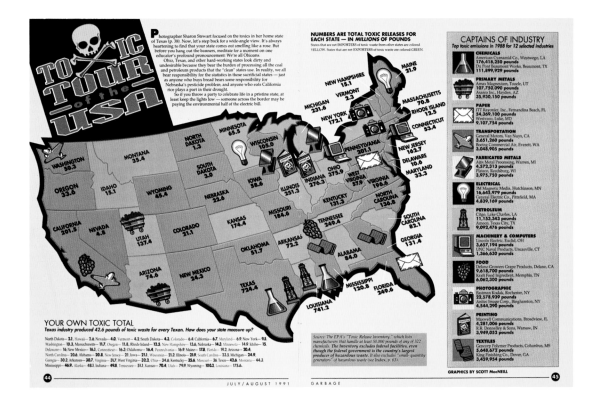

ARCHITECTURAL
PLANS & DRAWINGS

INSTRUCTIONAL DIAGRAMS
FOR PRODUCTS

SCIENTIFIC
ILLUSTRATIONS

Map locating the top polluters in the USA
by state and business with each state's pollution per person level.
アメリカの州や産業別でトップに位置する汚染源のデータを表した地図。

Map illustrating Phibro's marketing and distribution capabilities.
The smaller map illustrates the asset-based energy businesses concentrated in the Gulf Coast Region.
The globes show Phibro's office locations. From a Phibro Energy Inc. annual report.
ファイブロ社のアニュアルリポートより、同社のマーケティング能力や流通能力を表す地図、及び事務所の所在地を表す地球図。

STATISTICAL
TABLES &
GRAPHS

CHARTS & SCORES

MAPS

ARCHITECTURAL
PLANS & DRAWINGS

INSTRUCTIONAL DIAGRAMS
FOR PRODUCTS

SCIENTIFIC
ILLUSTRATIONS

U.S.NEWS & WORLD REPORT
USA 1992
D,I:Matt Zang

TIME MAGAZINE
USA 1992
AD:Nigel Holmes
D:Joe Lertola/Paul Pugliese/Steve Hart

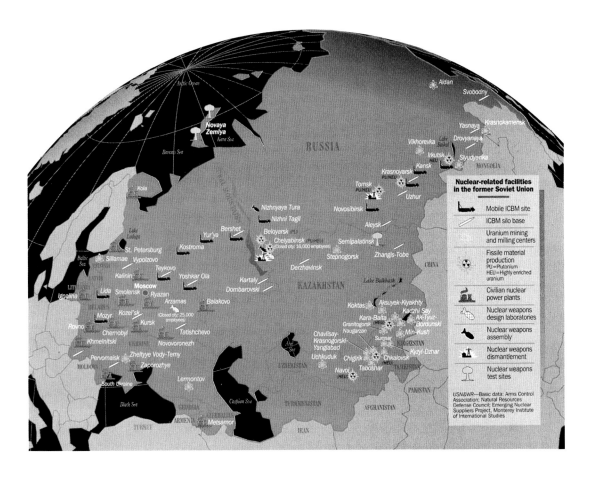

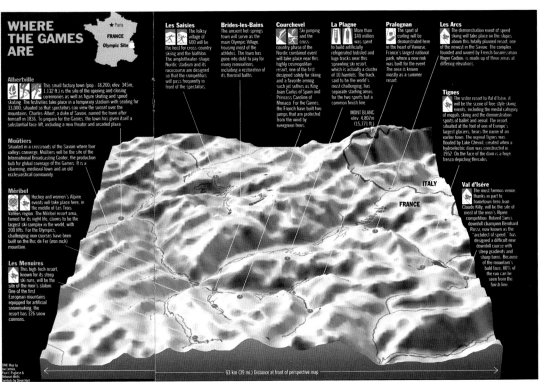

Map showing nuclear-related facilities in the former Soviet Union. From U.S. News & World Report magazine.

「USニュース ＆ ワールド・リポートマガジン」より、旧ソ連邦における核関連施設を示す地図。

Albertville Olympics map from Time magazine.

「タイムマガジン」より、アルベールビル・オリンピックの会場地図。

STATISTICAL
TABLES & GRAPHS

CHARTS & SCORES

MAPS

ARCHITECTURAL
PLANS & DRAWINGS

INSTRUCTIONAL DIAGRAMS
FOR PRODUCTS

SCIENTIFIC
ILLUSTRATIONS

TIME MAGAZINE
USA 1991
AD,D,I:Nigel Holmes
I:Joe Lertola/Paul Pugliese

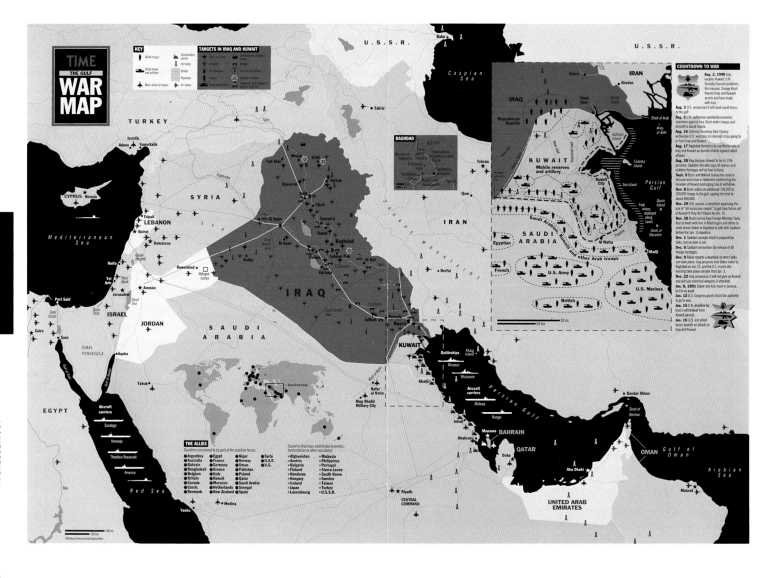

Map showing the positions of all the troops, air bases, oil fields, pipelines and ships involved in the 1991 Gulf War. From Time magazine.
「タイムマガジン」より、1991年の湾岸戦争に関連した軍隊、空軍基地、油田、パイプライン、船舶などの位置を網羅した地図。

STATISTICAL
TABLES & GRAPHS

CHARTS & SCORES

MAPS

ARCHITECTURAL
PLANS & DRAWINGS

INSTRUCTIONAL DIAGRAMS
FOR PRODUCTS

SCIENTIFIC
ILLUSTRATIONS

1. INHOUSE
ENGLAND 1991
CD,AD,D,I:Richard Schedler
P:Dave Denham

2. BRITISH TRUST FOR
YOUNG ACHIEVERS
ENGLAND 1991
CD,AD,D,I:Richard Schedler/
Marcus Kelly
P:Dave Denham

3. ALLIED INSURANCE BROKERS
ENGLAND 1992
CD,AD:Philip Kruger
D,I:Richard Schedler
P:Dave Denham

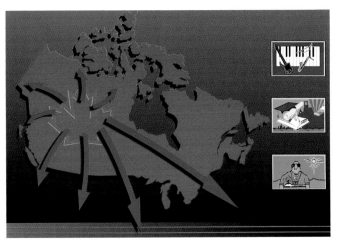

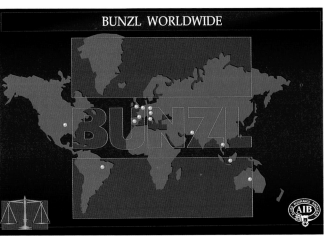

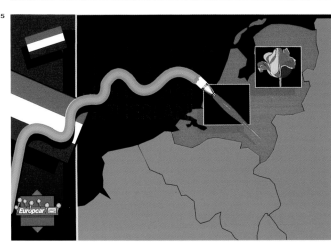

4. 6. BBC TELEVISION, NEWS
AND CURRENT AFFAIRS
ENGLAND 1991,1992
D:Kaye Huddy/Jean Cramond
DF:N/CA Graphic Design Department
BBC Television

5. EUROPCAR
ENGLAND 1992
CD,AD,D,I:Marcus Kelly
(The Presentation Co. Brussels)
P:Jerome Zimmerman

Visualized maps produced for corporate or TV presentation.
テレビ番組や企業のプレゼンテーションの映像用に制作されたマップ。

BRITISH STEEL PLC
ENGLAND 1992
CD:Geoff Aldridge
AD,I:Sally Mcintosh
D:Joseph Mitchell
I:Barry Brocklebank
DF:Communication by Design

STATISTICAL
TABLES & GRAPHS

CHARTS & SCORES

MAPS

ARCHITECTURAL
PLANS & DRAWINGS

INSTRUCTIONAL DIAGRAMS
FOR PRODUCTS

SCIENTIFIC
ILLUSTRATIONS

Giant route map of the round-the world yacht race "British Steel Challenge". Displayed at the British Pavilion in Expo'92.
Expo'92 の英国パビリオンに展示された、世界一周ヨットレース「ブリティッシュ・スティール・チャレンジ」の巨大なルートマップ。

ADVERTISING WOMEN OF NEW YORK
USA 1989
CD,AD,D,I:Keith Godard
D:Jamie Jett Walker
P:John T. Hill
DF:Studio Works

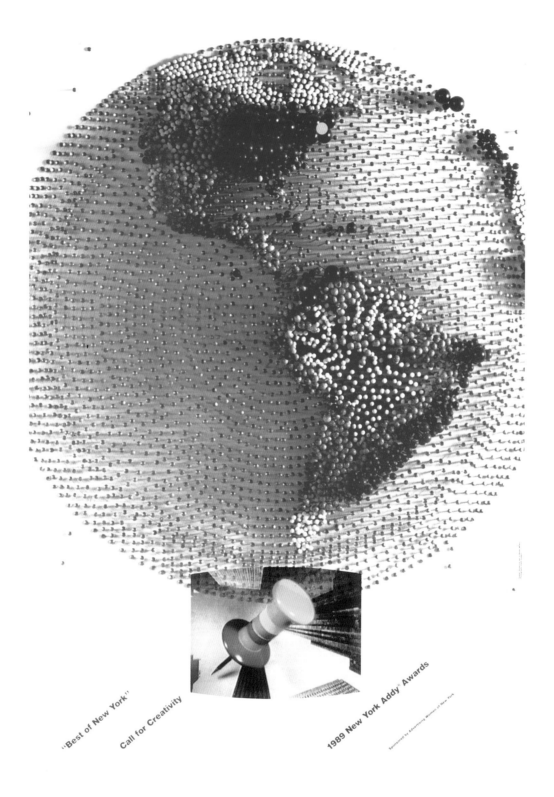

Global map is made up of pins representing the population of the western hemisphere.
The large dark pins represent over population and the small white pins represent no population.
ピンによる西半球人口地図。大きく濃い色のピンは人口過剰地帯、小さい白色のピンは無人口地帯を表している。

STATISTICAL TABLES & GRAPHS

CHARTS & SCORES

MAPS

ARCHITECTURAL PLANS & DRAWINGS

INSTRUCTIONAL DIAGRAMS FOR PRODUCTS

SCIENTIFIC ILLUSTRATIONS

STATISTICAL
TABLES & GRAPHS

CHARTS & SCORES

MAPS

ARCHITECTURAL
PLANS & DRAWINGS

INSTRUCTIONAL DIAGRAMS
FOR PRODUCTS

SCIENTIFIC
ILLUSTRATIONS

JOHN PORTMAN COMPANIES
USA 1991
AD:Lowell Williams
D:Bill Carson
I:Andy Dearwater
DF:Pentagram Design Ltd.

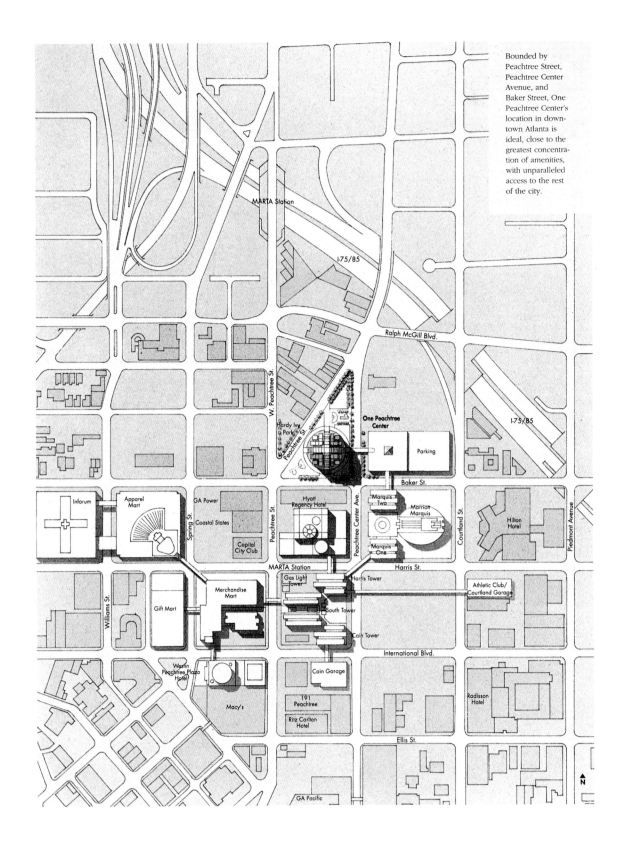

Bounded by
Peachtree Street,
Peachtree Center
Avenue, and
Baker Street, One
Peachtree Center's
location in down-
town Atlanta is
ideal, close to the
greatest concentra-
tion of amenities,
with unparalleled
access to the rest
of the city.

Location map of a high-rise building, One Peachtree Center, in Atlanta. From a promotional pamphlet.
プロモーション用パンフレットより、アトランタの高層ビル「ワンピーチツリー・センター」の所在地図。

STATISTICAL TABLES & GRAPHS

CHARTS & SCORES

MAPS

ARCHITECTURAL PLANS & DRAWINGS

INSTRUCTIONAL DIAGRAMS FOR PRODUCTS

SCIENTIFIC ILLUSTRATIONS

THE TURNER CORPORATION
USA 1990
AD:Lars Lofas
I:Alan Kikuchi
DF:The Turner Corp./In House

Illustration of the 220 buildings and ancillary facilities completed in Turner Ctiy in a single calendar year.
1年間にターナー市に完成した220のビルや付属施設の地図。

STATISTICAL
TABLES & GRAPHS

CHARTS & SCORES

MAPS

ARCHITECTURAL
PLANS & DRAWINGS

INSTRUCTIONAL DIAGRAMS
FOR PRODUCTS

SCIENTIFIC
ILLUSTRATIONS

REUTERS LIMITED
ENGLAND 1984
AD,D:Mervyn Kurlansky
D:Robert Maude
I:Roger Taylor/Richard Clifton-Dey
DF:Pentagram Design Ltd.

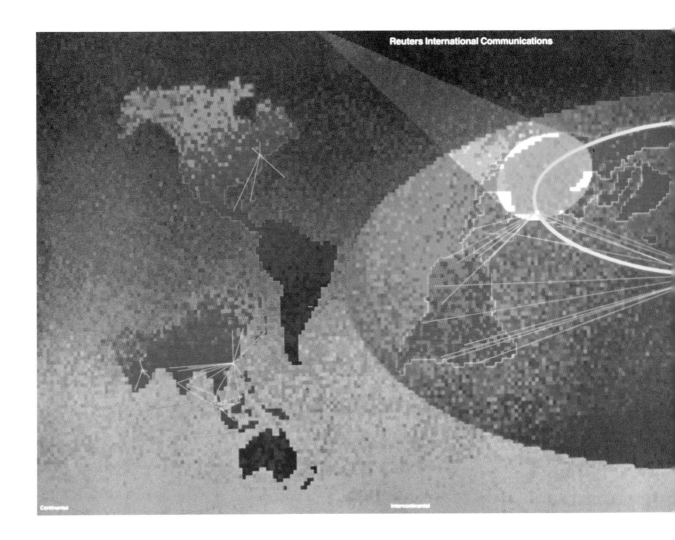

Communications map showing points of contact across the globe.
地球に張りめぐらされた通信ポイントを示す通信網の地図。

STATISTICAL
TABLES & GRAPHS

CHARTS & SCORES

MAPS

ARCHITECTURAL
PLANS & DRAWINGS

INSTRUCTIONAL DIAGRAMS
FOR PRODUCTS

SCIENTIFIC
ILLUSTRATIONS

SERVICES GROUP OF AMERICA
USA
AD,D:Jack Anderson
D:Mike Courtney
DF:Hornall Anderson Design Works

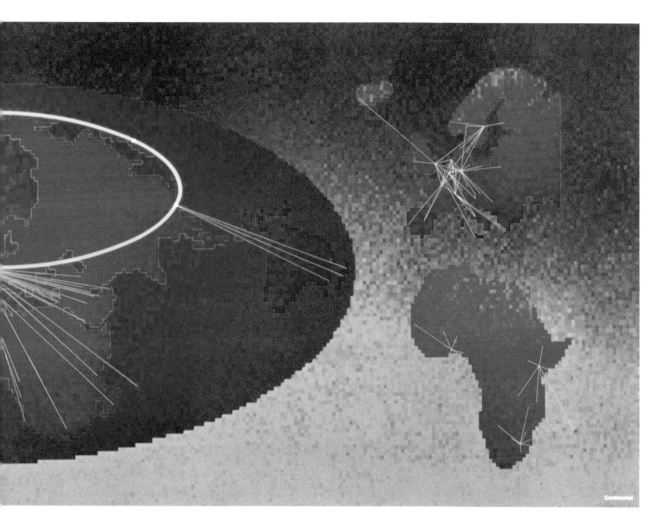

Wall map showing the member companies of Services Group of America.
サービスグループ・オブ・アメリカ社の会社所在地を示すウォール・マップ。

STATISTICAL
TABLES & GRAPHS

CHARTS & SCORES

MAPS

ARCHITECTURAL
PLANS & DRAWINGS

INSTRUCTIONAL DIAGRAMS
FOR PRODUCTS

SCIENTIFIC
ILLUSTRATIONS

MASTERCARD INTERNATIONAL, INC.
USA 1987
CD,AD,D:Stephen Wolf
I:Linda Puiatti
DF:Stephen Wolf Inc.

Connectivity map of a global telecommunications network. The map's graphic shape, two intersecting circles, recalls MasterCard International's corporate trade mark.
世界規模の電子通信ネットワークを表した地図。この地図の２つの円が重なり合っている形はマスターカード・インターナショナル社のブランドマークを象徴している。

STATISTICAL
TABLES & GRAPHS

CHARTS & SCORES

MAPS

ARCHITECTURAL
PLANS & DRAWINGS

INSTRUCTIONAL DIAGRAMS
FOR PRODUCTS

SCIENTIFIC
ILLUSTRATIONS

THE SEIBU GROUP OF
RETAIL ENTERPRISES
JAPAN 1981
CD,AD,D:Tetsuya Ohta

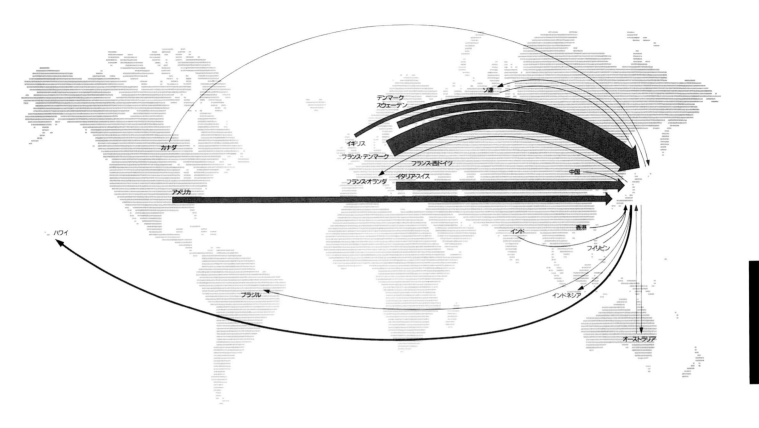

Map of the global penetration (export, import) of the Seibu Group of Retail Enterprises.
西武流通グループの世界展開（輸出量・輸入量）を解説する地図。

STATISTICAL
TABLES & GRAPHS

CHARTS & SCORES

MAPS

ARCHITECTURAL
PLANS & DRAWINGS

INSTRUCTIONAL DIAGRAMS
FOR PRODUCTS

SCIENTIFIC
ILLUSTRATIONS

THE SPACESHIP EARTH™ DYMAXION™ GLOBE

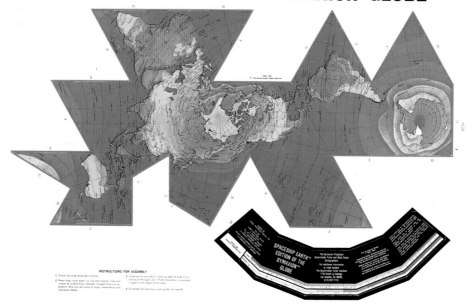

The dimaxion map invented by Buckminster Fuller; the most accurate way to show the size of areas and distances.

バックミンスター・フラーが考案した、面積や距離が最も正確に表されている世界地図「ダイマクシオンマップ」。

建築プラン

マップが区域や地域という、移動を前提とする大きな空間を描くことを基本としていたのに対して、ここに紹介する建築プランは、むしろ居住や販売、展示を目的とした、中規模以下の人造の空間を描いたものである。無論、建築プランのなかには、公園さらには都市といった大規模な空間を描くものも多いのだが、それらとマップの本質的な違いは、地図があくまで既存の空間の「案内」や「解説」を目的としているのに対して、プランは常に、その立案、設計といったクリエイティブな関心を背景に、検討、吟味、ないしはプレゼンテーションのために描かれている点にある。

いうまでもないことながら、ダイアグラムは二次元の表現である。マップという空間を描くダイアグラムもさることながら、プランには、二次元の画面に三次元の空間を描くことの興味があふれている。このことは、マップに関してもいえるのだが、マップが空間を広がりとして、むしろ二次元的に描く傾向が強いのに対して、プランには、立体的な箱状の空間を二次元にいかに再現してみせるかという造形的課題がある分だけ、空間の表現に関してはスリリングな視覚的な工夫に富んでいる。

もともと、ルネッサンス以降の西洋絵画の最大の関心も、三次元空間をいかに二次元の画面にだまし絵的に再現し得るかという、透視図法による遠近法の完成にあった。レオナルド・ダ・ヴィンチの名高い『最後の晩餐』や、ラファエロの『アテナイの学園』など、ルネッサンス絵画の最高峰の作品が、同時にきわめてすぐれた建築図であるのはそのためである。

したがって、建築プランには、そういった絵画的表現の魅惑のもっとも基本的な要素が含まれている。具体的には、立体感を表わすための影の表現の工夫、建築物の内部を屋根や壁を通して描く透視図法の工夫などが、デザイン上の見せ場になるが、あたかもそこに三次元空間があるかのような錯覚を起こさせる絵画的な美しさや完成度と同時に、どこにどのような空間があり、それらがどのような構造でつながっているのかという、空間の「仕組み」や「仕掛け」の明快な表示するという、ダイアグラム本来の視覚的な機能性というものを重視する必要がある。

ARCHITECTURAL PLANS & DRAWINGS

PLANS ARCHITECTURAL & DRAWINGS

Architectural plans are qualitatively and quantitatively different from maps. A map generally depicts a very large area, such as a territory or region, through which travel is implied. Architectural plans illustrate man-made structures which are on a smaller scale and which are intended as space for living, working or exhibiting things. Architectural plans do exist, of course, which deal with larger spaces such as parks and cities, but an essential difference remains; a map is always intended as a guide to and explanation of an already existing place. Architectural plans are always created as material either for the presentation of a project idea or as a guide to the actual construction of a project.

It goes without saying that a diagram is a two-dimensional image, and in the case of a map, the space described is, in essence, a two-dimensional plane. For the most part, it is simply a matter of scaling down the outlines of what is already there. Architectural plans, on the other hand, call for more interesting graphic solutions because they have to illustrate 3-D space on the 2-D surface. For the designer, this presents a number of challenges and options. Architectural plans will tend to demonstrate more clever visual contrivances where the expression of space is concerned, because that space must contain volume.

One of the main concerns in Western art after the Renaissance was how the artist could produce a 3-D effect on the surface of his canvas. This lead to the perfection of perspective drawings which employed a visual trick called the vanishing point. It is not surprising that masterpieces of Renaissance art such as "The Last Supper" by Leonardo Da Vinci and "School of Athens" by Raphael, in addition to being great paintings, are also superb examples of architectural drawing.

In architectural drawings, some of the basic elements of painterly technique are employed. Shadow is used, for example, to create a sense of depth and so forth, as well as illustrator's tricks such as cutaways to show the interior of a building through its roof or walls. Architectural plans, in other words, can serve as a show-place for design and illustration skills. Ultimately, however, aside from artistic beauty and illustrative tricks to create the illusion of 3-D space, the designer cannot lose sight of the original function of his drawing, which is that of a diagram. In architectural drawings, it is the structure and organization of space that we are interested in.

建築プラン

STATISTICAL
TABLES & GRAPHS

CHARTS & SCORES

MAPS

ARCHITECTURAL
PLANS & DRAWINGS

INSTRUCTIONAL DIAGRAMS
FOR PRODUCTS

SCIENTIFIC
ILLUSTRATIONS

MELVIN SIMON & ASSOCIATES
USA 1985
CD:Jon Jerde
D,I,DF:JPI

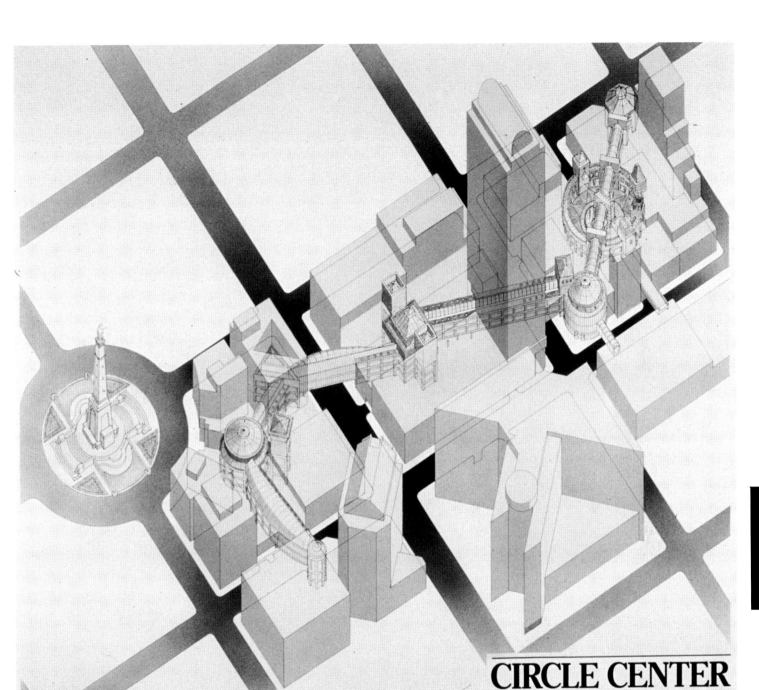

Two-dimensional isometric drawing for Circle Center, Indianapolis project, produced for a presentation.
プレゼンテーションのために制作されたインディアナポリス・サークルセンター計画のアイソメトリック。

STATISTICAL
TABLES & GRAPHS

CHARTS & SCORES

MAPS

ARCHITECTURAL
PLANS & DRAWINGS

INSTRUCTIONAL DIAGRAMS
FOR PRODUCTS

SCIENTIFIC
ILLUSTRATIONS

CUT AXONOMETRIC THROUGH SEQUENCE OF SPACES FROM MOSQUE TO FOUNTAIN.

11

Axonometric projection of a fountain for a mosque in Isfaham, Iran.
イラン・イスファハムのモスクに建設される噴水のアクソノメトリック。

STATISTICAL
TABLES & GRAPHS

CHARTS & SCORES

MAPS

ARCHITECTURAL
PLANS & DRAWINGS

INSTRUCTIONAL DIAGRAMS
FOR PRODUCTS

SCIENTIFIC
ILLUSTRATIONS

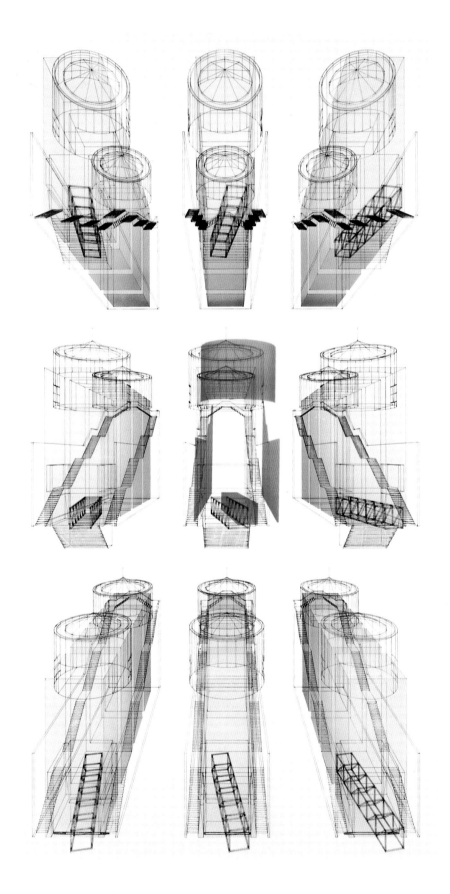

Diagram depicting 4-Torri Building in Takamatsu from 9 angles. From "Emerging Japanese Architects of the 1990's Exhibition".
「1990年代を代表する日本の新進建築家展」より、高松市4-Torriビルを9方向から描いたダイアグラム。

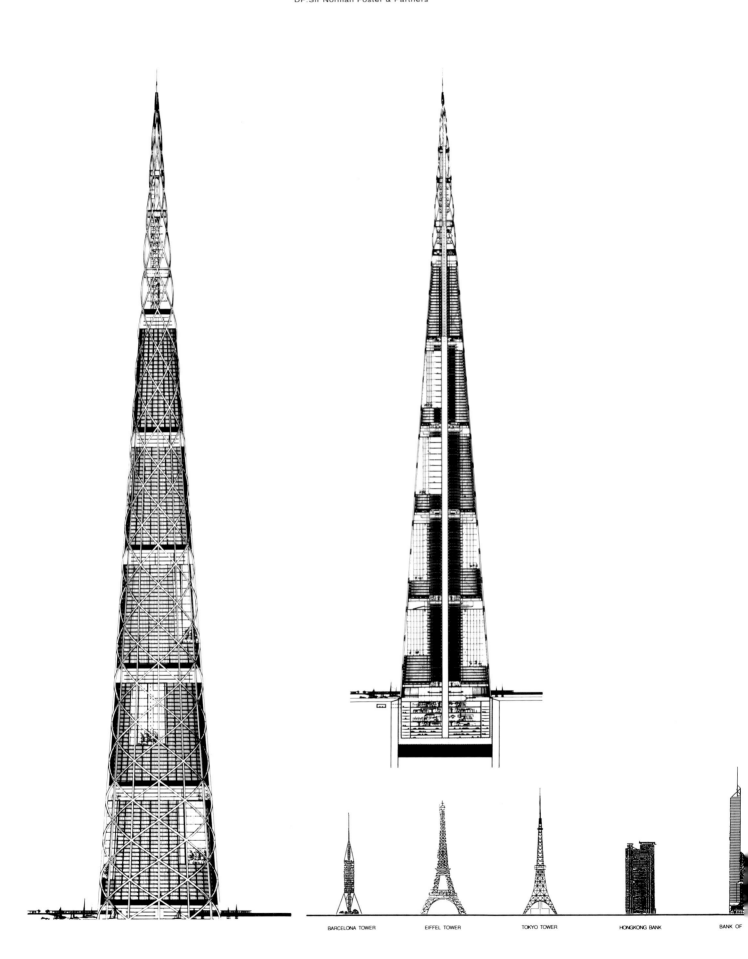

OBAYASHI CORPORATION
ENGLAND
CD:David Nelson/Chris Seddon
DF:Sir Norman Foster & Partners

STATISTICAL
TABLES & GRAPHS

CHARTS & SCORES

MAPS

ARCHITECTURAL
PLANS & DRAWINGS

INSTRUCTIONAL DIAGRAMS
FOR PRODUCTS

SCIENTIFIC
ILLUSTRATIONS

BARCELONA TOWER   EIFFEL TOWER   TOKYO TOWER   HONGKONG BANK   BANK OF

STATISTICAL
TABLES & GRAPHS

CHARTS & SCORES

MAPS

ARCHITECTURAL
PLANS & DRAWINGS

INSTRUCTIONAL DIAGRAMS
FOR PRODUCTS

SCIENTIFIC
ILLUSTRATIONS

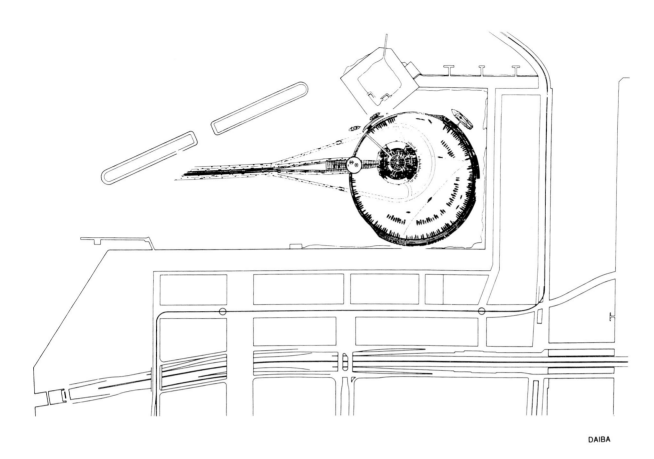

DAIBA

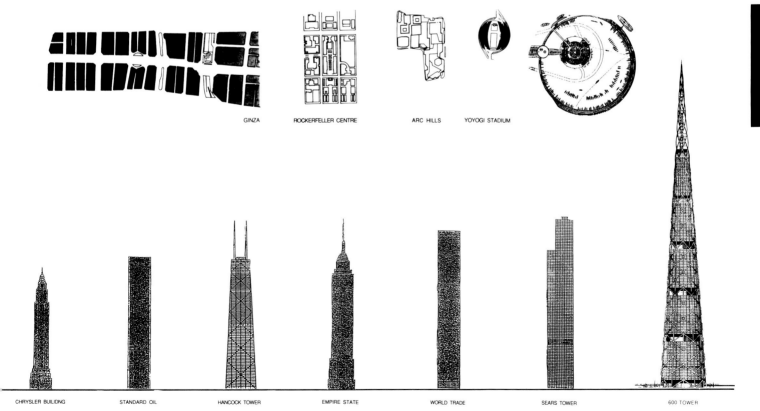

GINZA   ROCKERFELLER CENTRE   ARC HILLS   YOYOGI STADIUM

CHRYSLER BUILIDNG   STANDARD OIL   HANCOCK TOWER   EMPIRE STATE   WORLD TRADE   SEARS TOWER   600 TOWER

Illustration of the Millennium Tower project. An 800 meter-tall building with both intelligent office facilities and residential civic facilities.
インテリジェント・オフィス施設と住宅・都市施設を併せもつ全長800メートルの建造物ミレニアム・タワー計画の図解。

STATISTICAL
TABLES & GRAPHS

CHARTS & SCORES

MAPS

ARCHITECTURAL
PLANS & DRAWINGS

INSTRUCTIONAL DIAGRAMS
FOR PRODUCTS

SCIENTIFIC
ILLUSTRATIONS

AT & T
USA
AD:Louis Nelson
D:Chris Micelli/Dawn O'Keef
DF:Louis Nelson Associates Inc.

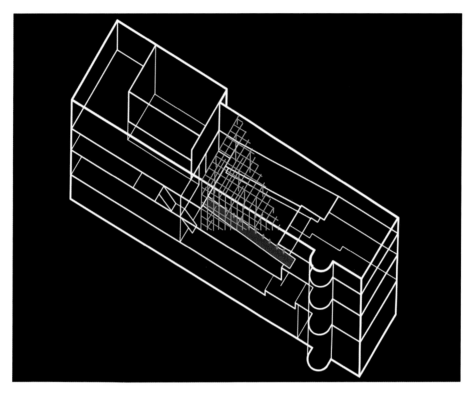

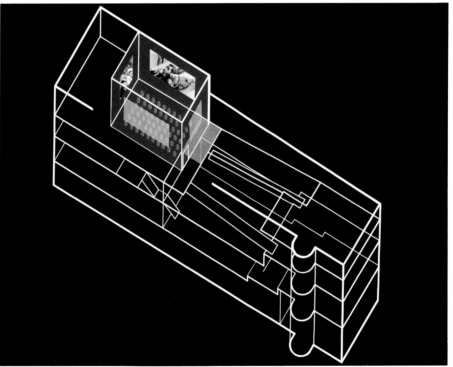

Dimensional diagrams illustrating the master plan for the AT & T, NY Communications Museum.
The diagrams show over 30,000 sq.ft. encompassing four levels, including all gallery spaces and adjacent areas.
3万平方メートル以上に及ぶ美術館/AT & Tニューヨーク・コミュニケーションズミュージアムの全ギャラリー空間、及び隣接区域を含むマスタープラン立体図解。

STATISTICAL
TABLES & GRAPHS

CHARTS & SCORES

MAPS

ARCHITECTURAL
PLANS & DRAWINGS

INSTRUCTIONAL DIAGRAMS
FOR PRODUCTS

SCIENTIFIC
ILLUSTRATIONS

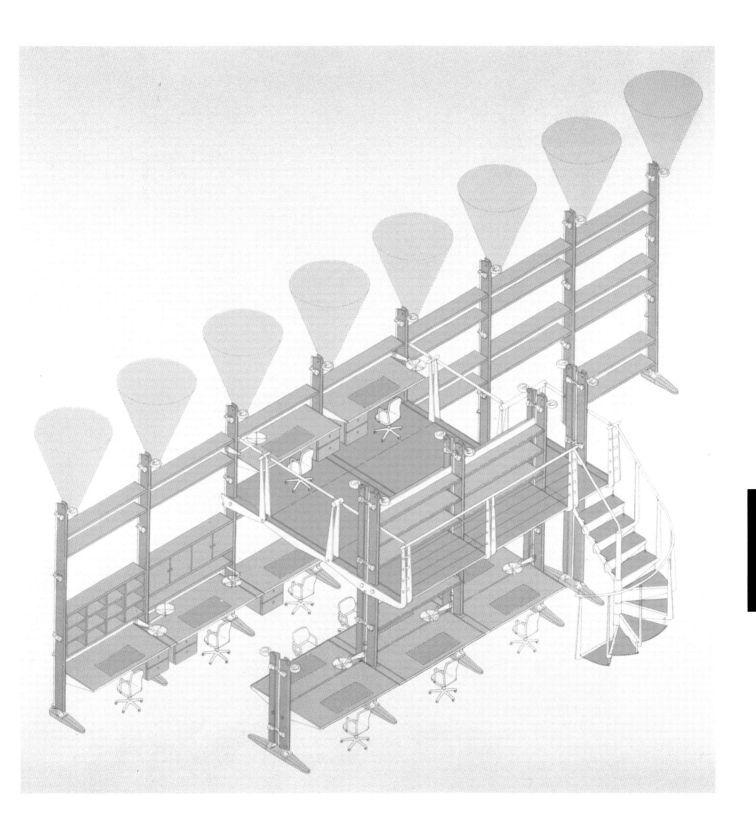

Isometric composition of Eco-iD "Evolution" freestanding structure and complete office which can be extended and reduced as required.
必要に応じて伸縮自在な家具システム「Eco-iDエボリューション」をとりいれた、事務所のアイソメトリック構成図。

STATISTICAL
TABLES & GRAPHS

CHARTS & SCORES

MAPS

ARCHITECTURAL
PLANS & DRAWINGS

INSTRUCTIONAL DIAGRAMS
FOR PRODUCTS

SCIENTIFIC
ILLUSTRATIONS

YUHUIN ART MUSEUM
JAPAN 1991
AD:Tatsuaki Yasuno
D:Susumu Utagawa
DF:T.Y.D. Inc.

STATISTICAL
TABLES & GRAPHS

CHARTS & SCORES

MAPS

ARCHITECTURAL
PLANS & DRAWINGS

INSTRUCTIONAL DIAGRAMS
FOR PRODUCTS

SCIENTIFIC
ILLUSTRATIONS

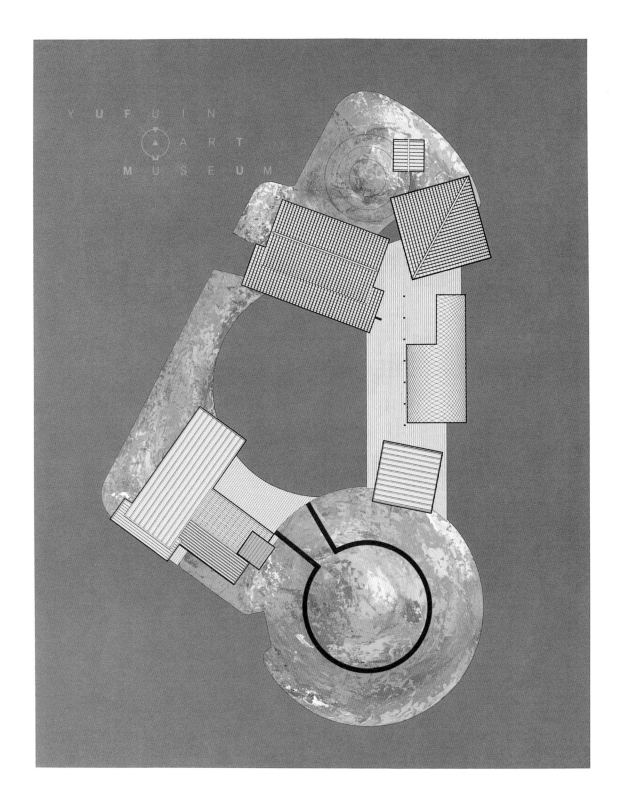

Architectural drawing for the Yuhuin Museum of Art in Oita Prefecture.

大分県「由布院美術館」の建築見取り図。

STATISTICAL
TABLES & GRAPHS

CHARTS & SCORES

MAPS

ARCHITECTURAL
PLANS & DRAWINGS

INSTRUCTIONAL DIAGRAMS
FOR PRODUCTS

SCIENTIFIC
ILLUSTRATIONS

SOLOMON R. GUGGENHEIM MUSEUM
AUSTRALIA 1991
CD:Pamela L. Myers
AD,D,I:Colin Rowan
DF:Powerhouse Museum Graphic Services &
The N.S.W Ministry for The Arts

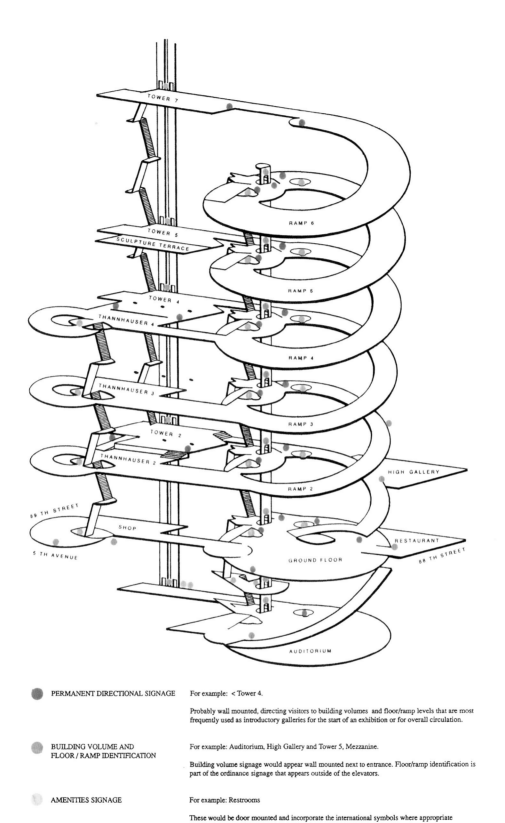

PERMANENT DIRECTIONAL SIGNAGE — For example: < Tower 4.

Probably wall mounted, directing visitors to building volumes and floor/ramp levels that are most frequently used as introductory galleries for the start of an exhibition or for overall circulation.

BUILDING VOLUME AND FLOOR / RAMP IDENTIFICATION — For example: Auditorium, High Gallery and Tower 5, Mezzanine.

Building volume signage would appear wall mounted next to entrance. Floor/ramp identification is part of the ordinance signage that appears outside of the elevators.

AMENITIES SIGNAGE — For example: Restrooms

These would be door mounted and incorporate the international symbols where appropriate

SERVICES — For example: Admissions, Coat check.

A building plan of the Solomon R. Guggenheim Museum prepared by the architectural company, Gwathmey Siegel, Associates.

ガスメイ・シーゲル建築会社が制作したソロモン・R・グッゲンハイム美術館の設計図。

STATISTICAL
TABLES & GRAPHS

CHARTS & SCORES

MAPS

ARCHITECTURAL
PLANS & DRAWINGS

INSTRUCTIONAL DIAGRAMS
FOR PRODUCTS

SCIENTIFIC
ILLUSTRATIONS

SOLOMON R. GUGGENHEIM MUSEUM
AUSTRALIA 1991
CD:Pamela L. Myers
AD,D:Colin Rowan

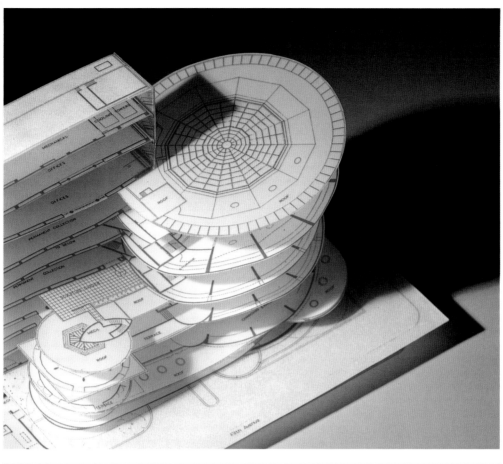

3-D diagram of the Solomon R. Guggenheim Museum showing the correspondence between volume and floor space.
ソロモン・R・グッゲンハイム美術館の床面積と建築物の容積との関係を示す立体ダイアグラム。

STATISTICAL
TABLES & GRAPHS

CHARTS & SCORES

MAPS

ARCHITECTURAL
PLANS & DRAWINGS

INSTRUCTIONAL DIAGRAMS
FOR PRODUCTS

SCIENTIFIC
ILLUSTRATIONS

THE SCIENCE MUSEUM, LONDON
ENGLAND 1991
CD:Sally Mcintosh
AD,D,I:Stuart Green
I:Barry Brocklebank
DF:Communication by Design

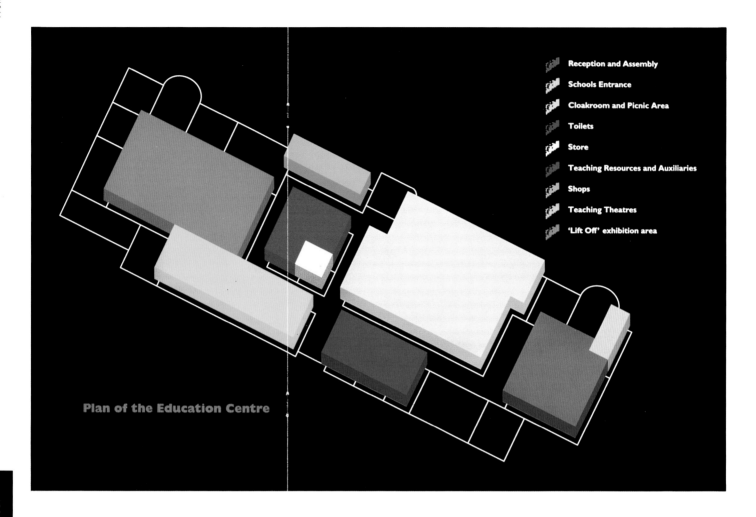

ロンドン科学博物館内部に新設される教育センターの間取り図。

Reception and Assembly

Schools Entrance

Cloakroom and Picnic Area

Toilets

Store

Teaching Resources and Auxiliaries

Shops

Teaching Theatres

'Lift Off' exhibition area

Plan of the Education Centre

Floor plan showing the area within the existing Science Museum, London to be developed as a new Education Center.
ロンドン科学博物館内部に新設される教育センターの間取り図。

STATISTICAL
TABLES & GRAPHS

CHARTS & SCORES

MAPS

ARCHITECTURAL
PLANS & DRAWINGS

INSTRUCTIONAL DIAGRAMS
FOR PRODUCTS

SCIENTIFIC
ILLUSTRATIONS

ESSEL'S AMUSEMENT PARK(S) INDIA LTD.
INDIA 1989
AD,D:Sudarshan Dheer
I:Narendra Vaidya
DF:Graphic Communication Concepts

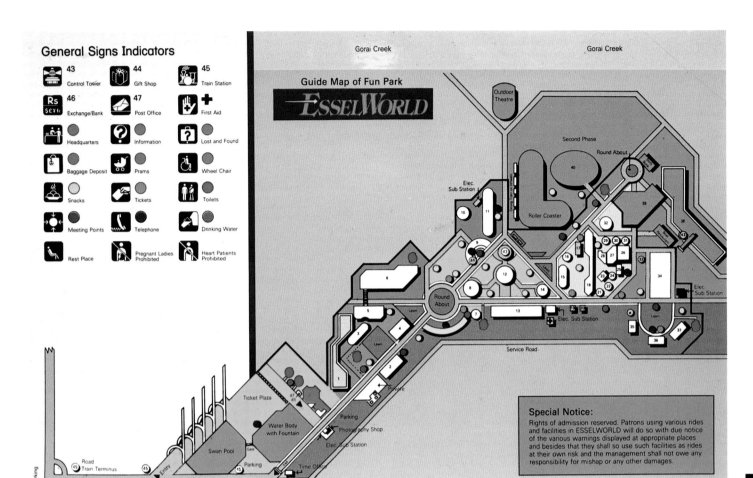

General Signs Indicators

43 Control Tower	44 Gift Shop	45 Train Station
Rs 46 Exchange/Bank	47 Post Office	First Aid
Headquarters	Information	Lost and Found
Baggage Deposit	Prams	Wheel Chair
Snacks	Tickets	Toilets
Meeting Points	Telephone	Drinking Water
Rest Place	Pregnant Ladies Prohibited	Heart Patients Prohibited

Guide Map of Fun Park
ESSELWORLD

Special Notice:
Rights of admission reserved. Patrons using various rides
and facilities in ESSELWORLD will do so with due notice
of the various warnings displayed at appropriate places
and besides that they shall so use such facilities as rides
at their own risk and the management shall not owe any
responsibility for mishap or any other damages.

Guide map using pictographs and signs to outline the facilities of Essel's Amusement Park in India.
インド・エッセル遊園地の施設をピクトグラムやサインで表した案内図。

NATIONS BANK
USA 1991
AD:Lowell Williams
D:Bill Carson
I:Andy Dearwater
DF:Pentagram Design Ltd.

STATISTICAL
TABLES & GRAPHS

CHARTS & SCORES

MAPS

ARCHITECTURAL
PLANS & DRAWINGS

INSTRUCTIONAL DIAGRAMS
FOR PRODUCTS

SCIENTIFIC
ILLUSTRATIONS

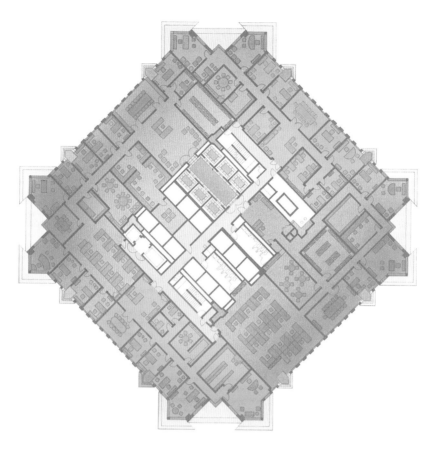

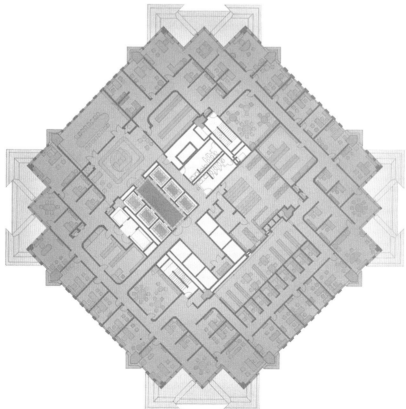

Part of the floor plan for a high-rise building, Nations Bank Plaza, in Atlanta. From a promotional pamphlet.
プロモーション用パンフレットより、アトランタの高層ビル「ネイションズ・バンクプラザ」のフロアープランの一部。

STATISTICAL
TABLES & GRAPHS

CHARTS & SCORES

MAPS

ARCHITECTURAL
PLANS & DRAWINGS

INSTRUCTIONAL DIAGRAMS
FOR PRODUCTS

SCIENTIFIC
ILLUSTRATIONS

CIRCUS CIRCUS ENTERPRISES, INC.
USA 1989
CD,AD,D:Don Kano
I:Carlos Delgado
DF:Kano Design Group

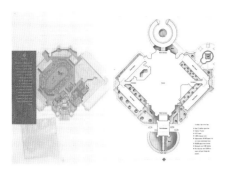

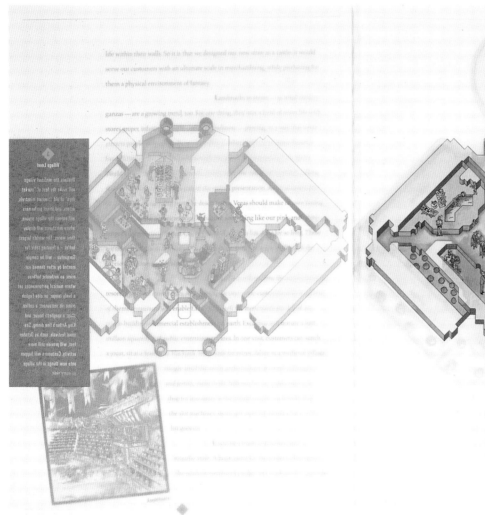

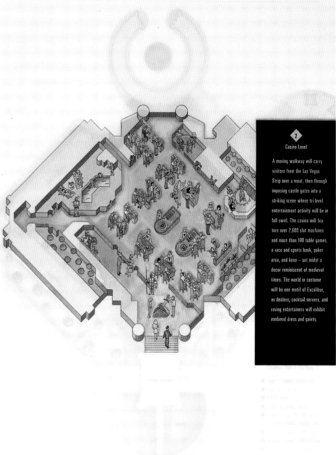

Casino Level

A moving walkway will carry visitors from the Las Vegas Strip over a moat, then through imposing castle gates into a striking scene where tri level entertainment activity will be in full swirl. The casino will feature over 2,600 slot machines and more than 100 table games, a race and sports book, poker area, and keno – set midst a decor reminiscent of medieval times. The world in costume will be one motif of Excalibur, as dealers, cocktail servers, and roving entertainers will exhibit medieval dress and gaiety.

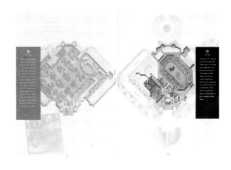

Diagrams showing the three levels of entertainment at Excalibur Hotel and Casino in Las Vegas, Nevada.
The illustrations were printed on translucent vellum with each level depicted and explained on separate sheets. From a Circus Circus Enterprises Inc. annual report.

サーカス・サーカス・エンタープライズ社のアニュアルリポートより、ネバダ州ラスベガスのエクスカリバーホテル＆カジノの3フロアの娯楽施設を表した図。
イラストレーションは半透明のベラム紙、フロア図は台紙に描き解説を加えてある。

JOHN PORTMAN COMPANIES
USA 1991
AD:Lowell Williams
D:Bill Carson
I:Andy Dearwater
DF:Pentagram Design Ltd.

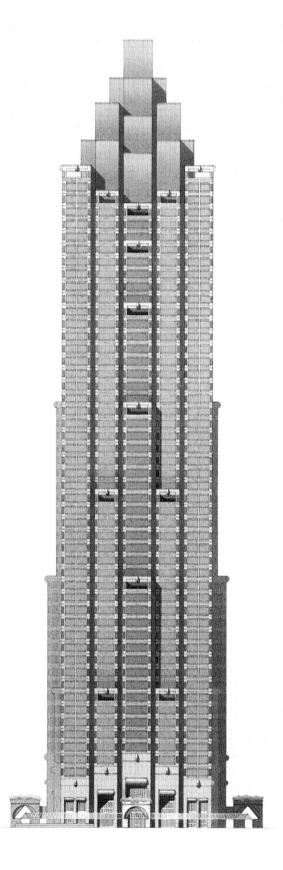

STATISTICAL
TABLES & GRAPHS

CHARTS & SCORES

MAPS

ARCHITECTURAL
PLANS & DRAWINGS

INSTRUCTIONAL DIAGRAMS
FOR PRODUCTS

SCIENTIFIC
ILLUSTRATIONS

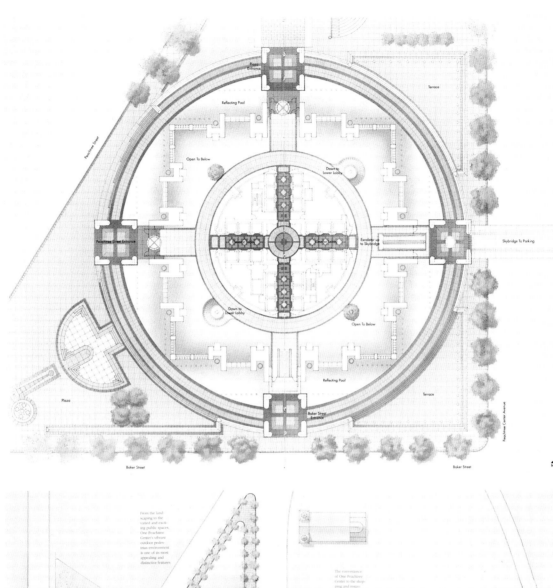

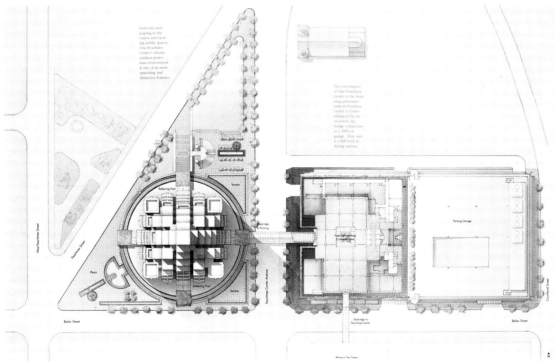

Elevation and site plan of a high-rise building, One Peachtree Center, in Atlanta. From a promotional pamphlet.
プロモーション用パンフレットより、アトランタの高層ビル「ワンピーチツリー・センター」の立面図、及び平面図。

VERLAG DAS BESTE

GERMANY 1985
CD:Rudi Schmidt
AD,I:Achim Kiel
DF:Pencil Corporate Art

STATISTICAL
TABLES & GRAPHS

CHARTS & SCORES

MAPS

ARCHITECTURAL
PLANS & DRAWINGS

INSTRUCTIONAL DIAGRAMS
FOR PRODUCTS

SCIENTIFIC
ILLUSTRATIONS

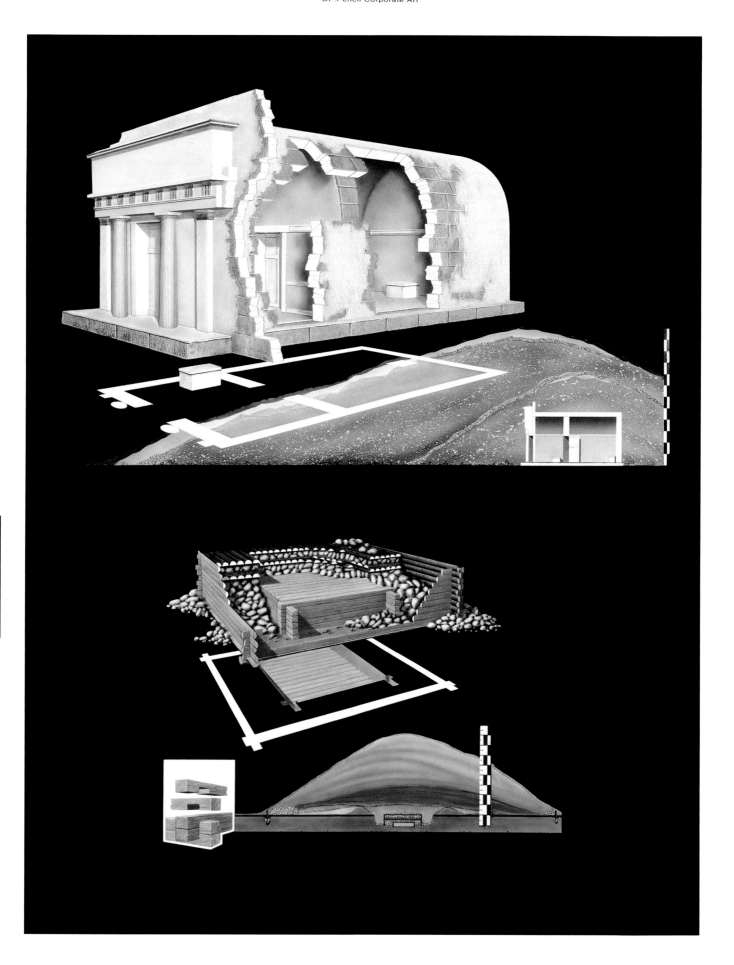

Diagrams of archaeological excavations showing the structure, proportions and lay-out of ancient burial sites.
古代埋葬場の規模、構造、及び配置などを示す考古学的発掘の図解。

製 品

いわゆる絵画と図解の違いは、絵画が多分に作者の心情を反映した「描写」的性格を重んじるのに対して、図解は、客観的な事実の冷静な「記述」としての性格を重んじる点にある。

本章で紹介する製品イラストレーションと、次章で紹介する科学イラストレーションはいずれも、こうした記述的意図をもって描かれた作品である。

本来、ダイアグラムとは、図と文字情報の共同による図解作品を指すもので、これらのイラストレーションの中には、画面中に文字情報を含まず、厳密な意味でのダイアグラムの範疇には属さない作品も含まれている。が、これらの作品に一貫して見られる記述的な意図というものは、その基本的な精神をダイアグラムと共有するものといえる。

製品イラストレーションは、文字通り、製品の仕上がり、ないしは構造を図解したものである。同じ用途に写真が使われることも多いが、製品を美しく見せる理想的なライティングや、細部の徹底した描写には、逆に「写真のように」精緻なイラストレーションの方が威力を発揮するケースというのが珍しくない。一般的な印象とは逆に、写真というメディアは細部の写実的な描写においては、ライティング、ピント、さらには被写体の仕上がりやコンディションと、実に多くの不確定要因が関わってくる分だけ、確実性に欠ける部分がある。その点、人間の手で細部を徹底的に吟味、修正しながら描けるイラストレーションは、描き手の技量さえ確かであれば、はるかに確実な結果を期待できることになる。加えて、製品の内部構造を示す断面図等においては、イラストレーションの表現力が断然まさっていることはいうまでもない。

これらのイラストレーションは、ある意味では一般の絵画をも上回る絵画技術を駆使しつつも、いわゆる絵画的な詩情を排した独特の知的な美学を示している点で、視覚表現ジャンルに特異な位置を占めている。

各時代の科学イラストレーションが、各時代の科学の状況を物語る貴重な視覚的証言であるのと同じように、製品イラストレーションは、産業革命以降の工業生産品に彩られた消費生活史を未来に保存する、貴重きわまりない視覚素材ということができるだろう。

INSTRUCTIONAL
DIAGRAMS
FOR PRODUCTS

INSTRUCTIONAL DIAGRAMS

FOR PRODUCTS

製品イラストレーション

The difference between fine art and illustration is that the former essentially reflects the artist's feelings and thoughts, whereas the function of the latter is the disinterested observation and recording of visual facts. The product illustrations introduced in this chapter and the scientific illustrations in the next chapter are artworks produced with just such a cool, descriptive intention.

Originally, the word "diagram" generally referred to illustrations which incorporate both graphic and text information. Among the illustrations introduced here, there are some which do not include any text. Strictly speaking, perhaps, they do not belong in the category of diagrams as it is normally defined. I dare say, however, that the intention to visually describe something from an objective viewpoint is certainly present, so these illustrations do have the essential spirit of diagrams.

A product illustration is, literally, an illustration of a finished product. It is not unusual to use photos for the same purpose, but it is often the case that a "photographically correct" illustration is more effective than a real photograph. In photography, the ideal lighting, which would show the beauty of the product and, at the same time, reveal it in all its detail, can be difficult to achieve. Contrary to the common assumption, photography is not always a visually reliable medium. When trying to reproduce details in photography, realism depends upon lighting, focus, the finish of the subject and a number of other factors, not all of which can be controlled by the photographer.

An illustration, on the other hand, can be produced very painstakingly, highlighting each detail as necessary. Control here depends upon human doggedness so that if the artist has certain level of technique, you can always expect a high quality illustration. Moreover, illustrations often have greater visual impact than photos, and are infinitely superior when it comes to cross-section views, exposing internal structures. This type of illustration is a genre in itself, in that it employs techniques which, in some ways, surpass those used in painting. It possesses a unique and intelligent esthetic, from which artistic or poetic sentiment has been banished.

Scientific illustrations are artifacts as well, bearing eloquent witness to the level of scientific advance in the era recorded. Product illustrations too, are extremely valuable visual documents which tell the story of consumerism and quality of life through the evolution of products manufactured since the industrial revolution.

STATISTICAL
TABLES & GRAPHS

CHARTS & SCORES

MAPS

ARCHITECTURAL
PLANS & DRAWINGS

INSTRUCTIONAL DIAGRAMS
FOR PRODUCTS

SCIENTIFIC
ILLUSTRATIONS

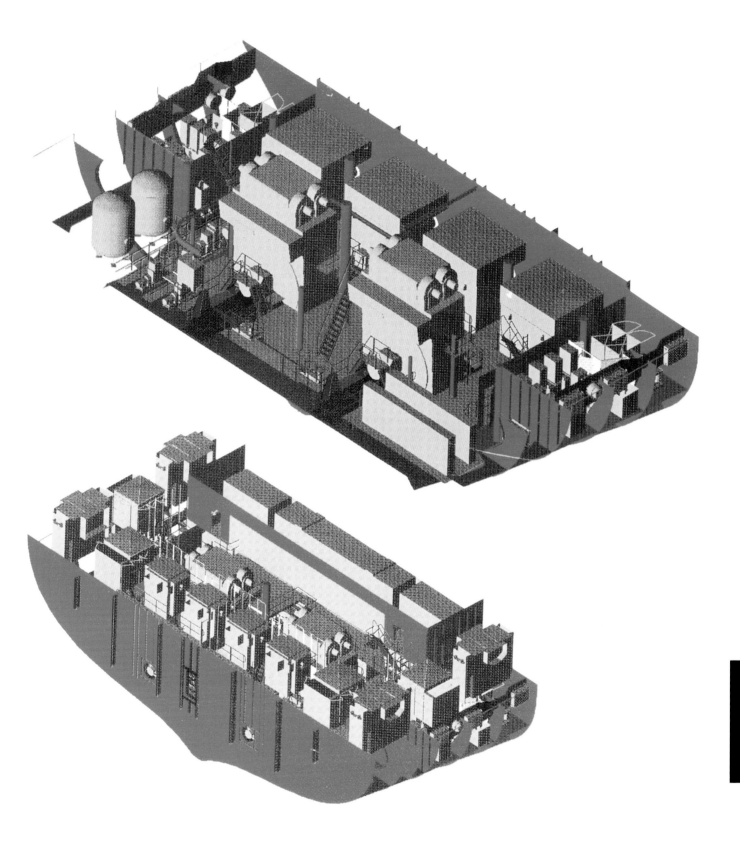

Spacial study of the axonometrics of the Crown Princess engine room. From GB progetti Magazine No. 3/4 1990.
「GB progetti マガジン」1990年3/4号より、クラウンプリンセスのエンジンルームのアクソノメトリック・スケッチ。

STATISTICAL
TABLES & GRAPHS

CHARTS & SCORES

MAPS

ARCHITECTURAL
PLANS & DRAWINGS

INSTRUCTIONAL DIAGRAMS
FOR PRODUCTS

SCIENTIFIC
ILLUSTRATIONS

HI-SHEAR INDUSTRIES, INC.

USA 1991
CD:Stephen Ferrari
D:Janet Scanlon
I:Steve Lyons
DF:The Graphic Expression, Inc.

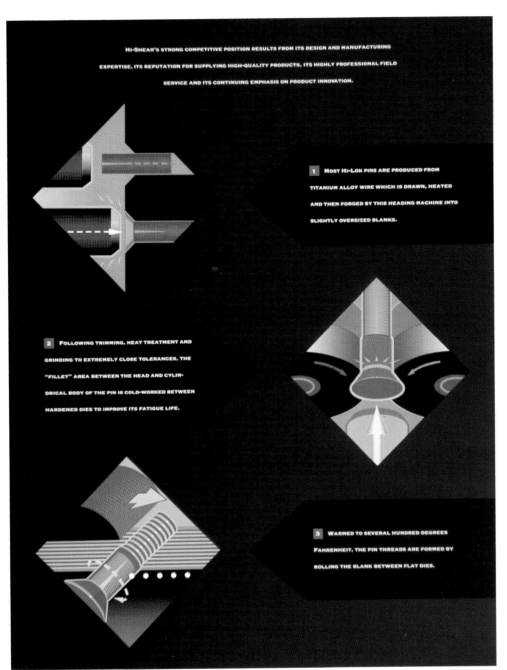

HI-SHEAR'S STRONG COMPETITIVE POSITION RESULTS FROM ITS DESIGN AND MANUFACTURING EXPERTISE, ITS REPUTATION FOR SUPPLYING HIGH-QUALITY PRODUCTS, ITS HIGHLY PROFESSIONAL FIELD SERVICE AND ITS CONTINUING EMPHASIS ON PRODUCT INNOVATION.

1 MOST HI-LOK PINS ARE PRODUCED FROM TITANIUM ALLOY WIRE WHICH IS DRAWN, HEATED AND THEN FORGED BY THIS HEADING MACHINE INTO SLIGHTLY OVERSIZED BLANKS.

2 FOLLOWING TRIMMING, HEAT TREATMENT AND GRINDING TO EXTREMELY CLOSE TOLERANCES, THE "FILLET" AREA BETWEEN THE HEAD AND CYLIN-DRICAL BODY OF THE PIN IS COLD-WORKED BETWEEN HARDENED DIES TO IMPROVE ITS FATIGUE LIFE.

3 WARMED TO SEVERAL HUNDRED DEGREES FAHRENHEIT, THE PIN THREADS ARE FORMED BY ROLLING THE BLANK BETWEEN FLAT DIES.

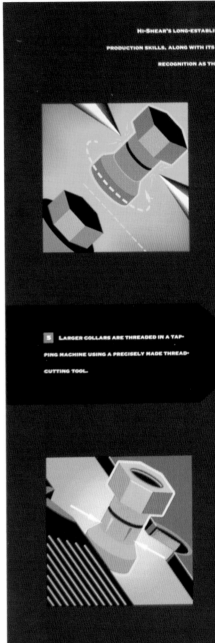

HI-SHEAR'S LONG-ESTABLI
PRODUCTION SKILLS, ALONG WITH ITS
RECOGNITION AS TH

5 LARGER COLLARS ARE THREADED IN A TAP-PING MACHINE USING A PRECISELY MADE THREAD-CUTTING TOOL.

STATISTICAL
TABLES & GRAPHS

CHARTS & SCORES

MAPS

ARCHITECTURAL
PLANS & DRAWINGS

INSTRUCTIONAL DIAGRAMS
FOR PRODUCTS

SCIENTIFIC
ILLUSTRATIONS

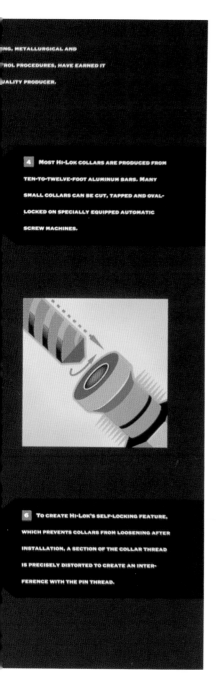

4 MOST HI-LOK COLLARS ARE PRODUCED FROM TEN-TO-TWELVE-FOOT ALUMINUM BARS. MANY SMALL COLLARS CAN BE CUT, TAPPED AND OVAL-LOCKED ON SPECIALLY EQUIPPED AUTOMATIC SCREW MACHINES.

6 TO CREATE HI-LOK'S SELF-LOCKING FEATURE, WHICH PREVENTS COLLARS FROM LOOSENING AFTER INSTALLATION, A SECTION OF THE COLLAR THREAD IS PRECISELY DISTORTED TO CREATE AN INTER-FERENCE WITH THE PIN THREAD.

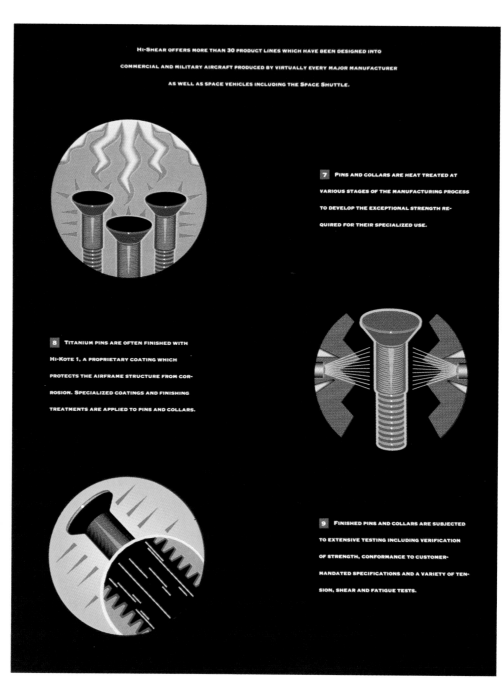

HI-SHEAR OFFERS MORE THAN 30 PRODUCT LINES WHICH HAVE BEEN DESIGNED INTO COMMERCIAL AND MILITARY AIRCRAFT PRODUCED BY VIRTUALLY EVERY MAJOR MANUFACTURER AS WELL AS SPACE VEHICLES INCLUDING THE SPACE SHUTTLE.

7 PINS AND COLLARS ARE HEAT TREATED AT VARIOUS STAGES OF THE MANUFACTURING PROCESS TO DEVELOP THE EXCEPTIONAL STRENGTH RE-QUIRED FOR THEIR SPECIALIZED USE.

8 TITANIUM PINS ARE OFTEN FINISHED WITH HI-KOTE 1, A PROPRIETARY COATING WHICH PROTECTS THE AIRFRAME STRUCTURE FROM COR-ROSION. SPECIALIZED COATINGS AND FINISHING TREATMENTS ARE APPLIED TO PINS AND COLLARS.

9 FINISHED PINS AND COLLARS ARE SUBJECTED TO EXTENSIVE TESTING INCLUDING VERIFICATION OF STRENGTH, CONFORMANCE TO CUSTOMER-MANDATED SPECIFICATIONS AND A VARIETY OF TEN-SION, SHEAR AND FATIGUE TESTS.

Diagrams of various manufacturing steps as part of an overall quality process. From a Hi-Shear Industries Inc. annual report.
ハイシアー・インダストリーズ社のアニュアルリポートより、製品の全体的な品質管理過程を表すために紹介された、いくつかの製造過程図。

STATISTICAL
TABLES & GRAPHS

CHARTS & SCORES

MAPS

ARCHITECTURAL
PLANS & DRAWINGS

INSTRUCTIONAL DIAGRAMS
FOR PRODUCTS

SCIENTIFIC
ILLUSTRATIONS

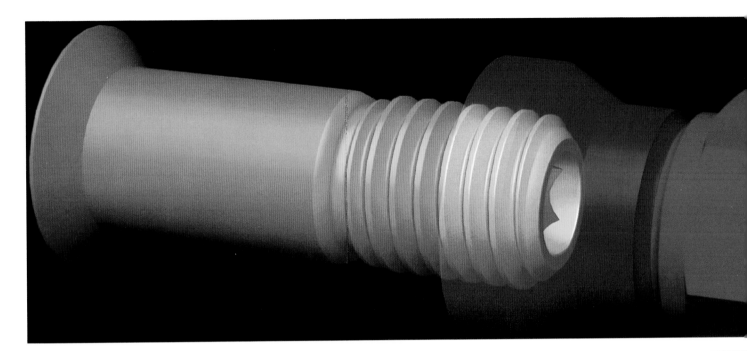

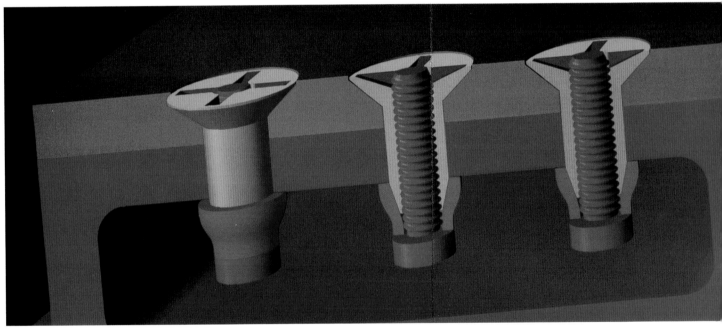

STATISTICAL
TABLES & GRAPHS

CHARTS & SCORES

MAPS

ARCHITECTURAL
PLANS & DRAWINGS

INSTRUCTIONAL DIAGRAMS
FOR PRODUCTS

SCIENTIFIC
ILLUSTRATIONS

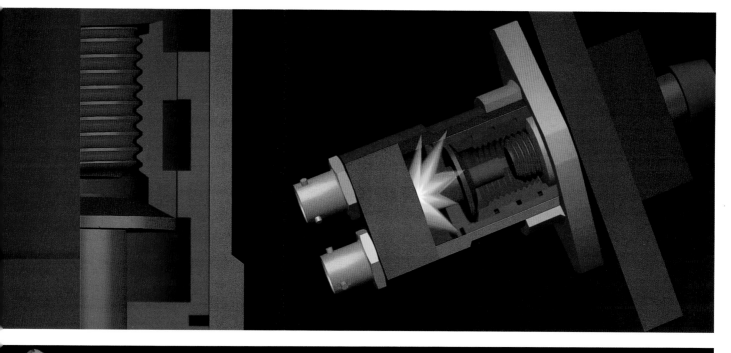

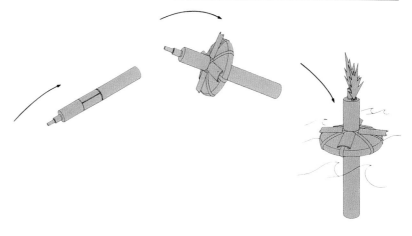

Illustration utilizing computer modeling to display the company's range of products. From a Hi-Shear Industries Inc. annual report.
ハイシアー・インダストリーズ社のアニュアルリポートより、会社の製品の適用範囲をコンピューター・モデリングを使って表すイラストレーション。

STATISTICAL
TABLES & GRAPHS

CHARTS & SCORES

MAPS

ARCHITECTURAL
PLANS & DRAWINGS

INSTRUCTIONAL DIAGRAMS
FOR PRODUCTS

SCIENTIFIC
ILLUSTRATIONS

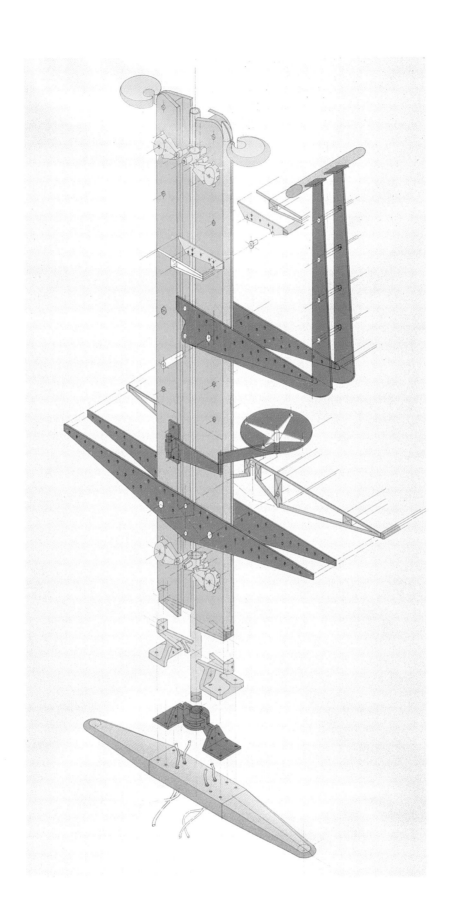

Isometric assembly of Eco-iD "Evolution" freestanding structure which can be extended and reduced as required.

必要に応じて伸縮自在な家具システム「Eco-iDエボリューション」のアイソメトリック組立図。

STATISTICAL
TABLES & GRAPHS

CHARTS & SCORES

MAPS

ARCHITECTURAL
PLANS & DRAWINGS

INSTRUCTIONAL DIAGRAMS
FOR PRODUCTS

SCIENTIFIC
ILLUSTRATIONS

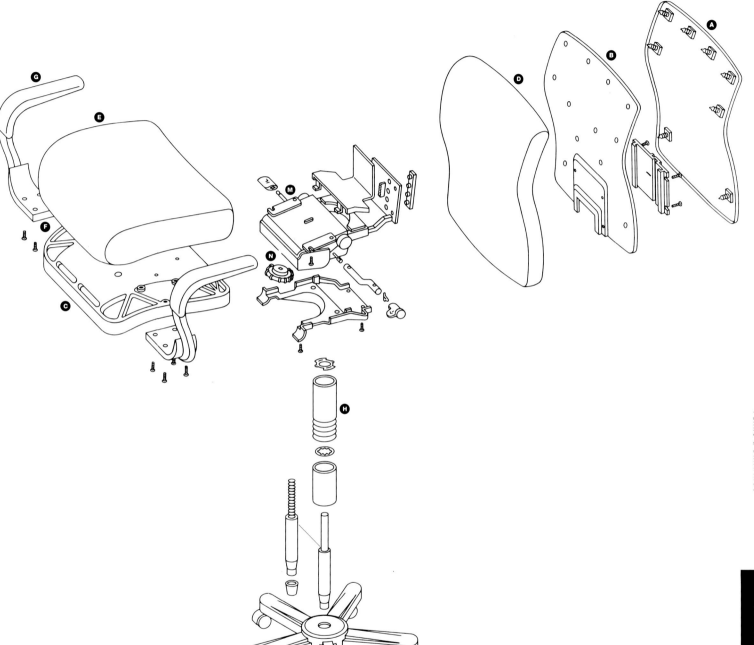

This "exploded view" of a Bulldog chair reveals details that are normally not visible and gives an understanding of how some of the many unique parts fit together.

「ブルドッグチェア」分解組立図。通常見えない部分を見せ、数多くの特殊な部品がどのように組み合わさっているかを解説している。

STATISTICAL
TABLES & GRAPHS

CHARTS & SCORES

MAPS

ARCHITECTURAL
PLANS & DRAWINGS

INSTRUCTIONAL DIAGRAMS
FOR PRODUCTS

SCIENTIFIC
ILLUSTRATIONS

MATSUSHITA ELECTRIC
INDUSTRIAL CO., LTD.
JAPAN 1991
CD:Mikio Mori
AD:Masato Okazaki
I:Takatoshi Oki

Technics CD player technical illustration. From a Matsushita Electric Industrial sales catalogue.
松下電機産業の製品カタログより、「テクニクスCDプレイヤー」のテクニカル・イラストレーション。

PIONEER ELECTRIC CORPORATION
JAPAN
CD:Isao Kobayashi
AD:Yukio Sekido
D:Masakatsu Nakamura
I:Ryo Ohshita

SONY CORPORATION
JAPAN
DF:Sony Corporation Advertising & Marketing
Communication Strategy Group

STATISTICAL
TABLES & GRAPHS

CHARTS & SCORES

MAPS

ARCHITECTURAL
PLANS & DRAWINGS

INSTRUCTIONAL DIAGRAMS
FOR PRODUCTS

SCIENTIFIC
ILLUSTRATIONS

Illustration of the turntable unit in a CD player "PD-T07".
From a Pioneer Electric Corporation sales catalogue.
パイオニア社の製品カタログより、CDプレイヤー「PD-T07」のターンテーブル部のイラストレーション。

Diagram showing the internal structure of a color television "Kirara Basso".
From a Sony Corporation sales catalogue.
ソニー社の製品カタログより、カラーテレビ「キララ・バッソ」の内部構造図。

STATISTICAL
TABLES & GRAPHS

CHARTS & SCORES

MAPS

ARCHITECTURAL
PLANS & DRAWINGS

INSTRUCTIONAL DIAGRAMS
FOR PRODUCTS

SCIENTIFIC
ILLUSTRATIONS

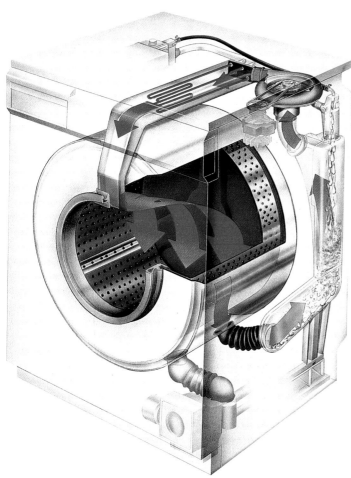

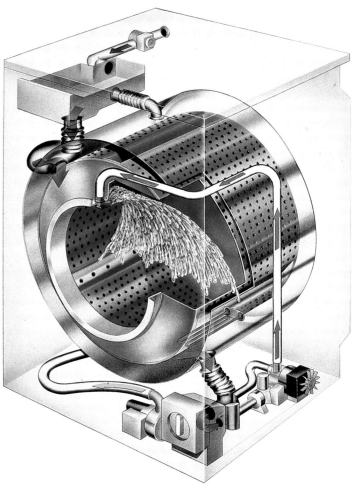

Illustration of the Zanussi ZTD900 washing machine, manufactured by Zanussi Elettrodomestici spa. in Italy. From MODO magazine #137.
「モードマガジン」137号より、イタリアのザヌッシ電気機器社の「ザヌッシZTD900洗濯機」のイラストレーション。

STATISTICAL
TABLES & GRAPHS

CHARTS & SCORES

MAPS

ARCHITECTURAL
PLANS & DRAWINGS

INSTRUCTIONAL DIAGRAMS
FOR PRODUCTS

SCIENTIFIC
ILLUSTRATIONS

HITACHI SALES CORPORATION
JAPAN 1989
D:Yoshiaki Yonejima

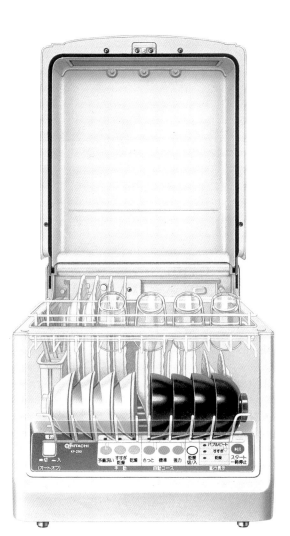
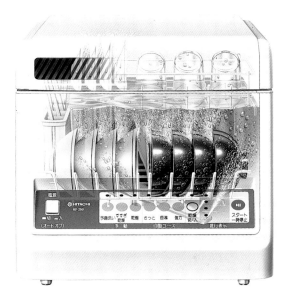

Illustration explaining the operating procedure for a home appliance dish washer/dryer "Arattokuwa". From a Hitachi Sales Corporation catalogue.
日立家電社の製品カタログより、家庭用食器洗い乾燥器「洗っとくわ」の操作手順の解説イラストレーション。

EUNOS INC.

JAPAN 1990

CD:Kazutomo Kanazawa

AD:Hiroyuki Fukusato

D:Mitsugu Muramatsu

I:Takashi Ohno/Takeshi Hosokawa

STATISTICAL
TABLES & GRAPHS

CHARTS & SCORES

MAPS

ARCHITECTURAL
PLANS & DRAWINGS

INSTRUCTIONAL DIAGRAMS
FOR PRODUCTS

SCIENTIFIC
ILLUSTRATIONS

STATISTICAL
TABLES & GRAPHS

CHARTS & SCORES

MAPS

ARCHITECTURAL
PLANS & DRAWINGS

INSTRUCTIONAL DIAGRAMS
FOR PRODUCTS

SCIENTIFIC
ILLUSTRATIONS

Illustrations of the engine and the chassis of the Eunos Cosmo automobile. From a Eunos Inc. sales catalogue.
ユーノス社の製品カタログより、自動車「ユーノス・コスモ」のエンジン部、及びシャーシ部のイラストレーション。

LOCKHEED CORPORATION
USA 1992
CD,AD:Carl Seltzer
D:Luis Alvarado
I:Jim Speas
DF:Carl Seltzer Design Office

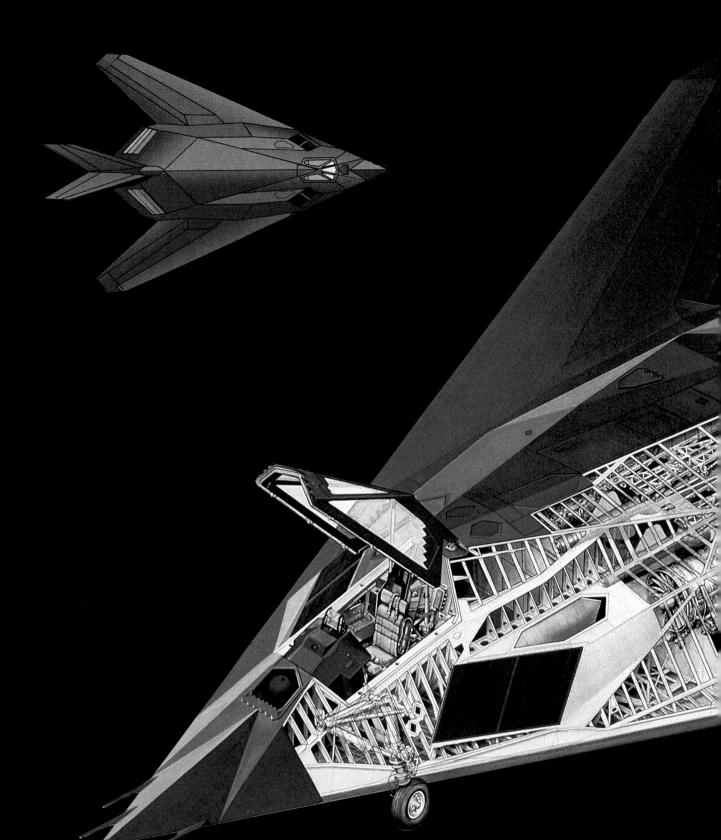

STATISTICAL
TABLES & GRAPHS

CHARTS & SCORES

MAPS

ARCHITECTURAL
PLANS & DRAWINGS

INSTRUCTIONAL DIAGRAMS
FOR PRODUCTS

SCIENTIFIC
ILLUSTRATIONS

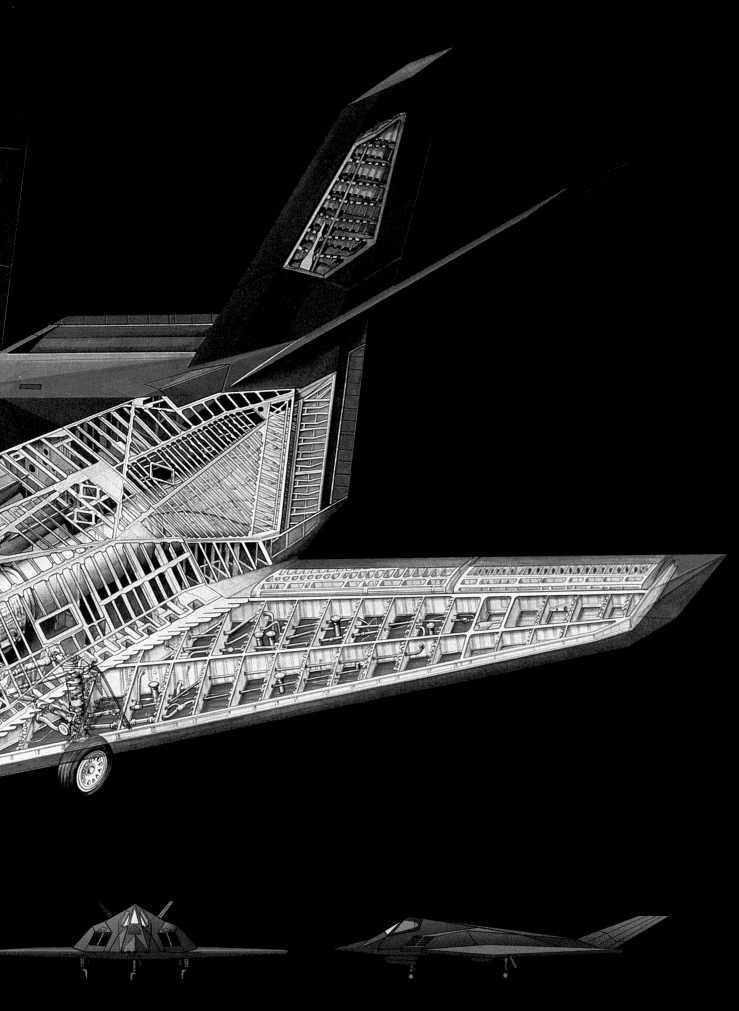

STATISTICAL
TABLES & GRAPHS

CHARTS & SCORES

MAPS

ARCHITECTURAL
PLANS & DRAWINGS

INSTRUCTIONAL DIAGRAMS
FOR PRODUCTS

SCIENTIFIC
ILLUSTRATIONS

The F-117 Stealth Fighter rose to worldwide fame during the Gulf War,
but this was the first time the U.S. Government permitted a cutaway view of this historic but once top-secret aircraft.
湾岸戦争で世界中の脚光を浴びた「F-117ステルス戦闘機」の断面図。かつては最高機密に属したこの戦闘機の内部の公開を合衆国政府が許可したのは初めてのことである。

STATISTICAL
TABLES & GRAPHS

CHARTS & SCORES

MAPS

ARCHITECTURAL
PLANS & DRAWINGS

INSTRUCTIONAL DIAGRAMS
FOR PRODUCTS

SCIENTIFIC
ILLUSTRATIONS

Illustration of a Jaguar automobile used on the package of a plastic model.
プラモデルのパッケージに印刷された、自動車「ジャガー」のイラストレーション。

イラストレーション
科学

科学イラストレーションの歴史は古い。

古代の天文図から、中世の化学図解、ルネッサンスの解剖図、そして近世以降の種々の科学書を飾る図解群は、そのまま科学という名の人間のあくなき探求心の足取りの、視覚化されたものといえる。

医学図解、天文図解、地学図解等が、科学イラストレーションの代表であるが、こうしたテーマやジャンルを問わず、なんらかの現象や知識を客観的かつ科学的な関心のもとに描いた図解作品はすべて、広い意味での科学イラストレーションに含まれると考えていいだろう。

もともと、絵画というものは、描かれた対象を視覚的に所有するための道具としての性格が強いものであった。したがって、人間は常に、自分が「欲しい」と思うものを描き続けてきたのである。原始時代、それは狩りの獲物であり、中世、それは神の恩寵であり、ルネッサンス期、それは理想的な人間像であった。

それぞれの動機は、それぞれに呪術、宗教、人文主義などと別の名前で呼ばれてはいるが、それらはすべて、なんらかのかたちで欲しいもの、手に入れたいものを描いているという点において共通している。

科学イラストレーションも例外ではない。それらの画面は、ある意味では、人間が「欲しい」と思うものの筆頭に挙げられるべき、知識というものへの思いの視覚化に他ならないのである。

したがって、科学イラストレーションの制作にあたっては、精緻な観察眼と確かな描画技術もさることながら、なにより、読者の知的関心の代理人あるいは読者の眼の代理人としての、好奇心に裏付けられた創造性というものが要求される。

近年、著しい発達を遂げたコンピュータ・グラフィックスなどは、かつて人間の手では決して描くことのできなかった画像を次々に実現してみせているわけだが、こうした描画技術の飛躍的な発展に直面するほどに、ダイアグラム・デザイナーは、この技術に見合うだけの、好奇心とイマジネーションというものを要求されることになるのである。

SCIENTIFIC
ILLUSTRATIONS

SCIENTIFIC ILLUSTRATIONS

The history of scientific illustrations goes back further than you might think. In Medieval times there were already astronomical and chemical illustrations. Later came the anatomical illustrations of the Renaissance period and, of course, ever more sophisticated illustrations have been appearing in various scientific publications since the beginning of the modern age. These are a direct reflection of the history of the human desire for knowledge, called science. When we talk about scientific illustration, we immediately think of medical drawings, geological diagrams and so forth. Regardless of theme or subject matter, however, if an illustration objectively depicts a certain phenomenon or body of knowledge with scientific interest, then, at least in the broader sense, it can be called a scientific illustration.

Originally, paintings functioned, in a visual sense, as a tool to take possession of the object depicted. Just as early humans made cave paintings of the animals they wanted to capture or kill, so people have always depicted the object of their desire. In the Medieval age it was God's love, and during the Renaissance it was the ideal image of man. The motivation for creating those images is not dissimilar to that of magical incantations, whether it is called religion, humanism, or something else, we depict what we want in order to call it forth.

Scientific illustrations are no exception; these images are the very visualization of the love of knowledge which has characterized the modern age. In producing a scientific illustration, creativity is driven by curiosity as the agent. The viewer's intellectual capacity is engaged and the reader's critical eye is assumed to be very sharp. Thus, for the designer, great powers of observation are required and a sure technique of rendering it in accurate detail. In this field, as in others, computer graphics have made a spectacular contribution and are embraced enthusiastically by most artists. Images now are being realized which, until recently, would have been difficult even to imagine, much less achieve. Diagram designers are facing quantum leaps in imaging technique and potential, but this does not necessarily make the job easier. Indeed, his artist's curiosity and imagination may be more challenged than ever by these exciting new tools.

科学
イラストレーション

ROCHE PRODUCTS LIMITED
ENGLAND 1971
CD,AD,D:Mervyn Kurlansky
D:Maddy Bennet
DF:Pentagram Design Ltd.

SCHOOL OF
VISUAL ARTS COMPUTER ILLUSTRATION PROJECT
USA 1991
I:Frank Fasano

STATISTICAL
TABLES & GRAPHS

CHARTS & SCORES

MAPS

ARCHITECTURAL
PLANS & DRAWINGS

INSTRUCTIONAL DIAGRAMS
FOR PRODUCTS

SCIENTIFIC
ILLUSTRATIONS

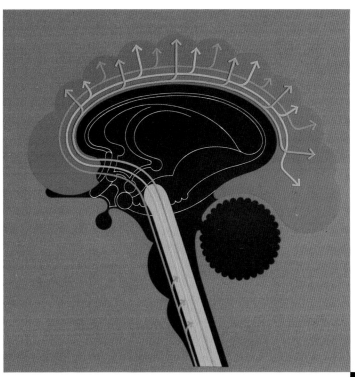

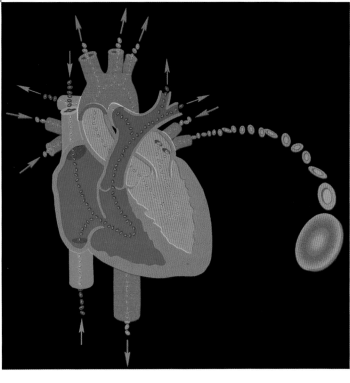

Illustration showing the main sensory pathway to the cortex indicated by arrows.
From a Roche Products Limited promotional brochure for a new tranquillizer.
ロッシュ・プロダクツ社の新精神安定剤プロモーション用パンフレットより、
大脳皮質への感覚の到達経路を矢印で示すイラストレーション。

Illustration of a heart with blood flow.
血液の循環経路を示す心臓のイラストレーション。

STATISTICAL
TABLES & GRAPHS

CHARTS & SCORES

MAPS

ARCHITECTURAL
PLANS & DRAWINGS

INSTRUCTIONAL DIAGRAMS
FOR PRODUCTS

SCIENTIFIC
ILLUSTRATIONS

AMERICAN HEALTH PARTNERS, INC.
USA 1987
AD:Will Hopkins/Ira Friedlander
D,I:Peter Bradford
I:Frank H. Netter
DF:Peter Bradford & Associates

*O'Shea got to the
hospital an hour after
his symptoms began.*

the edge of the bed for a few minutes,
the pain stopped. But it returned when
he resumed his shower. And this time,
it didn't go away.

Alarmed, O'Shea called a friend in
his parish and together they drove to
Seton Medical Center a few miles
south in Daly City. They arrived at the
emergency room a little more than an
hour after his symptoms had begun.
Cardiologist Colman Ryan needed only
one look at O'Shea's electrocardio-
gram to determine he was in the mid-
dle of a heart attack.

But there was still time to stop it.
First, Dr. Ryan sent O'Shea down to
the cardiac catheterization lab for a
coronary angiogram, an X-ray study
done with contrast dye injected
through a catheter into the coronary
arteries. The angiogram would reveal
the precise location of the blockage
and how extensive it was. The cardiol-
ogists could then try to unclog the artery and halt the attack.

Then Ryan beeped Dr. Richard Myler, one of the country's foremost ex-
perts in balloon angioplasty (also called
percutaneous transluminal coronary
angioplasty, or PTCA). Myler, who's
on staff at the hospital, had had success using PTCA as an emergency
measure to stop a heart attack in progress. (Normally, the procedure is
used to open vessels that are nar-
rowed but not completely closed, in
patients who aren't acutely ill.)

O'Shea's angiogram results came
in: The clot had completely blocked
the left anterior descending artery,
which supplies blood to the front of the
heart and to the wall that divides the
two beating chambers.

Ryan alerted an open-heart surgery
team in case emergency bypass surgery was needed. In emergency bypass, an arterial graft is used to detour

46

**During a heart
attack, a clot
blocks blood
circulation to
part of the
heart muscle.
Affected areas
die from insuf-
ficient oxygen
supply. Three
new methods
permit doctors
to restore
blood flow, and
thus cut short a
heart attack
and limit dam-
age. Clockwise:
TPA and other
clot-busting
drugs dissolve
the blockage;
in angioplasty,
a catheter is
snaked through
an artery to the
site and an
inflated bal-
loon at its tip
breaks up the
clot; emergency
bypass detours
blood supply
around the
obstruction.**

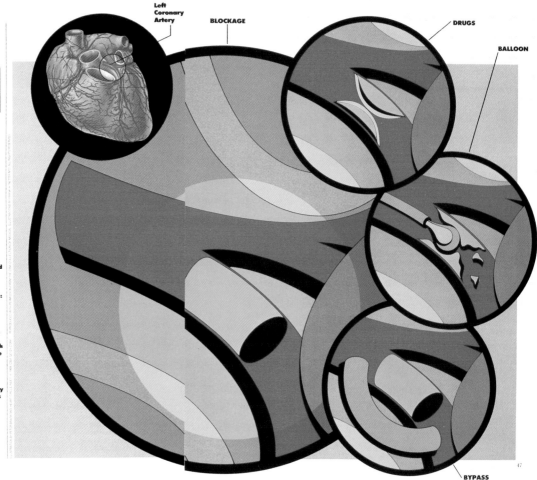

47

Illustration of three methods to restore blood flow to the heart and limit heart attack damage. From American Health magazine.
「アメリカン・ヘルスマガジン」より、心臓への血液の流入を修復しながら心臓発作による損傷を抑える3つの方法を解説したイラストレーション。

ACCESS PRESS, INC.

USA 1988

AD:Richard Saul Wurman

D,I:Lorraine Christiani

D:Peter Bradford

I:Michael Everitt

DF:Peter Bradford & Associates

CHARTS & SCORES

MAPS

ARCHITECTURAL PLANS & DRAWINGS

INSTRUCTIONAL DIAGRAMS FOR PRODUCTS

SCIENTIFIC ILLUSTRATIONS

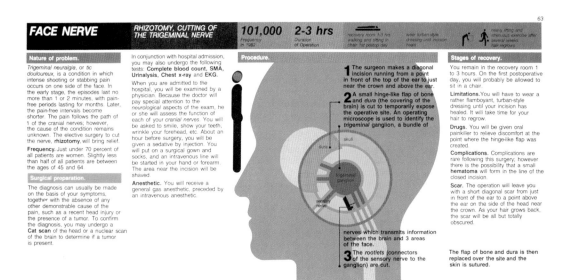

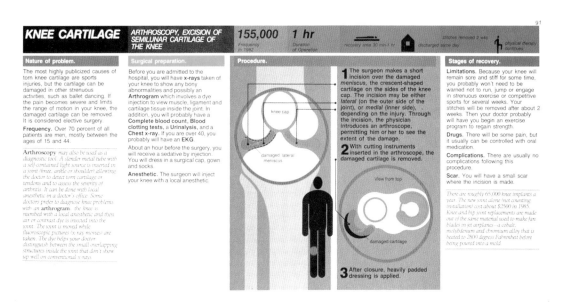

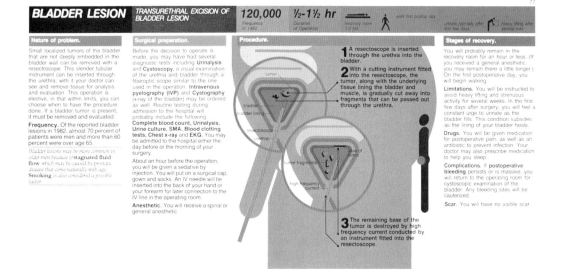

Illustrations for step-by-step explanations of common surgical procedure. From Medical Access Guide Book.

「メディカルアクセス・ガイドブック」より、外科手術の方法を段階をおいながら解説するイラストレーション。

STATISTICAL TABLES & GRAPHS

CHARTS & SCORES

MAPS

ARCHITECTURAL PLANS & DRAWINGS

INSTRUCTIONAL DIAGRAMS FOR PRODUCTS

SCIENTIFIC ILLUSTRATIONS

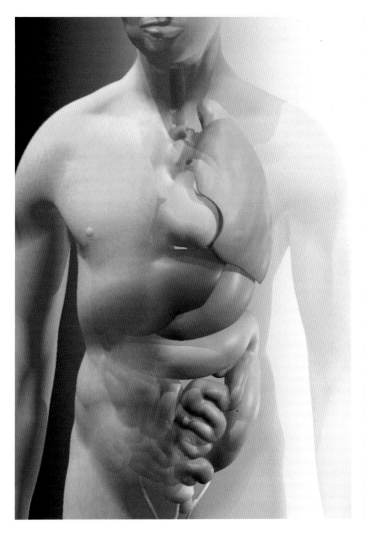
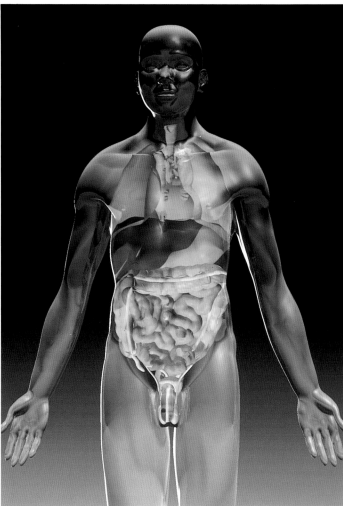

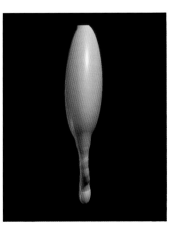
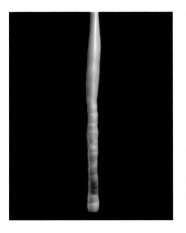

STATISTICAL
TABLES & GRAPHS

CHARTS & SCORES

MAPS

ARCHITECTURAL
PLANS & DRAWINGS

INSTRUCTIONAL DIAGRAMS
FOR PRODUCTS

SCIENTIFIC
ILLUSTRATIONS

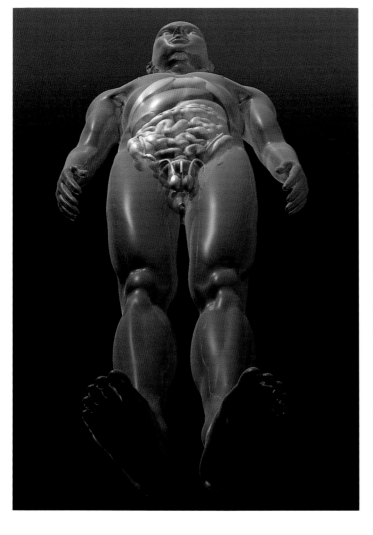
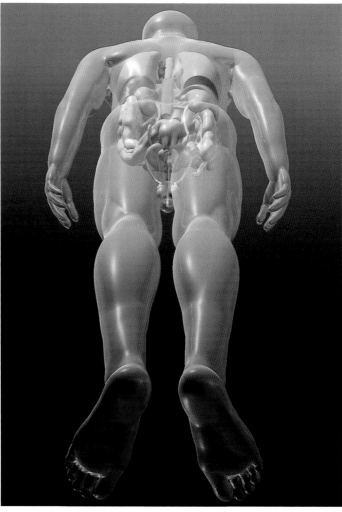

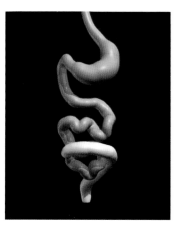
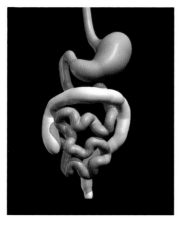
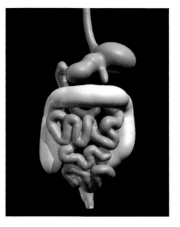
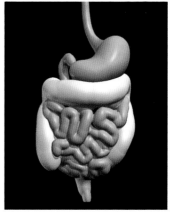

Computer-generated image of internal organs showing the development of the intestinal tract. From the TV program, "Human Body".

TV番組「人体」より、CGによる内臓透視図、及び腸管の進化過程図。

KRAMES COMMUNICATIONS
USA 1990
AD:Fran Milner
I:John Daugherty

SMITHKLINE BEECHAM
USA 1992
AD:David Holms
I:John Daugherty
DF:Frank J. Corbett

STATISTICAL
TABLES & GRAPHS

CHARTS & SCORES

MAPS

ARCHITECTURAL
PLANS & DRAWINGS

INSTRUCTIONAL DIAGRAMS
FOR PRODUCTS

SCIENTIFIC
ILLUSTRATIONS

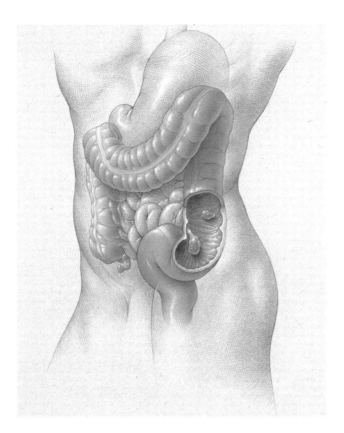

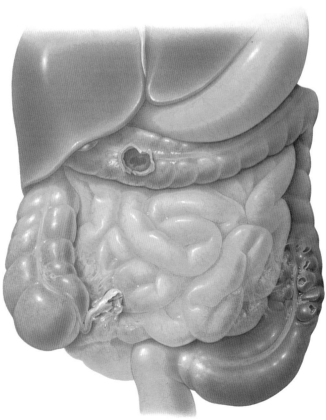

Cover illustration for a patient education booklet on polyps and colon cancer.
Two polyps are shown in the descending colon.
患者への教育用パンフレットより、表紙に使用されたポリープや結腸癌のイラストレーション。
傾斜する結腸に2つのポリープが見える。

Illustration promoting a leading antibiotic drug used to treat mixed bowel infections.
The illustration depicts a perforated gangrenous appendix,
a penetrating abdominal wound, ruptured diverticula,
a lower bowel obstruction and general abdominal peritonitis.
併発腸炎を治療する有力な抗生剤の広告用イラストレーション。
壊疽症、孔虫垂、貫通腹部創傷、腸閉塞、腹膜炎等が描かれている。

STATISTICAL
TABLES & GRAPHS

CHARTS & SCORES

MAPS

ARCHITECTURAL
PLANS & DRAWINGS

INSTRUCTIONAL DIAGRAMS
FOR PRODUCTS

SCIENTIFIC
ILLUSTRATIONS

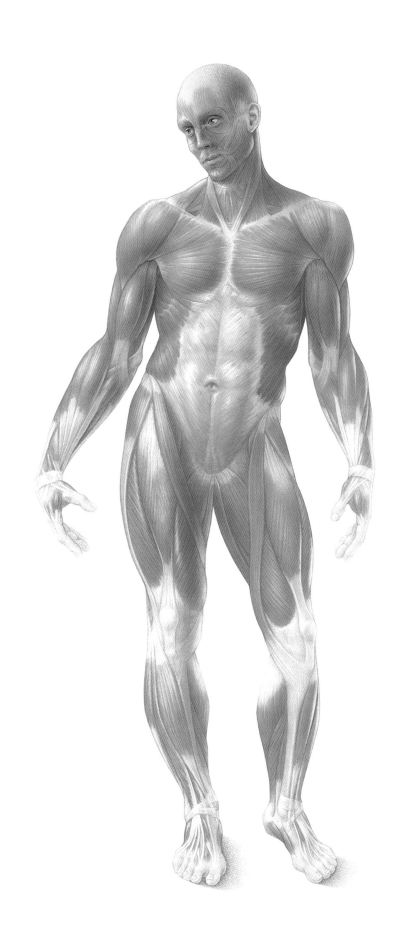

Anterior view of the muscles of the human body. The illustration, showing the adult human male in a classical pose,
was used in an advertisement to promote a feeling of strength and grace.
人体の筋肉図。力強さと優美さをそなえ、古典的ポーズをとるこの成人男性のイラストレーションは広告に使用された。

STATISTICAL
TABLES & GRAPHS

CHARTS & SCORES

MAPS

ARCHITECTURAL
PLANS & DRAWINGS

INSTRUCTIONAL DIAGRAMS
FOR PRODUCTS

SCIENTIFIC
ILLUSTRATIONS

PFIZER
USA 1990
AD:Edmund Puches
P,I:Bill Finewood
DF:Puches Design

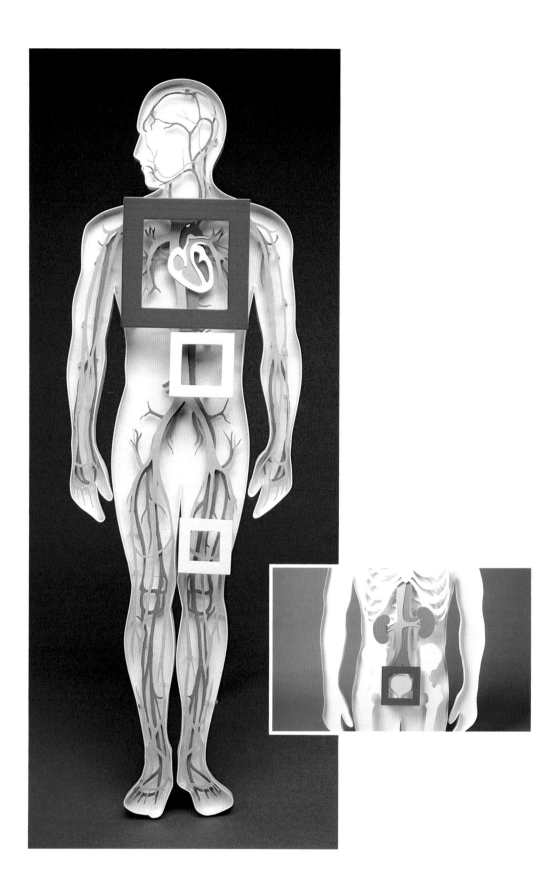

Illustration of cardiovascular system and urinary tract for Pfizer Technology Exhibit that shows pharmaceutical and hospital products.
医薬品、及び医療用品を紹介する「フィーザー社テクノロジー展」のために制作された心臓血管系と尿路の図解。

CENTOCOR, INC.
USA 1991
CD:Stephen Ferrari
D:John Ball
I:Michael Crumpton/
Martin Haggland/Micro Color
DF:The Graphic Expression, Inc.

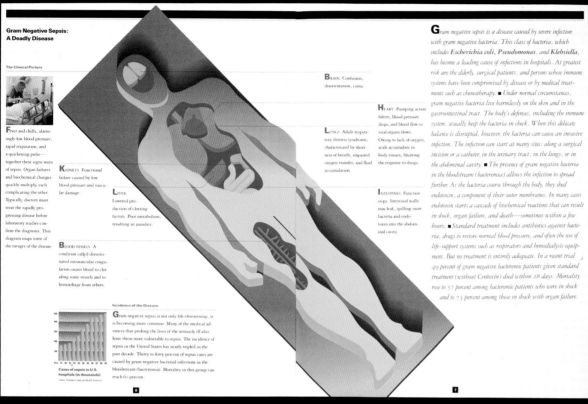

Gram Negative Sepsis: A Deadly Disease

The Clinical Picture

Fever and chills, alarmingly low blood pressure, rapid respiration, and a quickening pulse—together these signs warn of sepsis. Organ failures and biochemical changes quickly multiply, each complicating the other. Typically, doctors must treat the rapidly progressing disease before laboratory studies confirm the diagnosis. This diagram maps some of the ravages of the disease.

BRAIN. Confusion, disorientation, coma.

HEART. Pumping action falters, blood pressure drops, and blood flow to vital organs slows.

LUNGS. Adult respiratory distress syndrome, characterized by shortness of breath, impaired oxygen transfer, and fluid accumulation. Owing to lack of oxygen, acids accumulate in body tissues, blunting the response to drugs.

KIDNEYS. Functional failure caused by low blood pressure and vascular damage.

LIVER. Lowered production of clotting factors. Poor metabolism, resulting in jaundice.

INTESTINES. Function stops. Intestinal walls may leak, spilling more bacteria and endotoxin into the abdominal cavity.

BLOOD VESSELS. A condition called disseminated intravascular coagulation causes blood to clot along some vessels and to hemorrhage from others.

Incidence of the Disease

Gram negative sepsis is not only life-threatening, it is becoming more common. Many of the medical advances that prolong the lives of the seriously ill also leave them more vulnerable to sepsis. The incidence of sepsis in the United States has nearly tripled in the past decade. Thirty to forty percent of sepsis cases are caused by gram negative bacterial infections in the bloodstream (bacteremia). Mortality in this group can reach 60 percent.

Cases of sepsis in U.S. hospitals (in thousands)

*Gram negative sepsis is a disease caused by severe infection with gram negative bacteria. This class of bacteria, which includes **Escherichia coli, Pseudomonas, and Klebsiella,** has become a leading cause of infections in hospitals. At greatest risk are the elderly, surgical patients, and persons whose immune systems have been compromised by disease or by medical treatments such as chemotherapy. ■ Under normal circumstances, gram negative bacteria live harmlessly on the skin and in the gastrointestinal tract. The body's defenses, including the immune system, usually keep the bacteria in check. When this delicate balance is disrupted, however, the bacteria can cause an invasive infection. The infection can start at many sites: along a surgical incision or a catheter, in the urinary tract, in the lungs, or in the abdominal cavity. ■ The presence of gram negative bacteria in the bloodstream (bacteremia) allows the infection to spread further. As the bacteria course through the body, they shed endotoxin, a component of their outer membranes. In many cases endotoxin starts a cascade of biochemical reactions that can result in shock, organ failure, and death—sometimes within a few hours. ■ Standard treatment includes antibiotics against bacteria, drugs to restore normal blood pressure, and often the use of life-support systems such as respirators and hemodialysis equipment. But no treatment is entirely adequate. In a recent trial 49 percent of gram negative bacteremic patients given standard treatment (without Centoxin) died within 28 days. Mortality rose to 57 percent among bacteremic patients who were in shock and to 73 percent among those in shock with organ failure.*

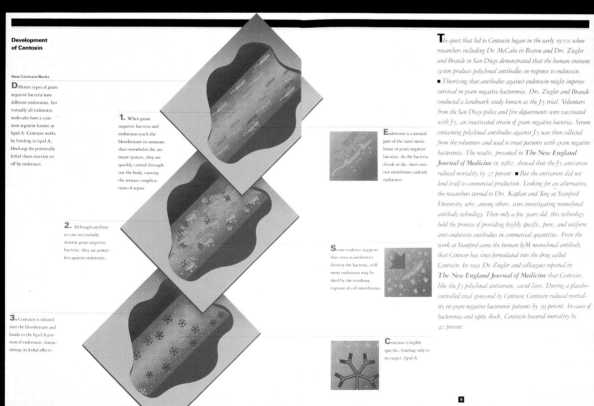

Development of Centoxin

How Centoxin Works

Different types of gram negative bacteria have different endotoxins, but virtually all endotoxin molecules have a common segment known as lipid A. Centoxin works by binding to lipid A, blocking the potentially lethal chain reaction set off by endotoxin.

1. When gram negative bacteria and endotoxin reach the bloodstream in amounts that overwhelm the immune system, they are quickly carried throughout the body, causing the serious complications of sepsis.

2. Although antibiotics can successfully destroy gram negative bacteria, they are powerless against endotoxin.

3. Centoxin is infused into the bloodstream and binds to the lipid A portion of endotoxin, diminishing its lethal effects.

Endotoxin is a natural part of the outer membrane of gram negative bacteria. As the bacteria divide or die, their exterior membranes unleash endotoxin.

Some evidence suggests that even as antibiotics destroy the bacteria, still more endotoxin may be shed by the resulting rupture of cell membranes.

Centoxin is highly specific, binding only to its target, lipid A.

*The quest that led to Centoxin began in the early 1970s when researchers including Dr. McCabe in Boston and Drs. Ziegler and Braude in San Diego demonstrated that the human immune system produces polyclonal antibodies in response to endotoxin. ■ Theorizing that antibodies against endotoxin might improve survival in gram negative bacteremia, Drs. Ziegler and Braude conducted a landmark study known as the J5 trial. Volunteers from the San Diego police and fire departments were vaccinated with J5, an inactivated strain of gram negative bacteria. Serum containing polyclonal antibodies against J5 was then collected from the volunteers and used to treat patients with gram negative bacteremia. The results, presented in **The New England Journal of Medicine** in 1982, showed that the J5 antiserum reduced mortality by 37 percent. ■ But the antiserum did not lend itself to commercial production. Looking for an alternative, the researchers turned to Drs. Kaplan and Tong at Stanford University, who, among others, were investigating monoclonal antibody technology. Then only a few years old, this technology held the promise of providing highly specific, pure, and uniform anti-endotoxin antibodies in commercial quantities. From the work at Stanford came the human IgM monoclonal antibody that Centocor has since formulated into the drug called Centoxin. In 1991 Dr. Ziegler and colleagues reported in **The New England Journal of Medicine** that Centoxin, like the J5 polyclonal antiserum, saved lives. During a placebo-controlled trial sponsored by Centocor, Centoxin reduced mortality in gram negative bacteremic patients by 39 percent. In cases of bacteremia and septic shock, Centoxin lowered mortality by 42 percent.*

STATISTICAL TABLES & GRAPHS

CHARTS & SCORES

MAPS

ARCHITECTURAL PLANS & DRAWINGS

INSTRUCTIONAL DIAGRAMS FOR PRODUCTS

SCIENTIFIC ILLUSTRATIONS

Diagram showing the attack of an infection on a human body and how a drug works against it. From a Centocor, Inc. annual report.
セントコア社のアニュアルリポートより、伝染病が人体を侵し、かつ医薬品がいかにそれに対処するかを表した図。

STATISTICAL
TABLES & GRAPHS

CHARTS & SCORES

MAPS

ARCHITECTURAL
PLANS & DRAWINGS

INSTRUCTIONAL DIAGRAMS
FOR PRODUCTS

SCIENTIFIC
ILLUSTRATIONS

CENTOCOR, INC.
USA 1987
CD:Charles C. Cabot Ⅲ
AD,D:Joel Katz
D,I:Dan Picard
I:Stacey Lewis
DF:Katz Wheeler Design

セントコア社のアニュアルリポートより、同社の医薬品が感染と戦う様子を描いているイラストレーション。

Antiplatelet Antibodies
Inside a blood vessel, squadrons of Centocor's antiplatelet antibodies scramble to occupy the over 40,000 fibrinogen docking sites on each of a group of activated platelets, blocking the formation of a potentially lethal blood clot.

Antiplatelet antibodies bind to the fibrinogen receptor sites on platelets, which are one of the primary components of blood clots. As a result, the fibrinogen rods that cause platelet aggregation cannot take hold, and the clot cannot form. We anticipate that this antibody will be used in conjunction with clot-dissolving enzymes.

Diagrammatic illustration for Centocor's annual report. It shows how this biopharmaceutical company's products fight off infection.
セントコア社のアニュアルリポートより、同社の医薬品が感染と戦う様子を描いているイラストレーション。

ARCO
USA 1991
CD:Ron Jefferies
D:Scott Lambert
P:Keith Wood
I:Hank Fisher
DF:The Jefferies Association

STATISTICAL TABLES & GRAPHS

CHARTS & SCORES

MAPS

ARCHITECTURAL PLANS & DRAWINGS

INSTRUCTIONAL DIAGRAMS FOR PRODUCTS

SCIENTIFIC ILLUSTRATIONS

ARCO's reformulation of gasolines adds the oxygenate methyl tertiary butyl ether (MTBE) while reducing the content of benzene (by more than 50 percent), aromatics and butane which causes evaporative emissions.

While EC-1 replaced leaded fuel for older cars and trucks, ARCO's EC-Premium is designed to meet the needs of late-model high-performance engines. These changes were achieved without increased cost to the consumer.

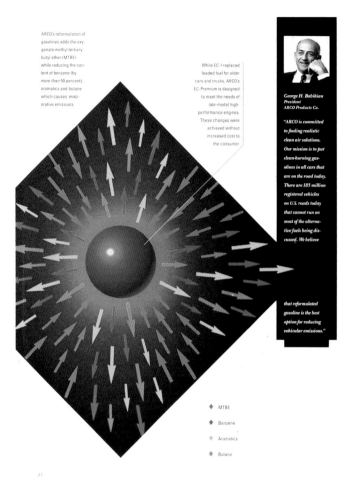

*George H. Babikian
President
ARCO Products Co.*
"ARCO is committed to finding realistic clean air solutions. Our mission is to put clean-burning gasolines in all cars that are on the road today. There are 185 million registered vehicles on U.S. roads today that cannot run on most of the alternative fuels being discussed. We believe that reformulated gasoline is the best option for reducing vehicular emissions."

◆ MTBE
◆ Benzene
◆ Aromatics
◆ Butane

ARCO Chemical has more than 20 years' experience with oxygenated fuels that have environmental and performance benefits. In the last 10 years, the Company has become the world's leading producer of MTBE.

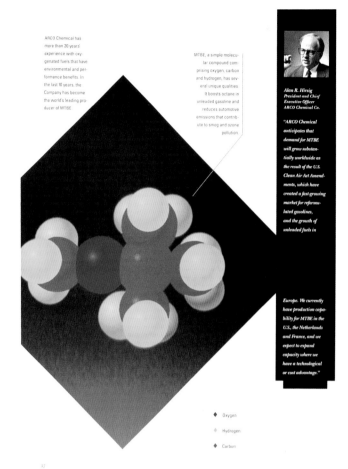

MTBE, a simple molecular compound comprising oxygen, carbon and hydrogen, has several unique qualities. It boosts octane in unleaded gasoline and reduces automotive emissions that contribute to smog and ozone pollution.

*Alan R. Hirsig
President and Chief Executive Officer
ARCO Chemical Co.*
"ARCO Chemical anticipates that demand for MTBE will grow substantially worldwide as the result of the U.S. Clean Air Act Amendments, which created a fast-growing market for reformulated gasolines, and the growth of unleaded fuels in Europe. We currently have production capability for MTBE in the U.S., the Netherlands and France, and we expect to expand capacity where we have a technological or cost advantage."

◆ Oxygen
◆ Hydrogen
◆ Carbon

Diagram showing the chemical make-up of clean burning ECI gasoline. The colored arrows represent different chemicals.
Diagram showing the molecular structure of MTBE, an additive which boosts the octane of unleaded gasoline and reduces automotive emissions. From an Arco annual report.
アルコ社のアニュアルリポートより、クリーンに燃焼するECIガソリンの科学的構成を表したイラストレーション。色別の矢印はそれぞれ異なった化学薬品を示している。
無鉛ガソリンのオクタン価を上げ、自動車排出物を減らすことができる添加剤MTBEの分子構造図。

GAKKEN

JAPAN 1982

CD:Yuji Yamanaka

I:Ukei Tomori

STATISTICAL
TABLES & GRAPHS

CHARTS & SCORES

MAPS

ARCHITECTURAL
PLANS & DRAWINGS

INSTRUCTIONAL DIAGRAMS
FOR PRODUCTS

SCIENTIFIC
ILLUSTRATIONS

Panoramic diagram of the Antarctic. From a science magazine and a program for a movie.
科学雑誌や映画のパンフレットに掲載された南極大陸パノラマ。

BLUE MOON STUDIO INC.
JAPAN 1992
AD,D:Masato Okazaki
I:Takatoshi Oki

STATISTICAL
TABLES & GRAPHS

CHARTS & SCORES

MAPS

ARCHITECTURAL
PLANS & DRAWINGS

INSTRUCTIONAL DIAGRAMS
FOR PRODUCTS

SCIENTIFIC
ILLUSTRATIONS

Illustration comparing the size of humans and dinosaurs.
人間と恐竜の大きさを比較したイラストレーション。

STATISTICAL
TABLES & GRAPHS

CHARTS & SCORES

MAPS

ARCHITECTURAL
PLANS & DRAWINGS

INSTRUCTIONAL DIAGRAMS
FOR PRODUCTS

SCIENTIFIC
ILLUSTRATIONS

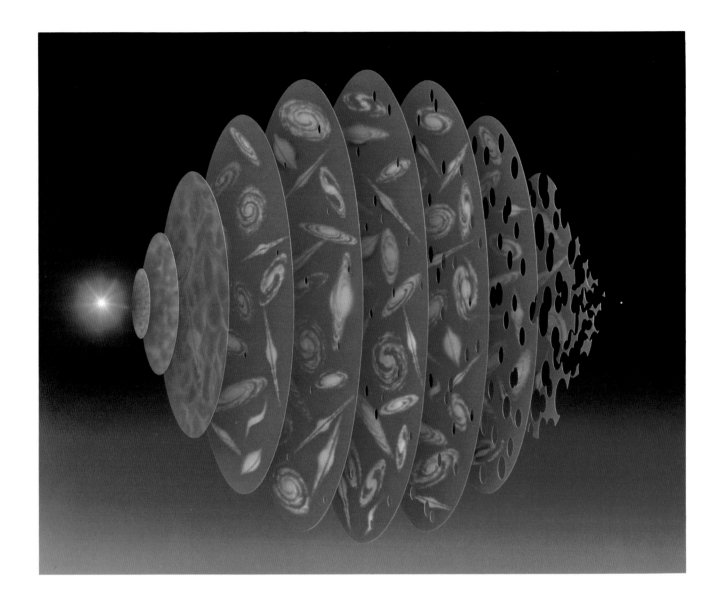

科学雑誌「ニュートン別冊/ブラックホール宇宙」より、宇宙はビックバン特異点に始まりビッククランチ特異点に終わるという"特異点定理"のイラストレーション。

Illustration of the "singular state" theory which postulates that the Universe started at the Big Bang singular state and will end at the Big Crunch singular state.
From a special edition of the scientific magazine "Newton".
科学雑誌「ニュートン別冊/ブラックホール宇宙」より、宇宙はビックバン特異点に始まりビッククランチ特異点に終わるという"特異点定理"のイラストレーション。

STATISTICAL TABLES & GRAPHS

CHARTS & SCORES

MAPS

ARCHITECTURAL PLANS & DRAWINGS

INSTRUCTIONAL DIAGRAMS FOR PRODUCTS

SCIENTIFIC ILLUSTRATIONS

SIGMA XI
USA 1991
AD,D,I:Linda K. Huff

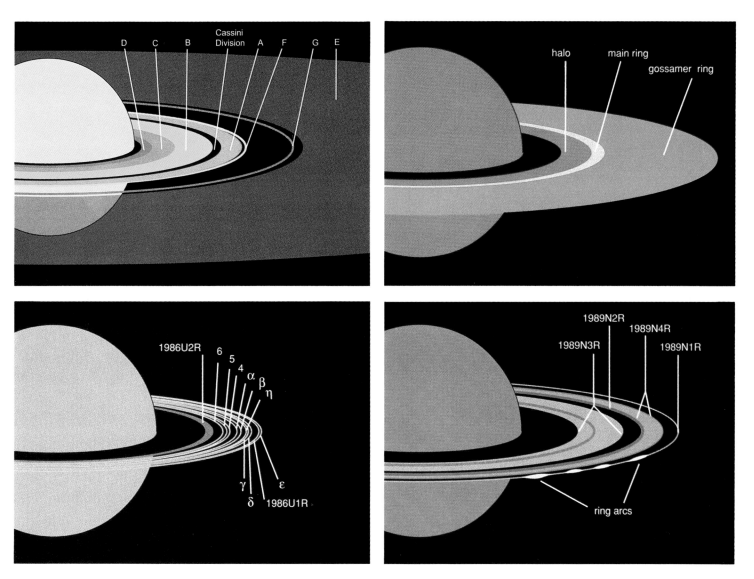

Diagrams of the ring systems of Jupiter, Uranus, Neptune and Saturn. Each planetary system has a unique complement of rings,
varying in width, height and density as well as the size and composition of its particles. From American Scientist magazine.
「アメリカン・サイエンティストマガジン」より、木星・天王星・海王星・土星の輪を表したダイアグラム。各惑星には幅・高さ・密度さらには大きさ・組成の異なった粒子からなる独特の輪がある。

STATISTICAL
TABLES & GRAPHS

CHARTS & SCORES

MAPS

ARCHITECTURAL
PLANS & DRAWINGS

INSTRUCTIONAL DIAGRAMS
FOR PRODUCTS

SCIENTIFIC
ILLUSTRATIONS

NORCEN ENERGY RESOURCES
USA 1991
AD:Kit Hinrichs
D:Piper Murakami
I:Helene Moore
DF:Pentagram Design Ltd.

GREAT CORAL REEFS
USA 1992
AD:Jeff Batzli
D:Susan Livingston
I:Scott MacNeill
DF:Micheal Friedman Publishing Group

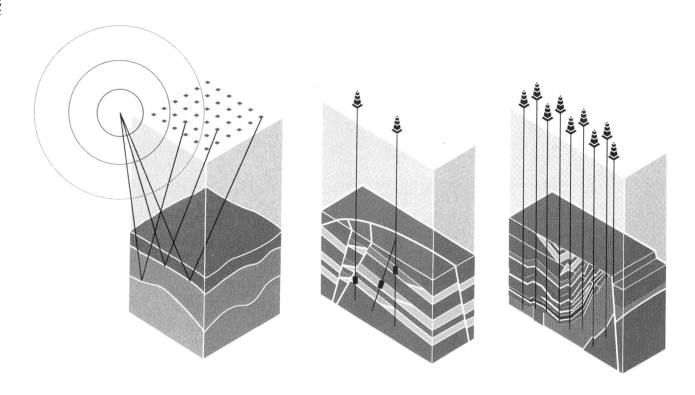

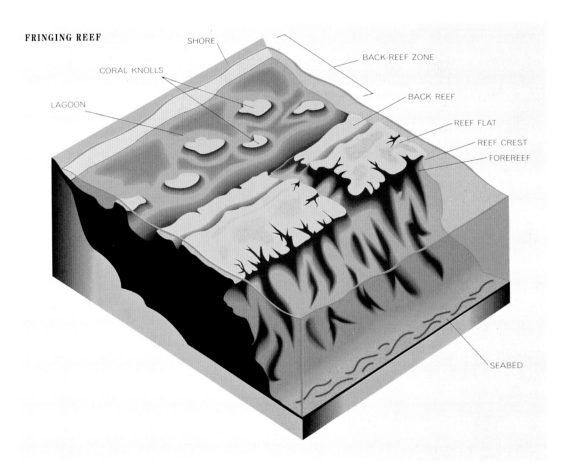

Cross-sectional view of sea-bed soil substrata showing layers rich in gas,
oil and indicating the earthquake factor. From a Norcen Energy Resources annual report.
ノーセン・エナジー・リゾース社のアニュアルリポートより、地震分析の様子、
及び海底や地底深くに存在するガス・オイルの地層等を表す地層断面図。

Illustration showing what a coral reef looks like, from its base,
to above the water line and pointing out its different features.
珊瑚礁の姿を海底から海面上まで描き、様々な特長を解説したイラストレーション。

INDEX

INDEX

DIAGRAM GRAPHICS

INDEX

DIAGRAM GRAPHICS

DIAGRAM GRAPHICS

ART DIRECTOR

Kazuo Abe

DESIGNER

Yutaka Ichimura

Kimiko Ishiwatari

Shinji Ikenoue

EDITOR

Yuko Yoshio

Tsutomu Hirata

EDITORIAL MANAGER

Masato Ieshiro

PHOTOGRAPHER

Shoichi Sato (Photo Studio Techne)

ENGLISH TRANSLATOR & ADVISER

Write Away Co., Ltd.

COORDINATORS

Roland Gebhardt Design (New York)

Sarah Phillips (London)

PUBLISHER

Shingo Miyoshi

EDITORIAL CONSULTANT

Fumihiko Nishioka

1992年11月 8日初版第 1版発行

発行所　ピエ・ブックス

〒170 東京都豊島区駒込4-14-6-407

Tel: 03-3949-5010

Fax: 03-3949-5650

製版・印刷・製本　(株)飛来社

〒162 東京都新宿区若松町38-23 和幸マンション

Tel: 03-5272-3651 Fax: 03-5272-3617

P·I·E Books, as always, has several new and ambitious graphic book projects in the works which will introduce a variety of superior designs from Japan and abroad. Currently we are planning the collection series detailed below. If you have any graphics which you consider worthy for submission to these publications, please fill in the necessary information on the inserted questionnaire postcard and forward it to us. You will receive a notice when the relevant project goes into production.

ピエ・ブックスでは、今後も新しいタイプの
グラフィック書籍の出版を目指すとともに、
国内外の優れたデザインを幅広く
紹介していきたいと考えております。
今後の刊行予定として下記のコレクション・シリーズを
企画しておりますので、
作品提供していただける企画がございましたら、
挟み込みのアンケートハガキに必要事項を記入の上
お送り下さい。企画が近づきましたら
そのつど案内書をお送りいたします。

A. POSTCARD GRAPHICS

A collection of various types of postcards including product advertising, direct mailers, invitations to events such as parties and fashion shows as well as birthday cards and seasonal greetings. In short all sorts of cards except the letter type which are mailed in envelopes.

A．ポストカード・グラフィックス

各シーズンのグリーティングカードをはじめとして、商品広告ＤＭ、パーティーやコレクション等のイベントのお知らせ、バースデイカードなど封書タイプを除く様々なポストカードをコレクションします。

B. ADVERTISING GREETING CARDS

A collection of letter-style direct mailers including sales promotional sheets, invitations to events such as exhibitions, parties and weddings. Some of these are quite simple, some have unusual shapes or dimensions (limited to cards inserted in envelopes).

B．アドバタイジング・グリーティングカード

販促用のＤＭ、展示会・イベントの案内状やパーティや結婚式などの招待状など、プレーンなものから形状の変わったもの・立体になったものまで封書タイプのＤＭをコレクションします。（封書タイプのものに限ります）

C. BROCHURE & PAMPHLET COLLECTION

A collection of brochures and pamphlets categorized according to the business of the client company. Includes sales promotional pamphlets, product catalogues, corporate image brochures gallery exhibitions, special events, annual reports and company profiles from all sorts of businesses.

C．ブローシュア＆パンフレット・コレクション

販促用パンフレット、商品カタログ、イメージ・カタログ、ギャラリーや展示会・イベントのパンフレット、アニュアル・リポート、会社案内など様々な業種のブローシュアやパンフレットを業種別にコレクションします。

D. POSTER GRAPHICS

A collection of posters, classified according to the business of the client. Fashion, department stores, automotive, food, home appliances and almost any sort of poster you might see on streets. Invitational posters for art exhibitions, concerts and plays as well as regional posters which will be seen for the first time outside of the local area where they were published.

D．ポスター・グラフィックス

ファッション、デパート、車、食品、家電など街角を飾る広告ポスター、美術展、コンサート、演劇などのイベント案内ポスター、見る機会の少ない地方のポスターなどを業種別にコレクションします。

E. BOOK COVER AND EDITORIAL DESIGNS

Editorial and cover designs for various types of books and magazines. Includes all sorts of magazines, books, comics and other visual publications.

E．ブックカバー＆エディトリアル・デザイン

雑誌、単行本、ヴィジュアル書、コミックなど様々なタイプの書籍・雑誌のエディトリアル・デザイン、カバー・デザインを紹介します。

F. CORPORATE IMAGE LOGO DESIGNS

A collection of C.I. materials mainly symbols and logos for corporations of all sorts, classified according to the type of business. In some cases, development samples and trial comps as well as the final designs are included. Includes logos for magazines and various products.

F．コーポレイト・イメージ・ロゴマーク・デザイン

企業やショップのシンボルマーク・ロゴマークを中心に幅広い業種にわたり分類しコレクションします。マークのみではなく展開例としてのアプリケーションも数多く紹介し、その他、雑誌や商品などの様々なロゴマークもコレクションします。

G. BUSINESS CARD AND LETTERHEAD GRAPHICS

A collection of cards such as the business cards of corporations and individuals as well as shopping cards for restaurants and boutiques, membership cards and various prepaid cards. This collection centers on business cards, letterheads and shopping cards of superior design.

G．ビジネスカード＆レターヘッド・グラフィックス

様々な企業や個人の名刺、レストランやブティックのショップカード、会員カード、プリペイドカードなど、デザイン的に優れたカードを名刺・ショップカードを中心にコレクション。またカードのみでなくレターヘッドも紹介します。

H. CALENDAR GRAPHICS

A collection of visually interesting calendars. We do not take into account the form of the calendar, i.e. wall hanging-type or note-type or desktop-type etc. So that the calendars represent the widest range of possibilities.

H．カレンダー・グラフィックス

ヴィジュアル的に優れたカレンダーをコレクションします。壁掛けタイプ、ノートタイプ、ダイアリー、日めくりタイプ、卓上タイプなど形状にはこだわらず幅広い分野の様々なタイプのカレンダーを紹介します。

I. PACKAGE AND WRAPPING GRAPHICS

A collection of packaging and wrapping materials of superior design from Japan and abroad. Includes related accessories such as labels and ribbons and almost anything else that comes under the heading of containing, protecting and decorating things.

Ｉ．パッケージ＆ラッピング・グラフィックス

商品そのもののパッケージデザインはもちろん、いろいろな物を包む、保護する、飾るというコンセプトで国内外の優れたパッケージ、ケース、ラッピング・デザイン及びラベル、リボンなどの付属アクセサリー類を幅広く紹介します。

Comme toujours, P·I·E Books a dans ses ateliers plusieurs projets de livres graphiques neufs et ambitieux qui introduiront une gamme de modèles supérieurs en provenance du Japon et de l'étranger. Nous prévoyons en ce moment la série de collections détaillée cidessous. Si vous êtes en possession d'un graphique que vous jugez digne de soumettre à ces publications, nous vous prions de remplir les informations nécessaires sur l'étiquette à renvoyer située à la carte postale questionnaire insérée et de nous la faire parvenir. Vous recevrez un avis lorsque le projet correspondant passera à la production.

Wie immer hat P·I·E Books einige neue anspruchsvolle Grafikbücher in Arbeit, die eine Vielzahl von hervorragenden Designs aus Japan und anderen Ländern vorstellen werden. Momentan planen wir eine Serie mit den nachfolgend aufgeführten Themen.

Wenn Sie grafische Darstellungen besitzen, von denen Sie meinen, daß sie in diese Veröffentlichung aufgenommen werden könnten, geben Sie uns bitte die nötigen Informationen auf der entsprechenden Antwortseite am füllen Sie die beigelegte Antwortkarte aus und schicken Sie sie an uns. Wir werden Sie benachrichtigen, wenn das entsprechende Projekt in Arbeit geht.

A. Graphiques pour cartes postales
Une collection de divers types de cartes postales, y compris la publicité de produits, l'adressage direct, des invitations à des événements tels que soirées et défilés de mode, ainsi que des cartes d'anniversaire et des voeux de saison. En bref, toutes sortes de cartes, à part le type lettre qui sera envoyé dans des enveloppes.

B. Cartes de voeux publicitaires
Une collection d'adressages directs style lettre y compris des feuilles de promotion de ventes, des invitations à des événements tels qu'expositions, soirées et mariages. Certaines d'entre elles sont très simples, d'autres ont des formes ou dimensions inhabituelles (limitées aux cartes insérées dans des enveloppes).

C. Collection de brochures et de pamphlets
Une collection de brochures et de pamphlets triées en fonction des affaires de la société client. Comprend des pamphlets de promotion des ventes, des catalogues de produits, des brochures sur l'image de la société, des expositions de galerie, des événements spéciaux, des compte-rendus annuels et des profils de sociétés de toutes sortes d'affaires.

D. Graphiques sur affiche
Une collection d'affiches, classées en fonction du secteur d'affaires du client. La mode, les grands magasins, l'automobile, l'alimentation, les appareils électro-ménagers et presque tous les types d'affiche que vous pouvez voir dans les rues. Des affiches invitant à des expositions d'art, des concerts et des pièces ainsi que des affiches régionales qui seront vues pour la première fois en dehors de la région où elles ont été éditées.

E. Designs de couverture de livre et d'éditorial
Des designs de livre et d'éditorial de divers types de livres et magazines. Comprend toutes sortes de magazines, livres, bandes dessinées et autres publications visuelles.

F. Designs de logo d'image de société
Une collection de matériaux d'image de société, principalement des symboles et des logos pour sociétés de toutes sortes ; classés en fonction du type d'affaires. Dans certains cas, sont inclus des échantillons de développement et également des compositions d'essai ainsi que les designs finaux. Comprend des logos pour magazines et divers produits.

G. Graphiques pour en-têtes et cartes de visite
Une collection de cartes telles que les cartes de visite de sociétés et d'individus ainsi que les cartes de fidélité de restaurants et de boutiques, les cartes de membre et diverses cartes payées à l'avance. Cette collection se concentre sur les cartes de visite, les en-têtes et les cartes de fidélité d'une qualité supérieure.

H. Graphiques pour calendrier
Une collection de calendriers visuellement intéressants. Nous ne tenons pas compte de la forme du calendrier, c.-à-d., type à accrocher au mur, type carnet ou type bureau, etc. de telle sorte que les calendriers représentent la gamme de possibilités la plus large.

I. Graphiques pour emballage et paquetage
Une collection de matériaux d'emballage et de paquetage de qualité supérieure en provenance du Japon et de l'étranger. Comprend des accessoires en relation tels qu'étiquettes et rubans, et presque tout ce qui est destiné à contenir, protéger et décorer des choses.

A. Postkarten-Grafik
Zusammenstellung verschiedener Postkartenarten, und zwar für Produktwerbung, Direkt Mailing, Einladungen zu Parties und Modenschauen sowie Geburtstagskarten und Karten zu verschiedenen Jahreszeiten. Also alle Arten von Karten, ausgenommen Briefkarten.

B. Werbe-Grußkarten
Zusammenstellung briefähnlicher Direkt-Mailings, wie z.B. verkaufsfördernde Texte, Einladungen zu Anlässen wie Ausstellungen, Parties oder Hochzeiten. Einige von ihnen sind recht einfach gemacht, andere fallen durch ungewöhnliches Aussehen oder Größe auf (Karten dürfen Umschlaggröße nicht überschreiten).

C. Zusammenstellung von Broschüren und Druckschriften
Diese Zusammenstellung von Broschüren und Druckschriften ist nach den Tätigkeiten der Kundenfirmen geordnet. Sie beinhaltet verkaufsfördernde Broschüren, Produktkataloge, Corporate-Image-Broschüren, Galerieausstellungen, besondere Veranstaltungen und Firmenprofile für alle Arten von Unternehmen.

D. Postergrafik
Eine Zusammenstellung von Postern, die nach dem Geschäftsgebiet des Kunden geordnet sind. Mode Kaufhäuser, Kraftfahrzeuge, Nahrungsmittel, Haushaltsgeräte und fast jede Art von Postern, die auf der Straße zu sehen sind. Einladungsposter für Kunstausstellungen, Konzerte und Theaterstücke ebenso wie Poster mit regionalen Themen, die zum ersten Mal außerhalb des Gebietes, in dem sie aufgehängt wurden, zu sehen sein werden.

E. Bucheinbände und redaktionelles Design
Bucheinbände und redaktionelles Design für verschiedenste Buch- und Zeitschriftentypen. Dies schließt alle Arten von Zeitschriften, Büchern, Comics und anderen visuellen Publikationen ein.

F. Corporate-Image-Logo-Design
Dies ist eine Zusammenstellung von C.I.-Material, und zwar hauptsächlich von Symbolen und Logos für Firmen aller Art, nach Geschäftsgebieten geordnet. In manchen Fällen sind die Arbeiten der Entwicklungsphase und Probeexemplare ebenso miteinbezogen wie das endgültige Design. Logos für Zeitschriften und andere Produkte sind miteingeschlossen.

G. Visitenkarten und Briefkopt-Grafik
Dies ist eine Zusammenstellung verschiedener Visitenkarten, z.B. für Firmen und Einzelpersonen, Kreditkarten für Restaurants und Boutiquen, Mitgliedskarten und Vorverkaufskarten. Diese Sammlung konzentriert sich vor allem auf geschäftliche Karten, Briefköpfe und Geschäftseigene Kreditkarten mit herausragendem Design.

H. Kalendergrafik
Eine Zusammenstellung von optisch interessanten Kalendern. Es ist für uns dabei unwichtig, ob es sich um die Form des Wandkalenders, Tischkalenders oder Notizbuchkalenders handelt, sodaß die größtmögliche Vielfalt an Kalendern gezeigt werden kann.

I. Grafik auf Verpackungen und Verpackungsmaterial
Eine Zusammenstellung von Grafik auf Verpackungen und Verpackungsmaterial mit herausragendem Design aus Japan und anderen Ländern. Dazugehörige Accessoires wie Etiketten und Bänder sind eingeschlossen, ebenso wie fast alles, was als Behälter für Produkte dienen kann, sie ziert oder schützt.

NEW TITLES

FROM

P•I•E BOOKS

GRAPHIC BEAT / LONDON-TOKYO Vol: 1 & 2

Pages: 224 (208 in color) Format: 225mm x 300mm

Binding: Hardbound with jacket Pub.date: Vol: 1 & 2: Available now

"The GRAPHIC BEAT" presents a compilation of graphic art created by 17 London and 12 Tokyo graphic designers who are continually breaking new ground, doing much to influence internationally the graphic trends of the past few years. Each designer has contibuted work not just in music but in all areas of design; posters, logotypes, catalogues, magazines and perhaps most importantly their personal expressions of art; Graphic or not. Features Malcolm Garrett, Russell Mills, Tadanori Yokoo, Peter Saville, Hajime Tachibana, Terry Jones, Neville Brody, Mic*Itaya, Garry Mouat, Yukimasa Okumura, Jamie Reid, Vaughan Oliver and many more.

CALENDAR GRAPHICS

Pages: 224 (192 in color) Format: 225mm x 300mm Binding: Hardbound with jacket Pub. date: Available now

Featuring approximately 250 calendars carefully selected from 500 entries produced in Japan and 20 other countries.

This book presents various types of calendars collected both from Japan and overseas. The formats include poster-type, book-type, daily and monthly tear-off types and even various 3-dimensional specialty calendars. Also featured are original collections from art museums which have not previously been shown widely, and calendars which can only be considered objets d'art. There are "POP" calendars, produced as music promotion graphics and commercially available calendars which are sold everywhere. In short, an unlimited variety. This book will afford you the boundless pleasure of leafing through some of the finest, most original calendar art ever created.

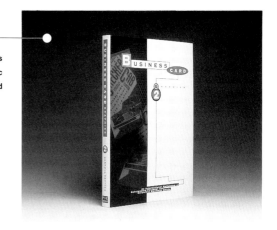

The Creative Index ARTIFILE Vol. 1

Pages: 224 (192 in color) Format: 225mm x 300mm Binding: Hardbound with jacket Pub. date: Available now

This first edition of ARTIFILE showcases the best works from 104 top graphic design studios from Japan and abroad. A variety of fields have been included such as advertising design, corporate identity, photography and illustration. All works are presented in striking full-color and include comments from the designers themselves. This annual publication is the perfect visual resource for all graphic designers looking for new perspectives.

BUSINESS CARD GRAPHICS 2

Pages: 224 (192 in color) Format: 225mm x 300mm Binding: Hardbound with jacket Pub. date: Available now

As an encore to the original BUSINESS CARD GRAPHICS, this new international collection presents 1,000 business cards selected on the basis of excellence in design. Emphasis has been given to cards used in creative fields such as graphic design and architecture. These exciting, trend-setting works are sure to be a source of inspiration for graphic designers and art directors.

T-Shirt GRAPHICS

Pages: 224 (192 in color) Format: 225mm x 300mm Binding: Hardbound with jacket Pub. date: Available now

Cool and casual, artistic and expressive, commercial & promotional...T-shirts, the garment of choice for millions, are all of these and more. Emblazoned with more than just a catch phrase or trendy design, T-shirts are an important promotional item bearing logos and brand names of corporations large and small.

The editors at P.I.E BOOKS showcase the entire spectrum of T-shirt graphics with this delightful collection of shirts gatherd from top designers worldwide. Categories include casual and designer T-shirts, shirts promoting exhibitions, concerts and events, shirts bearing logos, trademarks and brand names, self-promotional shirts from design agencies and others from schools, museums and organizations. Some 700 glorious designs in all, most in full-color.

T-SHIRT GRAPHICS is a valuable and inspirational visual sourcebook for all graphic and textile designers and also for corporate communications and C.I. specialist.